DUBLIN HANGED

DUBLIN HANGED

CRIME, LAW ENFORCEMENT
AND PUNISHMENT IN
LATE EIGHTEENTH-CENTURY DUBLIN

BRIAN HENRY

IRISH ACADEMIC PRESS

This book was set in 11 on 13 Janson Text
by Perro de Jong,
Utrecht, The Netherlands, for
IRISH ACADEMIC PRESS
Kill Lane, Blackrock, Co. Dublin

Photography by Brendan Dempsey,
the Photo Centre, Trinity College, Dublin.

Copy-edited by Dale Booker, Dublin

A catalogue record for this book
is available from the British Library.

ISBN 0-7165-2512-7

SPECIAL ACKNOWLEDGMENT

Publication has been made possible by grants from
The Arthur Cox Foundation,
The Esme Mitchell Trust,
and The Grace Lawless Lee Fund.

Printed in Ireland by
Colour Books Ltd, Dublin

*To my mother and to
the memory of my father*

THE ARTHUR COX FOUNDATION

Arthur Cox, solicitor, classical scholar and former President of the Incorporated Law Society of Ireland, was associated with the setting up of many Irish companies, not least the ESB. He was a specialist in company law and was a member of the Company Law Reform Committee which sat from 1951 and reported to the Government in 1958, ultimately giving rise to the Companies Act, 1963. When he decided to retire from practice as a solicitor in 1961 a number of his clients, professional colleagues and other friends, in recognition of his outstanding contribution to Ireland and his profession, thought that a fund should be established as a tribute to him, which fund would be used to encourage the writing and publication of legal text-books. There was a generous response to this appeal.

After his retirement he studied for the priesthood and was ordained in 1963. He went to Zambia to do missionary work. He died there in 1965 as a result of a car accident.

The Foundation was established to honour Arthur Cox and was for many years administered by Mr Justice John Kenny in conjunction with the Law Society. In paying tribute to the memory of Arthur Cox it is appropriate that tribute should also be paid to Mr Justice John Kenny, who died on 25 March 1987. John Kenny was a close personal friend of Arthur Cox and, like Arthur Cox, graced with distinction his own barristers' profession, as a chancery practitioner, and both the High Court and Supreme Court, as a judge. John Kenny was the encouraging force behind the publication of a number of Irish legal textbooks. Without his quiet drive and enthusiasm there would have been no Foundation. To both Arthur Cox and John Kenny we pay tribute.

The Law Society, as the continuing trustee of the Foundation, is pleased to have been able to assist in the publication of this book.

Michael V. O'Mahony
President,
The Incorporated Law Society of Ireland

December, 1993

Contents

List of Tables, Illustrations and Extracts

Abbreviations

Bolton Papers	Papers of Thomas Orde, 1st Baron Bolton, N.L.I.
Comm.	Commission of Oyer and Terminer
Common's jn. Ire.	*Journals of the House of Commons of the Kingdom of Ireland...*, (1613–1791, 28 vols., Dublin, 1753–1791; reprinted and continued, 1613–1800, 19 vols., Dublin, 1796–1800)
DA.MO.YR.	Day/Month/Year (newspaper references)
D.E.P.	Dublin Evening Post
D.Q.S.	Dublin Quarter Sessions
H.J.	*Hibernian Journal*
H.O.	Home Office Papers
K.Q.S.	Kilmainham Quarter Sessions
Lords' jn. Ire.	Journals of the House of Lords [of Ireland], *1634–1800* (8 vols., Dublin, 1779–1800)
Minute Book	*Minute Book of the Blackrock Association* N.L.I., MS 84
M.P.	Dublin Morning Post
N.L.I.	National Library of Ireland, Dublin
P.R.O.	Public Record Office of England

Parl. reg. Ire.	*The parliamentary register, or the history of the proceedings and debates of the House of Commons of Ireland* [1781–97] (17 vols., Dublin, 1782–1801)
Past & Present	*Past and Present* ... (London, 1952–)
R.I.A.	Library of the Royal Irish Academy
Statutes (Ire.)	*The statutes at large, passed in the parliaments held in Ireland* (1310–1800), 20 vols., (Dublin, 1765–1801)
U.K. Parl. Papers	*Journals of the House of Commons* [of England, Great Britain, or United Kingdom]
W.H.M.	*Walker's Hibernian Magazine*

Acknowledgments

I would like to express my gratitude to the Incorporated Law Society of Ireland, the trust advisers of the Esme Mitchell Trust and Trinity College, Dublin for their generous financial assistance. Without their aid, this book would not have been published.

In addition, I would like to thank the staff members of the Department of Early Printed Books at Trinity College, Dublin, the National Library of Ireland, the Royal Irish Academy and the National Archives of Ireland.

I am grateful to Dr Eamonn Hall at the Solicitor's Office of *Telecom Eireann*, who encouraged me to consider publication. In editing the drafts, Ms Dale Booker did a superb job (responsibility for all errors is mine). Mr Perro de Jong also deserves special mention for providing computer and technical assistance.

As this book is based on research undertaken at the Department of Modern History, Trinity College, Dublin between 1989 and 1992, I would like to thank again the people who assisted me in the completion of my PhD thesis. In particular, I would like to thank my supervisor, Dr David Dickson.

I would also like to mention my aunt, Mrs Marion Wright, who has always shown a keen interest in the subject matter of my research. Most important of all, I would like to thank my mother, Mrs Rita Anne Armstrong, who has supported my work over the past five years.

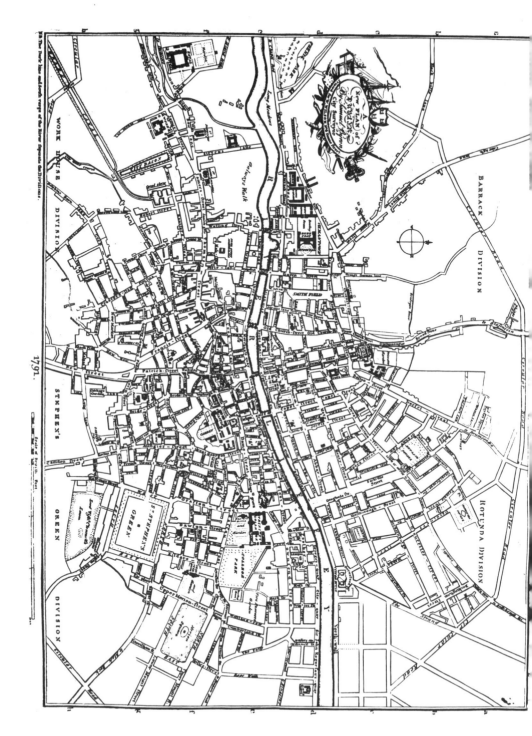

New PLAN of DUBLIN

1791.

BARRACK DIVISION

WORK HOUSE DIVISION

ST. STEPHEN'S GREEN DIVISION

ROTUNDA DIVISION

Introduction

The book is based on research carried out in the Department of Modern History, Trinity College Dublin, the aim of which was to undertake a quantitative and qualitative study of crime, the police and the courts in Dublin in the late eighteenth century.[1] A major obstacle had to be overcome: how to uncover a source that would most closely approximate the priceless court records destroyed in the disastrous fire at the Public Record Office in 1922. Several sources were examined and rejected before a satisfactory one was finally obtained. This was the *Hibernian Journal*, a legal-minded newspaper which was published three times a week in Dublin.

Violence was not an abnormal phenomenon in the late eighteenth century. Between 1780 and 1795, a total of 390 homicides were reported in the city and county of Dublin, including 189 murders, 82 suicides, 34 cases of manslaughter, 34 infanticides, 9 deaths from duelling, and 42 other fatalities, an average of over 24 violent deaths per year. Repetitive crime was rampant: the *Hibernian Journal* reported a total of 53 rapes (seven of which resulted in death), 337 assaults, 158 riots, and 22 cases of forcible enlistment. Housewives, children and young people were particularly vulnerable to violence. Major property theft was a daily occurrence: 3,600 robberies and burglaries took place and the three Dublin courts heard 1,300 prosecutions for theft. With a population of 180,000 people, Dublin city had become a modern consumer society. Merchants conducted a brisk trade in perfumes, gold watches, fashions, all of which were sold to a sophisticated gentry and to the swelling ranks of professionals with city residences. While the wealthier victims had the most to lose, crime excluded no class, rank or religion.

To cope with the rising tide of criminality, Dublin embarked on an ambitious plan to build a new prison in Green Street in 1773 at a cost of £16,000.[2] Work on the new prison proceeded at a snail's pace until the Gordon riots in London in June 1780, after which Newgate prison was completed within three months. It was believed that some

criminals who had escaped from London's Newgate prison during the
Gordon riots had made their way to Dublin. It was also feared that a
prison break of the kind seen in London would take place in Dublin.
Hence the prisoners at the city's "old" Newgate at the end of Thomas
Street were hurriedly transferred to the "new" Newgate in Green
Street in September 1780.[3] Having completed the prison in record
time, the Lord Mayor of Dublin summoned a general meeting of
parish officers to tackle the problem of crime.[4] In 1783, the ending of
the American War of Independence increased levels of crime with the
demobilisation of thousands of troops.

Against a backdrop of rising crime, the Irish Parliament passed
legislation to establish a centralised police force in March 1786; the
force arrived on the streets of Dublin in September, but survived for
only nine years. Up to this point, Dublin had been policed by a weak
parish watch system. In the early 1780s, the Dublin Volunteers tried to
inject new life into the old salt by establishing auxiliary forces. Even
the suburb of Blackrock organised a felons association to fight crime.
However with the collapse of the Volunteers in 1783, the parish watch
system was doomed to oblivion. In the summer of 1784, a crisis in law
and order shook the propertied classes and no merchant was safe from
the "tarring and feathering committee." In that fateful summer, the
Lord Lieutenant laid plans to dispose of the decrepit watch and establish a new police.

In March 1786, the Irish Parliament passed the Police Act which
launched the first centralised police force in the country six months
later. The teething problems of the police were many, especially its
extraordinarily high start-up costs and the odious obligations imposed
upon policemen made to enforce thousands of petty regulations which
had little to do with the fight against crime. The opposition seized
upon the problems to whip up a bitter campaign of hatred within
Dublin Corporation against the Castle. Eventually, the opposition
brought the police down in 1795.

Punishment for offenders varied from whippings, prison sentences,
transportation and of course the gallows. From 1784 to 1789, the
Dublin courts sentenced about 785 convicts to transportation to
North America, an average of 130 convicts a year. Transportation to
Australia began in 1791. Over the 16-year period, the courts hanged
between 199 and 242 convicted felons, including 189 verified hangings
of men and 10 verified executions of women, an average of at least 12

executions per year. In the city, hanging spectacles took place at Stephen's Green and at the front of Newgate prison in Green Street. In the county, hangings took place at Gallows Hill which was opposite Kilmainham gaol and at Kilmainham Commons near the Grand Canal bridge. In the mid-1780s, the Dublin courts adopted the harshest sentencing patterns: in 1784 and 1785, as many as 55 felons were executed. In 1783, the courts introduced the hanging drop-platform at Newgate and at Gallows Hill which was meant to break the necks of the condemned, but it failed as often as it worked. Two convicted females, one an arsonist in 1783 and the other a murderer in 1784, were burned at the stake at Gallows Hill and Stephen's Green.

A highly litigious period, the Irish parliament passed many private statutes by which offenders were to be punished by death. About 80 per cent of the Dublin hanged were indeed convicted under various statutes protecting the propertied classes against robbery and burglary. The legislation establishing the independence of the Irish Post Office in 1784, for example, resulted in the hangings of three letter carriers and five mail thieves within a few years. For many reasons, including the beginning of the French Wars in 1793 and the willingness of Parliament to impose increasingly harsh deterrents, levels of violence were substantially reduced in Dublin by the mid-1790s.

CHAPTER ONE

The Dublin Hanged

Public hangings of convicted felons were a common feature of life in Dublin in the late eighteenth century. In most cases, more than one felon was hanged and it was not unusual for four or five men to be hanged at the same time, one after the other. Hangings were well-publicised affairs and attracted huge numbers of people. Up to 1783, most hangings in the city took place at or near Stephen's Green and were characterised by a hanging procession. Riding in a cart, condemned felons were usually accompanied by their families, friends, supporters and ordinary bystanders, who hurried and jostled along the way from the "old" Newgate prison at Cutpurse Row and Francis Street to the "fatal tree" in the Green.

After 1783, hangings in the city took place at the front of Newgate prison (with the exception of an execution at Stephen's Green in August 1784). After the gallows were relocated to the north side of the city, the hanging processions came to an end. The condemned felons walked directly from the cells to a first-floor prison chapel, where a clergyman of their faith attended to their last spiritual needs. The felons would then walk out of the chapel through a large window which opened onto a gallows. Their family and friends would watch them from below.

Not everyone believed that an increase in hangings was an appropriate response to high levels of crime. In October 1781, a letter appeared in the *Hibernian Journal* suggesting that castration was a better form of punishment than the gallows. Signed by a "magistrate," the letter said,

> Will frequent executions contribute to their purpose? Experience shows the contrary. Their frequency renders them familiar; and the mob seems no more affected with this solemn scene, than a Puppet show. A terror is lessened. Villainy increases, and the necessity for execution is augmented by their multiplicity ... I am serious in proposing castration for the men whenever they com-

mit a crime … Intemperate lust is the most frequent cause of such crimes, and what more adequate punishment? 'Tis an operation not without a suitable degree of pain, sometimes danger, and perhaps the *New Gaol* would tremble more at the approach of such an execution, than at the parade of the gallows … Many of these wretches are more anxious about the safety of their bodies … Their bodies are themselves. The body relishes pleasure and enjoyment, and is the only object of their concern. The soul—they know nothing of it … Should a Capital C be marked on each Cheek, their contemptible infamous Punishment would be known to every one they meet.[1]

According to the *Hibernian Journal*, hangings became a more frequent occurrence in the city in the 1780s as compared to the 1770s.[2] Of the 12 felons hanged in the five years previous to July 1781, half were executed between March 1780 and July 1781. On Saturday 18 March 1780, four men were to be executed in Stephen's Green, but it was feared that a gang would disrupt the hanging procession. (Hangings were usually scheduled on Saturdays because they were the busiest market days in Dublin. Hence hangings on Saturday attracted larger crowds than hangings on Wednesdays or other days of the week.) This provoked an immediate reaction from the city sheriffs and three Volunteer Corps: the Dublin Volunteers, the Liberty Rangers and the Rathdown Horse Corps. (The Volunteers were an independent political party seeking to achieve commercial and constitutional reforms for Ireland.[3] Bearing arms, these patriots were also a quasi-vigilante force. Composed of members of the propertied classes, they supported the "civil order against lawless elements in both town and countryside.")[4]

On this occasion, however, the hanging procession of the four condemned men—Reid, Duffy, Farrell and Hickey—was disrupted due to a technicality in the law. Just before the hanging party was to set off from "old" Newgate in Thomas Street, the High Sheriff received a writ of error that spared Farrell and Hickey from the gallows. As the High Sheriff would have normally received this information much earlier, he ordered one of his sub-sheriffs to go to the home of Samuel Bradstreet, the Recorder of the Dublin Quarter Sessions, in Booterstown to authenticate the writ of error. As the clock ticked, a massive crowd assembled at old Newgate while the Volunteers kept order. When the sub-sheriff returned with the news that indeed two of the four condemned men had been spared, it was decided to confirm the legality of executing the other pair. More people gathered at old Newgate to hear the outcome of this decision. Finally, the sub-sheriff came back with the news that the hanging of Duffy and Reid could proceed.

Duffy and Reid, who had been convicted at the Dublin Quarter Sessions for a burglary of plate from a house on George's Quay, were put in a cart attended by the sheriffs while two columns of Volunteers were placed on either side of the cart and a detachment of horsemen closed both ends of the two columns.[5] In this fashion "they made a very solemn and silent procession to Stephen's Green," where the Volunteers formed a square around "the fatal tree" to prevent a "vast concourse of people" from disrupting the hanging. But the previous delays had taken their toll on Reid, aged 60, who "seemed totally absorbed in the horrors of his situation, and died in a wretchedness of mind not to be conceived." In contrast, Duffy, aged 27, maintained a calm composure to the end of the ordeal, turning to the sheriffs in reproach at "how any man could be brought to the place of execution without a clergyman." As the noose was being adjusted, he called out to a soldier in a regiment of Highlanders "to take care to put his body in the coffin." Duffy was then "turned off without any apparent concern."[6]

At the hanging of a butcher on Saturday 21 October 1780, the Volunteers ringed Stephen's Green to prevent those assembled from getting too close to the gallows. Just before Edward Kinshelagh was "launched into eternity," he declared before his family and friends his innocence of having robbed a dairyman on the North Strand. To demonstrate his innocence, he led the crowd in a prayer that "the gates of heaven might be shut against him if he was guilty." At the sight of his dead body the crowd, which had been worked up to a fever pitch of excitement and fury, broke through a phalanx of Volunteers in an effort to snatch the body and remove it to the front doorstep of the prosecutor's home, which was on the north side of the city. The sheriffs and the Volunteers reassembled with enough speed to prevent the mob from carrying out their plans and, in the aftermath of the incident, the Volunteers promised that the next body to be snatched would be dissected at the College of Surgeons.[7]

From the evidence it is not known whether Kinshelagh was innocent, but if a condemned felon declared the innocence of others who

Table 1: Hanged Count Dublin, 1780–1795
(242 executions: 199 verified and 43 unverified)

CM	Comm.: Men*	OM	Court unknown: Men
CW	Comm.: Women	OW	Court unknown: Women
DM	D.Q.S.: Men	TM	Total men hanged
DW	D.Q.S.: Women	TW	Total women hanged
KM	K.Q.S.: Men	TT	Total felons hanged
KW	K.Q.S.: Women		

Year	CM	CW	DM	DW	KM	KW	OM	OW	TM	TW	TT
1780	7	0	0	0	0	0	0	0	7	0	7
1781	8	0	0	0	0	0	0	0	8	0	8
1782	10	1	2	0	0	0	0	0	12	1	13
1783	3	1	3	0	8	0	1	0	15	0	16
1784	12	1	0	0	0	0	8	1	20	2	22
1785	6	0	4	1	19	0	3	0	32	1	33
1786	6	0	2	0	11	3	0	0	9	3	22
1787	8	0	2	1	7	0	0	0	17	1	18
1788	6	0	4	0	6	1	0	0	16	1	17
1789	5	0	7	0	3	0	0	0	15	0	15
1790	7	0	4	0	2	0	2	0	15	0	15
1791	1	0	4	0	5	0	0	0	10	0	10
1792	5	0	2	0	4	0	0	0	11	0	11
1793	9	0	3	2	6	0	3	0	21	2	23
1794	0	0	3	0	4	0	0	0	7	0	7
1795	0	1	1	0	3	0	0	0	4	1	5
Total	93	4	41	4	78	4	17	1	229	13	242

*The court, where two felons convicted of mail robbery were tried, was the King's Bench, which oversaw the proceedings of the Commission of Oyer and Terminer. (Source: *Hibernian Journal, Walker's Hibernian Magazine, Dublin Evening Post, Freeman's Journal*, Prisoners' petitions and cases.)

had been falsely accused, this was taken far more seriously. On Saturday 23 December 1780, George Lowe delivered a written declaration to a sheriff before he was hanged at Stephen's Green.[8] In his dying letter, Lowe acknowledged his guilt in a burglary of a Mr Norclift's house at Glasnevin, for which he had been convicted at the Commission of Oyer and Terminer in the same month.[9] (In 1729, the King's Bench created the Commission of Oyer and Terminer as a criminal court within the Court of King's Bench.[10] A judge from the King's Bench almost always presided over the criminal court, but the

Recorder of the Dublin Quarter Sessions occasionally presided over it as well. Although the term commission suggests a special inquiry on certain dates, the court was regularly sitting three times a year by the late eighteenth century.) In addition, Lowe declared that another man named Hall Fitzsimons was innocent of a separate house burglary. The previous July, the Commission of Oyer and Terminer had convicted Hall Fitzsimons of a burglary of plate from a Miss Hamilton in Glasnevin and sentenced him to death.[11] As no report of his hanging has ever been found, one may assume that the dying declaration exonerating him was taken seriously.

While Stephen's Green was a popular location for hangings, many others took place at a spot directly east of the Green, opposite a quarry along Baggot Street or the "Ball's-bridge Road" as it was sometimes called. While the high sheriffs considered this area a suitable ground for executions, it is unlikely that the residents shared the same opinion. A fire, which consumed 130 loads of hay opposite a gallows erected in the "Ball's-bridge Road," was caused by people carelessly smoking pipes under a rick of hay while watching the execution of a woman on Saturday 2 March 1782.[12] (The woman was found guilty of murdering her husband at the Commission of Oyer and Terminer in February 1782 and was hanged despite her sentence being initially respited at the recommendation of the jury.)[13] The fire at the hanging was put out by engines from St. Anne's parish.

In 1782 the number of hangings began to increase. On Saturday 20 July 1782, five men were hanged at or near Stephen's Green, in the largest group hanging that year.[14] More than three months later, huge crowds came to see the hangings of Thomas Heney and John Murray. A rumour circulated around town that the executioner was a woman.[15] Heney and Murray were convicted at the Dublin Quarter Sessions of the burglary of the home of George McCutchen, a timber merchant on Ellis Quay.[16] The two men were members of the same gang, many of whom were executed within weeks of each other. Despite the size of the gang and the number of their crimes, the community directed their fury against the alleged woman executioner. It was alleged that the high sheriffs had paid her an "unusual sum" of money for hanging the men. She was even denounced as "an outrage against the sex ... a proof of barbarism."[17] There were no further reports of women executioners, which suggests that this practice fell into disrepute.

Anger against keeping the gallows on the south side boiled over in the wake of a violent body-snatching riot on Saturday 21 December 1782. It was to be the last hanging in Stephen's Green, with the exception of a singular execution in August 1784, before the gallows were moved to the front of Newgate prison. Like other body-snatching riots, it involved a man well-known among the local criminal fraternity. Patrick Dougherty, a wine porter, was the leader of a large gang reported to have committed several armed robberies. At 10 o'clock at night on Tuesday 13 August 1782, Dougherty and George Coffey, both armed with pistols, robbed Thomas Moran, a wine merchant who lived on Lower Ormond Quay. The robbery occurred on Bachelor's Walk. They took his watch, seal, key, a pen-knife, a pair of silver shoe-buckles and his shoes.

During the incident, Moran was able to get a good look at the two men in the evening light of summer so that on Friday night, 4 October, Moran spotted Coffey on Bachelor's Walk.[18] Coffey was taken to prison and questioned for two hours until he confessed to the whereabouts of his leader. On the following day, Dougherty, "Captain of the Miscreants," was arrested at his lodgings in Abbey Street. Pistols and powder were found in his possession.[19] In December, at the Commission of Oyer and Terminer, Moran testified that Dougherty and Coffey robbed him at gun point of goods worth nearly £15. Having offered no defence, Dougherty was convicted (no report of Coffey's sentence appears) and sentenced to hang only three days later.[20] At the hanging, the Dublin Volunteers turned out in force to prevent a threatened outbreak of violence. They managed to keep the crowds back until after the hanging, when Dougherty's family and friends broke through a wall of men to rescue the body, which they defiantly carried to the house of his prosecutor, Moran.

In hot pursuit, a detachment of Volunteers rushed to Lower Ormond Quay, snatched the body back from the crowd, ran with it to the front gate of Trinity College and offered it to the professors of anatomy for dissection. In the end, the porters slammed the front door of the College in their faces. Afterwards, the family and friends of Dougherty recovered his body, whereby it was "taken for burial."[21] Although they did not succeed in their plan, the Volunteers' response to the mob's action illustrates the pervasive attitude of the propertied classes towards the common people. It also illustrates how science and medicine had become linked to the propertied classes and the punishment of hanging.[22] Surgeons were regarded with suspicion as their dissections prevented families and friends of deceased felons from waking their bodies.

No better example of the prevailing attitude towards the bodies of felons can be found than in a letter which appeared in the *Hibernian Journal*. The letter, written by "Heister," urged Parliament to pass legislation giving the right to amputate the limbs of convicted felons while still alive. The limbs would then be transplanted onto soldiers or sailors. Dated 15 June 1787, the letter was addressed to the College of Surgeons.

[I]f in this age means could be devised, by trying experiments upon our fellow creatures, who are become so hostile to society, as to be made by the laws of their country shocking examples of public justice; by amputating the limb of one man, and replacing it with the limb amputated from another; as the unhappy creatures are dead in law, good may result from evil, by the legislative tolerating to make experiments upon them, with a promise of a free pardon ... I am sure men and women of the same description in Ireland, would be better pleased to be given while alive for surgical improvements, the law concurring and granting a pardon should the experiment succeed ... I will suppose, government favouring the experiment, two operators with their assistants and apparatus apply the tourniquets upon the left or right thighs of two men or women, or a man and women if their limbs are proportioned, they are with two long bladed catlings to plunge the points seven inches below the parts, the limbs are to be taken off in oblique directions, upwards, forwards, and downwards, until the points penetrate the bones, they are to revolve the points round the skin, bringing the heels, the parts, the points, first entered, making neat circular flaps converging from the edges round the bones, the points of the catlings revolved; they are to retract the flaps, saw the bones, change the limbs, immersing them in warm water, sponge the blood, and unite the bones, they are with small pliers to draw the mouths of the crural arteries together, giving the pliers to their assistants, while they unite them by the glovers suture, uniting the rest of the great blood vessels in like manner ... the patients [convicts] will be thrown into violent convulsions; but these considerations should not prevent them [doctors] persisting in the experiment ... The bones and muscles not uniting, the nerves and veins not inosculating, the flaps growing flabby and mortifying, and discharging a foetid ichor absorbing in the mass, contaminating the blood and juices, the patients growing hectic and convulsed, under these melancholy circumstances, it will be a pleasing reflection to them, that their lives are prolonged for offering up prayers to their Almighty Redeemer, that their mal-practice are expiated for transgressing the law; and that by dying fervent in spirit, they may expect eternal salvation. Although many lives may be lost in its attainment, they will be more than sufficiently compensated by the high advantage resulting to our fleets and armies.[23]

In the aftermath of the Dougherty hanging, the Lord Lieutenant ordered that hangings were to take place on the city's north side, at the front door of Newgate prison in Green Street from January 1783. Thus ended the centuries-old hanging processions in the city. The decision was not made on the spur of the moment. In December 1781, a year earlier, there was a proposal to move the place of execution to Newgate because "the dress and apparatus of it ... makes an impression on the mind."[24] As a penal institution Newgate was a complete failure, but as a venue for public hanging spectacles it became an immediate success. From January 1783, convicted felons were hanged high up against a prison wall facing eastwards where turrets jutted out on both sides. The spectacle created was far more dramatic than any seen at Stephen's Green. Friends and family lost any power they once had and were reduced to helpless spectators, jostling for position amongst the thousands of strangers. Meanwhile, the hangman held the power in his hand: an iron lever which, when pulled, opened the false step on the platform to plunge the condemned felon to his or her death.

Ironically, the decision to move the gallows was justified on the grounds that hanging processions had become too public an affair and that nothing was to be gained by "bringing unhappy wretches through a city, amid the sighs, and too often the commendation, pity, and tears of the common people."[25] In reality, the location of the new gallows was far more accessible to the "common people" as Green Street was surrounded by small shops and in close proximity to one of the biggest food markets in Dublin, the Ormond fruit and vegetable market. Tens of thousands of people took time off from their shopping or selling to descend on Green Street and observe the hangings.

Patrick Lynch was the first felon to be hanged at the new gallows on Saturday 4 January 1783. Only the day before, he had been tried at the Dublin Quarter Sessions and convicted under the 1778 Chalking Act for robbing one Mr Dowling and firing two pistol shots at his face.[26] (The Chalking Act was first passed in 1774 and made it a felony to kill or maim with intent to do so. Those convicted under it were to suffer death without benefit of the clergy, a medieval term which came to mean loss of legal recourse. In 1778, the Chalking Act was amended and those convicted under it were to have their bodies, after hanging to death, delivered to the surgeons in Dublin or the anatomists at Trinity College, Dublin for dissection or anatomisation.)[27]

In Patrick Lynch's case, Counsellor Masset argued that the defendant's pistol had gone off by accident and hence his crime did not come within the meaning of the Chalking Act, which specifically requires proof of intent. When this line of argument was flatly rejected, Masset asked Samuel Bradstreet to arrest the judgement against Lynch. The defence counsellor wanted to present his arguments before the 12 judges of the King's Bench for their decision as to whether justice was being served in Lynch's case. After consideration, Bradstreet turned down Masset's request and sentenced his client to death.[28] A member of a large gang, Lynch had been tried for several robberies, including the burglary of George McCutchen's house.

With fewer than 24 hours between Lynch's trial and his hanging, city scavengers had no time to clean up the streets surrounding Green Street "as not a creature could get a sight of that spectacle without being over their ankles in mire."[29] When Lynch appeared on the front steps of Newgate, the executioner tied a noose round his neck with the rope attached to a mechanical apparatus on the first landing. Lynch was suddenly hoisted up in the air by a pulley affixed to the window just above the front door. The body swung from noon till four in the afternoon, during which time thousands of people pressed forward from the streets leading into Green Street to view the spectacle. Many adjoining streets were made impassable throughout the entire day. After the hanging, his body was cut down and delivered over to the surgeons for dissection. As a result of criticisms of Lynch's hanging, it was decided not to hoist convicts up "like woolsacks" or to suspend their bodies for more than an hour at future hangings.[30]

Work began on the construction of an elaborate iron platform attached to the middle first-floor window of Newgate, overlooking

Green Street.[31] In March 1783, the modified machine in the gallows was completed. Meanwhile, local Dublin wits, who used to call the gallows on Baggot Street a "picture frame" and "puzzling sticks," now called the new gallows at the front of Newgate the "city crane" and the "fall of the leaf."[32] The gaoler at Newgate had copied the new drop platform from the gaoler at Kilmainham, who employed such a device to hang three men at Gallows Hill (the site on which Kilmainham gaol now stands) on Saturday 18 January 1783.[33] The deaths of the three felons upon the sudden release of the false bottom were deemed "much easier" than the death suffered by Lynch.[34]

Newgate's second victim, the first felon to be hanged from a new drop platform, was Patrick Mathews, aged 20. Mathews had been a member of a gang led by Nicholas Nugent. The gang, which included Peter O'Hara and John Larney, committed many robberies in Dublin. In July of that year, the Commission of Oyer and Terminer convicted Nugent, Larney and O'Hara and sentenced them to death.[35] The three men were hanged in Stephen's Green on Saturday 11 August 1781. Mathews escaped a certain death by fleeing to England, where he disguised himself as a naval officer. He was still wanted in Dublin, however, for the same robbery of which Nugent had been convicted—stealing £200 from a carman named McKennan in a Dublin whiskey cellar.[36] In September 1782, Mathews was arrested at a "ragfair" in England and charged not only with the £200 robbery, but also with the murder of a Mrs Rigmaiden of Co. Meath in June 1781.[37] He was conveyed to Dublin, where he was identified by McKennan at Newgate prison.

At his trial for the robbery (he was not indicted for the Rigmaiden murder) in early March 1783, Mathews was not permitted to testify before the jury at the Commission of Oyer and Terminer. Nevertheless, he was convicted and sentenced to death on Saturday 8 March. After his conviction, serious doubts arose about whether justice had been served at his trial. Having successfully appealed for an arrest of judgement, counsel for Mathews entreated the King's Bench to consider whether a "subject can with any safety go to trial if he is precluded from the benefit the Law allows him of proving an *Alibi*, and take every other fair advantage of the Crown in pleading, which ought to be allowed the Prisoner?"

Needing more time to debate this question, the King's Bench pushed back the Mathews hanging to the following Saturday. The

Lord's Chief Justices, however, did not inform the hangman of their decision to postpone the hanging until the last minute. Meanwhile, Mathews had prepared himself for the worst:

> Without seeming any Ways impenitent or hardened, he prayed alternatively, had two Boys read to him, eat heartily, recited his Adventures chearfully [*sic*], and confessed the Justice of his Sentence; He seemed to have no Dread of Death; and when the Account of his Respite was communicated, did not discover a single Extravagance of Joy. Such a character bred up in Virtue, and in a more dignified Station, might challenge the Fortitude of Sir Thomas Moore, and the Resignation of Anne Boleyne.[38]

In the end, the King's Bench did not find fault with the Commission's original ruling. On Saturday 15 March, Mathews prepared once again to meet his death. His second walk to the gallows proved far more difficult than the first. His earlier respite "was productive of very great distraction, he declaring to the last, that he was, on the day first appointed for his execution, much better prepared for another world."[39] The hangman tied the noose around Mathews' neck, pulled the lever and the false metal bottom opened wide to fell its first victim. Mathews dropped like a stone and died instantly.[40] A pick-pocket was detected amongst the large crowds attending the novel hanging and was given a severe ducking at Ormond Quay.[41]

Over two consecutive weekends in August 1783, five people were hanged, four men and a boy, all likely members of the same gang. Tens of thousands of people descended on Green Street to see the hangings. The first hanging day involved two men who were no strangers to the courts. One was Christopher Burgess, who had been arrested in Red Cow Lane in November 1782 by Michael Toole, the under-gaoler of Newgate. Disguised as a countryman, Burgess was found with 17 false keys and pick-locks in his possession and was charged with the burglary of a home in Channel Row.[42] In December 1782, at the Commission of Oyer and Terminer, he was convicted and sentenced to serve in the navy.[43] But a month later, the American War of Independence ended and the process of demobilisation began for thousands of men, including Burgess and other convicted men, who were discharged by the navy on the Dublin quays in February 1783.[44]

After his two-month absence from Dublin, Burgess began to commit crimes again. In March, he was charged with the burglary of a hatter in Temple Bar.[45] In July 1783, at the Dublin Quarter Sessions, he and an accomplice named Patrick Godfrey were convicted of robbing tobacco and wine from Simon Christie's warehouse in Church Street.[46] Burgess attempted to escape from prison by sawing off his irons, but George Roe, keeper of Newgate, managed to secure him in time.[47] On Saturday 2 August, Burgess and Godfrey were hanged, but the executioner failed to adjust the noose properly around the neck of Godfrey. Burgess died instantly, but it took Godfrey 25 minutes to die. He clung onto the body of Burgess for most of the time, but his strength eventually gave out before a crowd estimated at 10,000 people, their "feelings … during this shocking conflict … better conceived than described."[48] While the newspaper may have exaggerated the number of people at the hanging, the details of the event seem too compelling an account to be an over-exaggeration of the torture and trauma suffered by the felon and the crowd.

On Saturday 9 August, two men and a boy—James Egan, one Woods and John Short (aged 14)—were executed at Newgate before an "immense multitude."[49] In July 1783, Egan and Short had been convicted at the Commission of Oyer and Terminer for the robbery of James Moore Davis (the details surrounding the trial of Woods are not known).[50] The Davis robbery in December 1782 led to the formation of the Blackrock Felons Association in the same month. At the hanging, the crowd was shocked at the sight of John Short, so "small in stature," and a "universal and loud … shriek" filled Green Street. Short, it was said, was one of the youngest and smallest persons ever to have been hanged in Dublin.[51]

In the execution madness that gripped Dublin in the mid-1780s, at least eight innocent men were hanged. On Saturday 20 March 1784, Hugh Feeney and John Murphy were executed at Gallows Hill, just minutes before the hangman received word that the Lord Lieutenant had reprieved the two from execution. "They were instantly cut down, but the lamp of life being extinguished, every effort used for their recovery proved ineffectual."[52] This unfortunate event must have been viewed with great concern by the legal establishment, given the publicity surrounding it. Feeney and Murphy had been convicted at the Commission of Oyer and Terminer for the burglary of Luke Gardiner's house in Phoenix Park.[53] In January 1784, while Gardiner was away in London, a gang numbering 14 people organised a convoy of carts to remove a vast quantity of possessions, including valuable clothing, from Gardiner's house.[54] After Feeney and Murphy were sentenced in March 1784, serious doubts arose about the safety of the conviction. A respite order delayed their hangings from 15 to 20 March. The subsequent reprieve indicates that new evidence had exonerated the men from any guilt in the crime.

Four months later, Gallows Hill was the scene of another hanging of three innocent men. This mistake, however, only came to light over a year later. In January 1784, Mr Magrath was robbed of his watch, coat, and buckles at the Royal Hospital wall. The robbers made Magrath recite the Lord's prayer before one of them attempted to stab him.[55] Henry Binns, John Mullen and his brother Peter Mullen were convicted of the robbery and were executed at Gallows Hill on Saturday 24 July 1784. Before they were hanged, the three men "in the most solemn manner, declared their innocence."[56]

Their innocence was attested to about 15 months later, when John Hugan acknowledged that he had robbed Magrath and had prevented one of his accomplices from killing him. In a written statement given to the sheriffs on Saturday 22 October 1785 just before his hanging, along with Daniel Devay and William Shanley for the robbery of Thomas Bolts on Glasnevin Road in August 1785, Hugan declared that his gang had carried out the Magrath robbery and that Henry Binns and the two Mullen brothers had nothing to do with it.[57] Hugan's statement disturbed many critics of the harsh penal code. In 1785, approximately 33 people were hanged in Dublin, compared to 22 in the previous year. One critic argued that Hugan's letter "should serve as a warning both to jurors and prosecutors not to be too positive in cases where the life of a man is concerned."[58] In short, five innocent men were hanged at Gallows Hill in a space of four months in 1784.

Three innocent men were hanged in January 1785, but the evidence took seven months to come to light. On Saturday 23 July 1785, Thomas Cartwright, Michael Shoughnessy, Jeremiah Reily, Charles Fallon and James McMahon were hanged at Gallows Hill.[59] The details of the trials of the last four are not clear, but it seems they had robbed Mr Hanlon's bleach green at Bluebell. We only know for certain that the Kilmainham Quarter Sessions convicted Cartwright of robbing Mr Monaghan's bleach green at Kimmage.[60] Attended by two Catholic priests, the five men confessed to many burglaries, including the burglary of both Christian Nash's house in Kimmage and Thomas

Murphy's house in Kilmacud, each situated beyond the southern boundaries of the city. Three men had already been hanged for these crimes at Gallows Hill on Saturday 22 January 1785. The three—Edward Doyle, Roger Mathews and Nicholas Eager—had indeed declared their innocence till their dying breath.[61] Meanwhile the hanging of the five men on Saturday 23 July 1785 went badly wrong as their body weight proved too much strain on the gallows, causing it to collapse as soon as the drop platform was released. While the men lay "half strangled on the ground," the executioner was determined to continue on with the business: he hanged them in separate bunches.[62] Two of the bodies were still in a stable on the following day without kin to bury them.[63]

In addition to the eight innocent men hanged at Gallows Hill between March 1784 and January 1785, at least two other innocent men were hanged at the front of Newgate prison in April 1791. Chief Inspector William Shea arrested a returned convict named Garret Ryan for robbing Jonathan Taylor of his bank notes, cash, a hat and watch, all amounting to £70, in Thomas Street in March 1791.[64] It is not clear what became of Ryan, but Shea may have obtained false information from him. In early April 1791, the Dublin Quarter Sessions convicted Laurence Lynch and John McDermot of the Taylor robbery and both were sentenced to hang at the front of Newgate prison on Saturday 23 April 1791.[65] While the two men steadfastly maintained their innocence of the crime for which they were to suffer, they admitted many other crimes "for which they deserved death."[66]

Confirmation of their innocence came to light in the form of a dying declaration long after their execution. In September 1792, just as he was about to be hanged, a convicted felon named George Robinson admitted that he had robbed Jonathan Taylor and that Lynch and McDermot had been entirely innocent of the crime.[67] He also admitted to robbing Mr Fagan's house in Co. Westmeath, thereby exonerating a convicted felon named Sullivan, who was hanged at Mullingar for the crime. In all, the evidence indicates that at least 10 men were innocent of the crimes for which they were hanged, representing five per cent of the verified hangings in the 16-year period.

In addition, many convicted felons were hanged for the most trivial offences. An examination of one case indicates that the courts adopted tougher sentencing practices for repeat offenders. In September 1781, the Dublin Quarter Sessions convicted Margaret Savage of stealing 18 yards of black calico worth about £2, the property of Elizabeth Conway. Savage was sentenced to prison for three years. Less than a year later on 21 August 1782 she, together with 29 female and 2 male offenders in prison with her, petitioned the Lord Lieutenant for a royal pardon. Almost all the protesting prisoners had recently been convicted of property theft, mainly of clothing. Acting on the petition, the clerks of the peace noted that Savage and the 31 others listed in the petition had " showed signs of reformation and contrition." [68]

Five years later, however, Savage committed another theft and on this occasion her luck turned against her. In September 1787, she and a 15-year-old male accomplice robbed a second-hand rag vendor named Mary Purcell of 18 shillings at pistol-point.[69] In the following month, the Dublin Quarter Sessions sentenced her to hang at the front of Newgate prison on Saturday 17 November 1787.[70] (Her hanging conflicted with the state funeral procession of the Duke of Rutland. This prompted the *Hibernian Journal* to report that Savage's "wretched situation seemed to have less effect upon her than the neglect of the populace, in not gracing her exit with their appearance on so deplorable an occasion.")[71]

Four years after the Savage hanging, the Dublin Quarter Sessions hanged another felon for a minor theft. In December 1791, Denis George, the Recorder of the Dublin Quarter Sessions, heard the case of an English sailor named John Philips who was indicted for robbing Patrick McGowen of his coat and hat. At trial, the jury convicted the mariner, but recommended him as an object of mercy "in the consideration of the apparent severity in depriving a wretch of life for so trivial a robbery."[72] The Recorder ignored the recommendation of the jury and sentenced him to death.

Philips, aged 50, lived in London with his wife and five children and, with no family or friends in Dublin, had been unable to raise the necessary cash to employ counsel for his defence. A month after his conviction, he managed to find the means to have a petition drawn up and sent to the Lord Lieutenant, appealing for mercy on the grounds that he had been intoxicated at the time of the robbery and showed no criminal intent. The Lord Lieutenant would in all probability have respited his hanging if he had received it in time. On the back of the petition was written, "has any thing been done in this?" A stark answer followed, "was executed the 14th—Received 31st Jan 1792."[73] Philips was hanged at the front of Newgate on Saturday 14 January 1792.

Neither guilt nor innocence nor the triviality of the crime committed seemed to matter much to the crowds who flocked to Green Street to see the hanging machine devour one felon after another. On Saturday 15 October 1785, a huge throng turned out to see the execution of James Ennis, who was convicted of killing his mother with a razor. During the hanging, a number of people "impelled by the weight of the crowd, fell into a cellar, and many of them were danger ously hurt."[74] Shortly after the Ennis hanging the courts took some short-lived steps to put an end to the public spectacles in Green Street, which were now dangerously out of control. Three changes were introduced: the gallows were moved from the platform at the front of Newgate to the inside court within the walls of the prison, the public was not allowed to enter the prison at the time of the hangings, and the hangings took place only in the presence of the remaining convicted felons, the judges and city sheriffs.[75]

The first two men to be hanged within the walls of Newgate were William Ready and Maurice Fitzgerald, convicted of separate robberies. In early October 1785, Ready was arrested for the burglary of eight coach windows at Richard Daly's stables in Drumcondra.[76] Also arrested was Thomas Deacon, charged with receiving the stolen glasses. Both were committed to Newgate to face trial.[77] Later in the month, the Commission of Oyer and Terminer convicted both of them, sentencing Deacon to prison for 12 months and Ready to death.[78] As for Fitzgerald, his gang had robbed Robert Ahmuty, a merchant in Dublin, and two other people with him on Santry Road in early September 1785. The Dublin Volunteers managed to secure one of the gang, who was committed to Newgate.[79] At the end of the month, Alderman Richard Moncrieffe arrested Fitzgerald, but charged him with the burglary of a quilt owned by James Gillsenear.[80] In the end, the Commission of Oyer and Terminer convicted Fitzgerald for the robbery of Ahmuty and sentenced him to death.[81] Ready and Fitzgerald were due to hang on Saturday 5 November 1785, but whether the sentences were carried out remained a mystery until a report appeared in the *Hibernian Journal* two weeks later citing the "good effects" of the private executions of the two men as "a very inconsiderable croud [*sic*], if compared with those on former occasions, attended." [82]

The practice of hanging people inside Newgate without any publicity came under heavy criticism almost immediately. Arguing against "the omission of the usual notoriety as to day and hour," a critic praised "the salutary consequences resulting to society from the terror which public executions impress on minds prone to evil."[83] Eventually such criticism put pressure on a prominent Dublin judge to call for the restoration of public executions. Charging a grand jury at the Commission of Oyer and Terminer in May 1785, Judge Robinson condemned the "private manner . . . [of execution which] divested it of its horrors." Robinson claimed that public executions were "productive of more awe and terror in the breasts of evil-doers" than private executions.[84] This was followed up by calls for "the awful preliminaries which ought to attend public executions."[85] Meanwhile, the Police Act of 1786 provided fresh impetus for a tougher attitude against crime. In December 1786, public executions returned to Green Street.

Hangings in Co. Dublin were widely publicised before, during and after the short-lived ban in the city. In November 1785, John Farrell broke into the cabin of John Browne, aged between 80 and 90, grabbed the old man and held him over an open fire to make him confess where his money was kept.[86] The heat from the fire was so intense that one of his eyes started to fall out.[87] At the Commission of Oyer and Terminer, Alderman William James suggested that Farrell be hanged near the site of the crime on Tallaght Hill.[88] Farrell was indeed a dangerous offender. At a previous Commission of Oyer and Terminer he had been convicted of assaulting two girls, needle-makers in Cook Street, and sentenced to two months in prison where, it was alleged, he planned the burglary of Browne.[89] On Saturday 31 December 1785, Farrell was hanged and gibbeted at the Seven Mile Stone.[90] On the morning of his execution, a troop of horse guards from the garrison escorted him to Tallaght Hill, where thousands, including many from the surrounding counties, waited to see him hang.[91] A farmer from Blessington, Co. Wicklow was robbed of 18 shillings by a gang of highwaymen on his way home from the execution. Along with another farmer, the victim pursued the gang to Hollywood Glen, below Blessington, but they escaped.[92]

A similar execution had taken place on Gallows Hill only three months earlier. In September 1785, Robert Jameson stabbed to death James Kelly, a mathematician and a stone-cutter, in a bleach green near Chapelizod. A coroner's inquest returned a verdict of wilful murder.[93] Jameson attempted to flee the area, but Lieutenant Stevenson, a member of the Dublin Volunteers, captured him at a distance of 20 miles from Dublin.[94] He had Kelly's watch in his possession.[95] An elegy, composed in memory of Kelly, appeared in the *Hibernian Journal* on 26 September:

> Friend of my infant years, alas! too late,
> Accept the tribute tender friendship pays;
> Ah! who can stop the harsh decrees of fate,
> Or trace its mazy dark mysterious ways!!
>
> With thee full many a studious hour I spent,
> Ranging the vernal fields of classic lore;
> And sought the pleading light that SCIENCE lent,
> When still they happier genius ran before.
>
> Now thou'st fallen!—thy gentle spirit fled!—
> Fallen by the ruffian hand of murdering force!
> Who knew thee living, must lament thee dead!
> And weep the end of thy ill-fated course!
>
> Ah! what avails it that in early youth,
> When emulation fir'd the rising mind,
> We drew the puzzling lines of mystic truth,
> And many a fellow student left behind.
>
> Or sometimes, when the sun with parting rays,
> Sent forth our shadows on the level ground,
> We mark'd the insects in the solar blaze,
> With the eager eyes and rhapsody profound.
>
> The same concerns in life we both pursu'd;
> Together studied, and together grew;
> With the same talents were we both endu'd,
> Equall'd by many, yet excell'd by few.
>
> A long farewell be to thy sable shrowd;
> Thy guiltless blood aloud to Heaven shall call,
> For speedy vengeance on the murderers' head
> That caus'd, alas! thy too untimely fall.[96]

In March 1786, the Commission of Oyer and Terminer convicted

Jameson and on Saturday 18 March, he was hanged on Gallows Hill and his body was gibbetted on a tall wooden beam.[97] Over a week later, the gibbet was chopped down, but the gaoler of Kilmainham re-erected it.[98] Three weeks after the hanging, the gibbet was again attacked, but on this occasion the wooden beam on which the gibbet was nailed was dragged down the hill and thrown into the River Liffey and his corpse was stripped of its irons and buried in a shallow grave on Gallows Hill.[99]

Hanging days in Green Street caused considerable chaos for local residents. In March 1785, some of the residents petitioned Dublin Castle to remove the place of execution from Green Street to the rear of the prison.[100] Over the next few years, the local community kept up their opposition to the gallows at regular intervals. Complaints were often voiced in the wake of hangings that went badly wrong. One such execution was that of Patrick Malone on Saturday 27 October 1792. He had been convicted at the Dublin Quarter Sessions of the robbery of June Haughton.[101]

In preparing the correct length of rope for the hanging, the hangman assumed that Malone was lighter than he really was. When the hangman released the false bottom to the gallows, Malone dropped farther than the rope's strength would allow. The rope snapped on the uptake, plunging him onto the steps of Newgate with the noose tight around his neck. While Malone was loosening the noose, soldiers standing guard at the gallows fired their rifles into the air to prevent a possible rescue attempt on the condemned man. Thousands of people turned foot and stampeded through the narrow streets. One spectator was killed and many others were injured. Malone was carried back into Newgate alive, where it was decided to draw up a petition to have his sentence respited and this was immediately despatched to the Lord Lieutenant for his signature. But Malone's plea for mercy was rejected on the grounds that no appeal on his behalf had been made before. At his second hanging, a shorter length of rope was fed into the machine and this time the rope did not break.[102]

As many as 22 people were hanged in 1793, compared with 9 in the previous year, a dramatic increase of nearly 150 per cent. In the same year, Dublin saw the effects of a severe food shortage and the onset of the French wars. In April 1793, several riots and mutinies occurred in the city as military parties began to recruit young men to serve in the French wars.[103] In addition, a number of food riots swept the Liberties throughout the summer as hungry people looted food supplies coming into the city from the country.[104] Dublin was not alone in facing a severe economic recession and war panic in 1793; a French invasion scare also swept London in 1793. As a result, two innocent men were hanged, drawn and quartered in London on the mere suspicion of their being members of a society which advocated republican ideas.[105]

In Dublin, the government organised a massive hunt for a group of Defenders, a recently formed republican organisation,[106] who were alleged to have murdered a prominent counsellor named William Grady.[107] On Monday night, 11 March 1793, Grady was robbed of his purse by five men in Park Street near Lower Merrion Street. One of the robbers shot him with a pistol and he died of his wounds four days later.[108] Grady was apparently a member of the Volunteers, who attended his body to St. James's church.[109] Several men were captured in Co. Wicklow and Co. Offaly. On Friday 28 June 1793, the Commission of Oyer and Terminer convicted John Delany and Laurence Penrose and the latter's brother Patrick Penrose, both of whom were Quakers, of the murder of Grady.[110] The Commission of Oyer and Terminer also convicted Edward Boyce, who was connected with the Defenders, for firing a loaded pistol at a policeman with intent to kill.[111] Four days later, the four men were hanged under the Murder Act of 1791, which ruled that convicted murderers must be hanged within four days of their trial.[112] Boyce and Delany were hanged together, followed by the two Penrose brothers who, "before they were turned off, took an affecting leave of each other."[113]

In the turbulent events of the mid-1790s, Newgate saw many more hangings designed to deter the growth of the Defenders.[114] In December 1795, for example, the Commission of Oyer and Terminer convicted James Weldon, a member of the Meath Defenders who had infiltrated a militia regiment in Dublin.[115] On Wednesday 2 March 1796, Weldon was executed at the front of Newgate prison before thousands of people, "numerous beyond example." After he was hanged, his body was drawn back up onto the platform for decapitation, where the hangman made "many ineffectual strokes of the axe and applications of the knife," before holding the "head of a traitor" before the crowds.[116] Such examples of repression most likely prevented the Defenders from gaining a wide following in Dublin.[117]

An examination of the Dublin hanged sheds light on the evolution of law and order in Dublin. In the 16 years between 1780 and 1795, as many as 242 convicted felons were hanged in the city and county of Dublin, an average of 15 hangings per year. The number of annual hangings increased steadily up to 1787, after which they began to decrease. In 1793, the hanged count rose upward to its mid-1780s height. The hanged count describes a pattern consistent with the economic fluctuations and the effects of war and peace during this time. A subsistence crisis seriously affected living conditions for poor people in Dublin from 1782 to 1784.[118] At the same time, the American War of Independence came to an end in 1783 and thousands of de-mobilised troops considerably swelled the population of the city. Both these factors contributed to an increase in social disruption and crime in the early to mid-1780s.

Dublin was comparable to London for the number of hangings in this period. Between 1783 and 1787, the Old Bailey in London was responsible for the hangings of 348 convicted felons, up 82 per cent over the previous five years.[119] The Surrey assizes hanged 42 felons in 1783, 1784 and 1785, compared with the hangings of only seven felons in the three previous years, a huge increase of 500 per cent.[120] The three Dublin courts hanged approximately 71 felons in 1783, 1784 and 1785, compared with the hangings of 28 felons in the three previous years, a sharp increase of 154 per cent. One year in particular stands out above the rest. In 1785 the number of hangings reached an all-time record: the Old Bailey hanged 97 felons, the Surrey assizes hanged 23 felons, compared with only 11 the year before, and the three Dublin courts hanged as many as 33 felons, compared with 22 in the previous year.

By 1787, the number of hangings in Dublin began to slacken. Dublin's new police force completed their first full year of operation in that year. The hanged count briefly surged in 1793, when approximately 23 felons were hanged, but this was a year in which food riots and mutinies of enlisted soldiers swept the city. By 1795, the number of hangings was reduced to its lowest level in 16 years.

The Commission of Oyer and Terminer hanged more felons than the other two courts. The Kilmainham Quarter Sessions also took a severe approach towards crime, particularly under Serjeant-at-Law John Toler, who chaired the sessions from 1782 to October 1789.[121] During Toler's eight-year chairmanship, the Kilmainham Quarter Sessions convicted and hanged as many as 52 felons. The Dublin Quarter Sessions, which heard far more trials than the other two courts, hanged the least number of felons.

CHAPTER TWO

Women and Crime

Women were reported to have committed approximately 700 crimes and to have been defendants in about 485 trials in the 16 years between 1780 and 1795. Most of these crimes involved property theft, but there were some serious crimes as well. It was reported that women perpetrated over two dozen murders and attempted murders and, indeed, four women were convicted and executed for homicide.

One case in particular stands out, the murder of a young girl by her mistress. In May 1781, a dairy woman beat a 12-year-old servant girl named Molloy to death with a hammer in Charles Street. The killer, who lived in Phoenix Street, was arrested and conveyed to Newgate prison.[1] At her trial in July 1781, the Commission of Oyer and Terminer acquitted her due to lack of evidence.[2] Her acquittal did not go unnoticed. A writer condemned the acquittal in the *Hibernian Journal*, claiming the employer had paid money to buy off key prosecution witnesses and denouncing the Commission of Oyer and Terminer for not demanding security from the dairy woman for her future good conduct.[3]

Infanticide, a crime almost always perpetrated by women, claimed 34 lives between 1780 and 1795, an average of 2.1 deaths a year. Not only were the bodies of new-born infants discovered with regularity, but the bodies of small children up to the age of four-years-old were found.[4] Bridget Farrell, a wet nurse, was convicted of starving the child of one Mr Tobin, a crier for the Chancery Court, in May 1783. The Dublin Quarter Sessions sentenced Farrell to three months in gaol, fined her £20 and ordered her to be whipped three times from Kilmainham gaol to Mount Brown.[5]

In one year alone, 1790, nine infanticides were reported in Dublin. In September 1790, the body of a week-old infant was found floating in the Dodder river with 20 corking pins sticking out of its head.[6] Hired killers were regularly employed to commit infanticide. In July 1790, a hired woman succeeded in killing an infant in a field near Kevin Street by dashing it against the ground several times and breaking its bones.

She then threw the lifeless body into a ditch. Justice Robert Wilson arrested her and the mother who had hired her. They were remanded to Kilmainham gaol to stand trial, but were apparently released.[7] The failure of Dublin's three courts to prosecute the two women was not unique. Not a single woman was executed for infanticide.

Society, however, condemned infant killers and angry mobs often took the law into their own hands. In 1781, a man happened to see "an extraordinarily masculine woman" pressing a bundle with her knee into the River Liffey at Arran Quay as he watched from an upper window. Hearing an infant cry, he ran outside to rescue the child. It was discovered that the child's mother had employed the woman to kill her son. A crowd tied up the muscular female, lowered her onto a coal vessel in the river, suspended her over its side and ducked her repeatedly in the water, before allowing her to escape.[8] In October 1794, the bodies of 10-day-old twins were taken out of the Poddle Hole, where they had lain for about two days. In response, the *Hibernian Journal* condemned "their wretched and inhuman" killer for a crime "at the base idea of which the human mind revolts."[9]

In addition to infanticide, women committed suicide in the face of unwanted pregnancies and a wide variety of other misfortunes. Between 1780 and 1795, the *Hibernian Journal* reported 82 suicides—an average of 5.1 suicides per year. There were 46 male suicides and 35 female suicides. Certain years were worse than others; suicides claimed the lives of at least 28 men and women in 1788, 1789 and 1790—an average of 9.3 victims a year. The largest proportion, over 27 per cent of the suicides, were committed in the Liberties, the poorest section of the city.

In July 1781, a pregnant woman hanged herself at Loughlinstown, Co. Dublin, having been "got with child by a person in that neighbourhood."[10] Women who suffered a loss of marriage prospects also committed suicide. It is not known if some of these were pregnant at the time. In April 1786, a woman jumped to her death in the River Liffey while reportedly suffering from "a fit of disappointment in love."[11] In December 1790, a woman threw herself into the Liffey near Barrack Street, after gambling away her "little all."[12]

In December 1787, a woman, half-starved for want of food, attempted to commit suicide by throwing herself and her child into the Liffey. A policeman named Maguire stopped the woman from carrying out her plans. He conveyed her before Richard Moncrieffe, divisional justice of the Rotunda division, "who, in conjunction with the Rev Mr Anderson of Liffey Street chapel, collected a sum of money."[13]

Collections for such victims show that the police were sympathetic to suicide victims. In August 1789, Divisional Justice of the police John Carleton prevented a woman, who was "very decent looking ... but with a distress and melancholy painted in her countenance, that no language can describe," from returning to her lodgings, where only hours earlier she had been discovered hanging by the neck. After Carleton warned her "against a repetition of her crime," she was summarily committed to the House of Industry. As in the Maguire case, a collection was raised on her behalf.[14]

In December 1790, Chief Inspector William Shea investigated the death of Mary Fitzgerald, who died of self-strangulation. Fitzgerald's body was found with a ribbon tied twice round her neck in a house in Maiden Lane.[15] In August 1790, a woman poisoned herself to death, leaving a note stating that a recent love affair had failed.[16] In May 1790, a woman hanged herself after her first husband, a seaman who made contact after having disappeared years earlier, threatened to break up her second marriage. A letter he wrote to her caused a minor crisis when it got into the hands of her new husband.[17] Rather than face divorce proceedings, she hung herself with a child's rocket, thereby leaving almost no mark of violence and temporarily delaying a coroner's verdict.[18]

Both the murder and the suicide rates tended to fluctuate quite sharply. In 1788, the *Hibernian Journal* reported 12 suicides, a doubling over the previous year. This seems to have given cause for public concern, particularly among chemists who did not want to become unwittingly involved in abetting such crimes. In July 1788, a woman asked for white arsenic at an apothecary's shop. After he observed "her to sigh heavily and look dejected," her request for the deadly poison was turned down. As a warning to other apothecaries to guard against future requests of this sort, the chemist reported the episode to the *Hibernian Journal*.[19] In October 1788, there were reports of calls being made on parliament to pass legislation that would prevent people who had committed suicide from obtaining a Christian burial.[20] The evidence indicates that the same authorities allowed church burials for wealthy suicides. In other words, one's status in society had a bearing on most aspects of entitlement in Dublin, from birth to death.

Surprisingly, women were actively involved in the crime of rape;

one of only two felons who were convicted and hanged for rape was female. In July 1795, the Commission of Oyer and Terminer heard the case of Sarah Delany, aged 50, who was charged with being present, aiding and abetting a male in the rape of Ann Mathews, aged 10, in Essex Street the previous May. Before returning their verdict, the jury was anxious to find out whether the victim was a prostitute. Mr Pollock, a clerk of the crown and a juror, inspected the victim's lodgings, which were found to be vile, and questioned her parents, who were respectable people. On the first and second floors of her house in a lane near Ormond market, the family kept pigs and poultry. They lived on the third floor, which was sparsely furnished with a stool and a bed without its feathers, which had been sold to meet their bills. The victim lived with her blind father, a former Custom House porter who reportedly had lost his sight from the strain of carrying heavy loads. The victim's "general employment was to lead her father about the streets" of Dublin. The mother, who testified in court, said she had always instructed her daughter "in the duties of religion." It was thus determined that the victim was not a prostitute and had not been abandoned by her loving parents, an important consideration for the jury. In fact, the jury donated £30 to the victim and her family, which indicates that juries had the power to compensate victims of crime. As for the offender, she was found guilty and sentenced to death. On Wednesday 22 August 1795, Rev. Mr O'Brien read prayers to the condemned woman in the first-floor chapel at Newgate. She then walked through the opened chapel window onto the "fatal board" where she was "launched into eternity."[21]

By coincidence, at the same Commission of Oyer and Terminer in July 1795, a female servant named Barbara Walsh was charged with aiding and abetting in the rape of a young girl named Maria Larkin. It transpired that in the previous May, the victim, aged 11 or under, was raped in the presence of Miss Walsh before the rapist absconded.[22] At trial, the prosecution suffered from two disadvantages: the mother of Maria Larkin failed to appear in court and the girl's testimony was not allowed to be sworn under oath due to her tender years. In the end, the girl was allowed to tell the court her story. One afternoon while begging for bread, she was enticed into the house of a wealthy citizen in Smock Alley and repeatedly raped on a carpet in front of a fireplace in the kitchen with the full consent of the female servant, who could hear her screaming from an upstairs room. Indeed, the female servant locked the door of the house, thereby forcing the girl to spend the night.

Maria Larkin managed to return to her mother's lodgings in Copper Alley on the following afternoon, but did not tell her mother of the attack until symptoms of a sexually transmitted disease appeared on her body. Her mother, a shirt mender for soldiers at the garrison, thought it was a "scalding", but a surgeon who testified at the trial recognised the illness for what it was, treating it with a "course of mercury." The surgeon described her disorder as "dreadful." During most of the trial, the young girl kept her composure, but lost it at the thought of the punishment which awaited Walsh if convicted, exclaiming to the jury, " do not touch her, because it was the man that did it all to me." In the end, the jury acquitted Walsh of the rape.[23]

Many rape victims were young girls who, like Maria Larkin, were abandoned by their parents and left to their own devices. Brothel keepers organised the most vulnerable children into a fast-growing sex trade, the source of much violence in Dublin. Brothel-keepers employed brutal tactics to exploit their sex workers. In February 1781, a prostitute was murdered in the Temple Bar area, after which the parish watch called in a brothel keeper and other suspected persons for questioning.[24] In October 1781, a 17-year-old woman from Belfast was murdered at her lodgings in Stephen Street. A coroner's inquest returned a verdict of wilful murder.[25] The Belfast sex worker had refused "to accommodate" Ann McDonagh, a brothel keeper who exploited a stable of prostitutes in Little Booter Lane. Angry with the murders of two sex workers within nine months, local residents attacked McDonagh's brothel, but this apparently had little impact. In July 1782, McDonagh beat a street prostitute so badly that she lost one of her eyes.[26] This incident suggests that the parish watch system was neither strong enough nor willing to tackle the problem of prostitution. The same could also be said of the new police. In April 1791, a crowd of people destroyed "Mother" Beatly's house of ill fame in Ross Lane after a girl had been lured in by the owner. When policemen intervened to prevent further damage, the mob pelted them with stones.[27] In July 1791, soldiers pulled down at least four brothels in Fleet Lane and Crown Alley after one of the local bullies working in the sex trade taunted them.[28]

Four years later rioters attacked brothels over a two-week period in response to the above-mentioned rape of Ann Mathews. On the first night, crowds attacked brothels in Strand Street and, on the following night, brothels in Liffey Street. Four nights later, they attacked houses of ill-fame in Trinity, Cope, Fleet, and Townsend Streets.[29] A week later, a brothel in Great Ship Street was attacked.[30]

The many brothels in the city, particularly in the Temple Bar area, were the scene of violent behaviour perpetrated against the most vulnerable members of society. Young women, many of whom had migrated to Dublin from the surrounding counties, were exploited as sex workers for clients who preferred girls because they were more likely to be free of disease. Women who were enlisted in the sex industry could expect little sympathy. Convictions for the raping of prostitutes were difficult to obtain and, if they were obtained, sentences were seldom carried out. In May 1786, Richard Moncrieffe, who was to become a divisional justice of the new police five months later, arrested Mary Neal, aged 12, Morgan Donnelly, Thomas Keating and James King. The latter three were charged with raping and robbing Mary Hogg, a prostitute, near Ringsend.[31] In August 1786, the Dublin Quarter Sessions convicted and sentenced them to hang, but their sentences were never carried out, according to the *Hibernian Journal*.[32]

In July 1788, the Commission of Oyer and Terminer heard the trial of Maria Lewellin, a brothel keeper, charged with aiding and abetting in the rape of the same Mary Neal.[33] Before the trial, Robert Edgeworth, one of Lewellin's sex workers, managed to organise the arrest and imprisonment of John and Anne Neal, her father and mother, to prevent them from testifying at the trial. (Apparently, Anne Neal died in Newgate prison as a result of abuse at the hands of the gaol keeper, George Roe.)[34] Despite Edgeworth's attempt to prevent the prosecution of his one-time employer, Mary Neal's testimony was sufficient for the jury to convict Lewellin, who was sentenced to death. The safety of her conviction was called into question after allegations came to light that Neal had been a habitual sex offender. Indeed, Neal was actively engaged in criminal activity, most likely prostitution, for years before the Lewellin case, according to the crime index.[35]

Allegations that Neal was a prostitute were most likely substantiated given that the Lord Lieutenant pardoned Lewellin on the morning scheduled for her hanging in November 1788.[36] Even though Lewellin was pardoned, a conviction did arise from the Lewellin case. In the following month, the Commission of Oyer and Terminer convicted Edgeworth of "subornation of perjury." The court sentenced him to a year in gaol, two times at the pillory, and a fine.[37] Angry crowds turned out at the pillory opposite the Tholsel on both occasions. At the first punishment, Edgeworth's head and hands were locked into stocks on a purpose-built platform, providing the crowds with a good target for their rotten eggs and snow-balls.[38] In July 1789, when Edgeworth was pilloried a second time, the event turned into a confrontation between the crowds and the military. Crowds threw "rotten eggs, oranges, potatoes, old shoes, brickbats, dead cats, mud, and filth of every sort" at both Edgeworth and the soldiers who were keeping them away from the platform.[39]

After the introduction of the new police in 1786, the number of reported rapes declined sharply, and indeed no rapes were reported between 1792 and 1795. It is not known what effect the police had on rapes which occurred within the family, but at least one serious case of domestic violence occurred during this period. In July 1792, at the Commission of Oyer and Terminer, William Byrne was indicted for murdering his wife. It transpired that no murder had taken place, but that the crime he had committed could have led to death.[40] Anne Byrne was beaten with such force and frequency that when she suddenly fled from Dublin to Dundalk, she did not tell her neighbours of her whereabouts and one of them was led to believe she had been murdered. Anne's mother and sister, who came to her rescue, apparently duped a neighbour into pressing charges against the husband for murder. It would seem that they believed a certain Michael Walsh "was the only person who could bring him to justice."

On the day of the trial, much to the surprise of the judge and jury, Anne walked into the court. Even after her identity had been established, the trial continued. Bernard Madden, a neighbour who knew Byrne for only a year, testified to the extent to which Anne Byrne had suffered from her husband. Madden said he had "frequently seen her with black eyes from the ill-usage of the prisoner and has no manner of doubt but this is the woman." Madden's statement indicates that he and the other neighbours were aware of the beatings, but were not prepared to press charges against her husband for assault. After the court was satisfied that no murder had been committed, William Byrne was acquitted of the charges. Before discharging him, however, the court warned him to "take your wife home and treat her in a more becoming manner."

Indeed, women subjected to violence within the family risked intimidation and pressure if they took legal action. In August 1792,
Letitia Morgan prosecuted her son at the Dublin Quarter Sessions for
an assault. She apparently came to regret her action as she pleaded
with the judge "not to oblige her to give evidence against her unfortunate child."[41] Denis George, the Recorder of Dublin, threatened to
levy a fine on her if she did not testify. She then told the court how her
son Charles Morgan, a watch-maker, struck her on the forehead with
an iron poker, inflicting a serious injury.

At the time of the assault she "gave him no other provocation
whatsoever, than asking him why he poked out the fire." Furthermore,
Morgan "threatened to stab his sister for reproving him for his treatment to his mother."[42] Morgan offered no defence for his behaviour
nor showed any remorse, walking away from the dock "muttering new
threats against his aged parent."[43] After the jury found him guilty,
George sentenced him to six months in gaol and to keep the peace for
seven years. This was a harsh sentence by the standards of the day,
suggesting that the court wanted to make an example of Morgan.
Compared to the leniency shown by the courts towards wife-beaters,
this sentence indicates that they drew limits at mother-beating.

Whatever about outright physical attack, Dublin society during this
period seemed to tolerate low-level intimidation against women and
other weaker members of society. This intimidation sometimes took
the form of public humiliation by means of paid advertisements in the
press. In the 16 years between 1780 and 1795, the *Hibernian Journal*
published advertisements impugning the character of 10 wives, one
daughter, 14 servants, and 10 apprentices. They were singled out for
improper conduct, misbehaviour and an assortment of petty crimes.
Although this character assassination usually went unanswered, two
wives responded in kind against their husbands by placing counter-
advertisements. In September 1784, William Wilkinson warned shopkeepers not to give credit to his eloped wife.[44] Sarah Wilkinson,
however, charged her husband as a wife-beater and a thief, who had
deserted her and their four "destitute" children.[45]

An almost identical set of advertisements appeared in September
1789: John Redmond warned shopkeepers not to give credit to his
wife.[46] Driven to the necessity of defending her character publicly, Jane
Redmond defended her character in a counter-advertisement: "As there
is nothing of so much consequence to a woman as her character, I hope

I shall be acquitted in the eyes of the world in justifying mine."[47]

One of the most spectacular examples of public humiliation of a woman in the press was the case of Robert Parvisol. Four days before he was due to stand trial for assaulting his daughter, he published a long (26 inches) and scurrilous statement, in which he denied not only allegations of assault but also allegations of incest. In the public statement, he denounced the character of his daughter with the intent to prejudice the public, the judge and the jury before the trial.[48] Parvisol said this about his daughter, Anne:

> What is this daughter, so weak in point of understanding as not to be many degrees removed from a fool … this daughter, they say, I made love to, whose person from the wickedness of her heart, and deformity of her mind, was so disgusting to me, that I solemnly declare, I could look on the most forbidden of God's creations with a more favourable eye than her.[49]

Long before this letter was published, rumours of the incest had begun to circulate in their neighbourhood just north of Oxmantown Green. Anne Parvisol was evicted forcibly from her father's home and, without any means to support herself, went to live with an ex-servant in Dirty Lane. On 4 March 1785, she returned to the family home, but her father beat her on the front doorstep and then kicked her into the street in full view of neighbours. After the assault, she lodged examinations against him, which led to a trial at the Kilmainham Quarter Sessions on 8 April 1785.

Before the trial, John Toler, chairman of the Kilmainham Quarter Sessions, cleared the court-room of all women, which may have included some witnesses for the prosecution.[50] In presenting its arguments, the prosecution, led by Counsellor Smith, said that he had "the clearest and most indisputable evidence" upon which to obtain a conviction against Robert Parvisol for incest. Toler, however, charged the jury to consider only the indictable offence of assault before them and not to consider any "other circumstance." Although Parvisol was only indicted for assault, incest became the focal point of the trial. This became clear when Anne was cross-examined by the defendant's counsel:

> Q. How long is it since you left your father's?
> A. I left it in June, 1784.

Q. What was your reason for leaving your father's house? Why did you not live with him as a child should have done?

A. He forcibly turned me out, and refused to give me either support or protection.

Q. Did he assign any reason for this severity?

A. I do not know. I do not remember to have ever heard him assign any.

Q. Before you left your father's house, did he not, in a conversation with you, desire that you would tell him who were the authors of the scandalous reports propagated in the neighbourhood, that he was the father of a child of which you were then pregnant? And did he not threaten you, that, if you did not tell him, he would turn you out of doors?

A. Such conversation did pass.

Q. Did you tell him the authors?

A. No. I did not know then.

Q. Did he not ask you who was the father of the child?

A. He did.

Q. Did you tell him?

A. No!—he knew it but too well; he wanted no information on that score.

Q. And was it because you refused to answer his questions, or what else do you conceive to have been his reasons for banishing you [from] his house?

A. I believe his reason to be, because I would not agree with him in endeavouring to gloss over and hide from the world an action, which has made me for the last three years, the most wretched miserable object in God's creation, and, if he has the least compunction, the least feeling, must have stuck his own pillow also with thorns.

Not surprisingly, the jury found Robert Parvisol guilty of assault and Toler sentenced him to gaol for 30 days and fined him one mark.[51] With her father in gaol, Anne Parvisol was able to gain access to the house, which was one of her main objectives.[52]

Dublin in the late eighteenth century was a society where violent crimes against women were frequent and tolerated. In December 1790, a servant watering his master's horse near Barrack Street pulled the body of a woman from the River Liffey and laid it against a wall.

The following morning the body had been stripped of all its clothing "and remained for a considerable time stark naked, until a little straw was thrown over it." A newspaper said that this betrayed "a barbarous propensity in the manners of the common people" and called on parishes to erect mortuaries "to preserve decency on such unfortunate occasions."[53]

An estimated 97 women were murdered according to the *Hibernian Journal*. This is approximately 25 percent of all the 390 homicides reported in the newspaper during the 16-year period. In July 1788, the body of a partially dismembered woman was dumped on George's Quay. The victim had been stabbed repeatedly with a small sword, her breasts and ears cut off and her body pushed down the embankment walls into the River Liffey where it lay unmoved by the tide. Alderman John Exshaw conducted a coroner's inquest and returned a verdict of wilful murder.[54] No more was heard about this crime in the newspaper, but it is clear that Dublin had a serious problem with violent crimes against women.

It was reported that 12 husbands murdered their wives, but in many other cases it was not clear how the victims met their deaths. Indictments were never easy to obtain in murder cases. In October 1780, a coroner was informed that the body of a woman who had been buried only a week earlier was the victim of a murder. Hugh Carmichael, the coroner, exhumed the woman's body from a freshly dug grave at a church yard in Killester, beyond the northern outskirts of Dublin.[55] An inquest discovered marks of violence on her neck, shoulders and breasts, indicating that she had been strangled to death. Although the inquest established that she had been murdered, the verdict stated the murder was done by person(s) unknown. Afterwards, suspicions arose about the woman's husband, who was subsequently arrested and committed to Newgate.[56] Examinations were lodged against the husband, but apparently he was not brought to trial; neither the coroner's inquest nor the evidence was strong enough to indict him.

Only one known wife-killer was hanged. In January 1785, a publican in Cabinteely named Foye murdered his wife.[57] The Blackrock Felons Association paid two guineas to one Dan Browne to prosecute him. In addition, the association paid five guineas to a witness named Mary Garrigan "for her ... integrity in resisting any attempt made to withdraw her evidence in the trial."[58] Another guinea was paid to a surgeon who inspected the body of the victim. At the Kilmainham Quarter

Sessions, Foye was tried, convicted and hanged on Wednesday 9 March.[59]

A few years later, in September 1791, a farmer named Murtagh Gately from Yellow Wall (near Malahide) in Co. Dublin struck his wife Jane over the head with an iron hammer, knocking her to the floor. Nine days later, a surgeon was finally called to treat her fractured skull. The doctor prescribed bark, a prescription that her husband did not bother to fill, and Jane Gately died 14 days after the attack. In December, the Commission of Oyer and Terminer tried the husband for the murder.[60] He had already been tried and acquitted for a previous assault in January 1791.[61] At the trial, it was revealed that he "had been in the habit of beating her about the body." An uncle of the deceased gave an eye-witness account of the brutal attack and the surgeon also gave damaging testimony. After deliberating for almost an hour and a half, the jury found him guilty of murder, though they also recommended him as an object of mercy. Justice Boyd, however, refused to accept the verdict and demanded that the jury reduce the sentence to manslaughter. After retiring for only two minutes, the jury accepted the judge's wisdom. The judge then sentenced him to be burnt in the hand, to spend 12 months in gaol and to keep the peace for seven years.

Less than a year later, Justice William Downes, who presided at the Commission of Oyer and Terminer, pardoned Gately and, at the same sitting, heard the case of another wife-killer named John Woods.[62] On Easter Monday 10 April 1792, Woods murdered his wife Anne Woods by driving an iron chisel through her spine at the base of the neck with such force that he severed her head from the backbone. Woods had made the chisel in his capacity as a pump-borer for the Pipe Water Commission in Dublin.[63] The trial turned on the lusty friendship between a regimental musician and the deceased rather than on the brutal murder. Two "eminent distillers" named John Edwards and James Trant, who had previously employed Woods as a plumber, provided the court with good character references, the latter claiming that Woods was "of a gentle and humane disposition." In his summing up, the judge said that the wife's adulterous behaviour had driven the offender "to the most frantic pitch of rage and indignation" and that he had committed the crime "in a state of temporary madness." After retiring a short time, the jury returned a verdict of manslaughter. The judge then sentenced him to be burnt in the hand and to be incarcerated for six months.[64]

Pressures were brought to bear on prosecuting witnesses in cases of wife-killing. On 22 June 1794, John Echlin beat his wife to death in their apartment in Thomas Court. Alarmed by the struggle, John Groves entered the Echlin lodgings to find Elizabeth Echlin "expiring on the ground" with "violent bruises and contusions … in several parts of the body." Elizabeth Echlin managed to talk to Groves just before she died, upon which he immediately lodged examinations with Thomas Emerson, divisional justice of the district. Groves pressed charges against Echlin for murder.

What Groves said in court, however, was rather different. At the Commission of Oyer and Terminer a month later, Groves testified that John Echlin had beaten Elizabeth several times in the past, but that he had not beaten her on the day of her death. Groves also testified that the deceased told him just before her death that "she had been beat abroad." This conflicted with his sworn statement to Emerson, which was produced and read in court. Unmoved by the telling of his previous statement, Groves persisted in his prevarication. Angry at his cowardly refusal to testify, the judge arrested him on charges of perjury. With no other prosecution witness, the case against Echlin collapsed and he was acquitted.[65] This case exemplifies just how difficult it was to obtain convictions against wife-killers.

Nine of the 34 people killed by manslaughter were women, which is over 25 percent of all cases of manslaughter. In January 1786, Mary Hodgins was shot and killed by Laurence Delany. Both were servants of a grocer named Mr Farrell in High Street. A coroner's inquest returned a verdict of accidental death, but Delany was arrested for firing a gun illegally.[66]

In December 1786, a clerk at the house of pawnbroker Thomas Armitage in Skinner's Row accidentally shot a woman who was waiting in a queue to pledge some items. (A parliamentary report indicated that the number of pawnbrokers actually doubled in 1787 and that turnover among them improved dramatically, a sign that the local economy was on the road to a recovery that lasted for the next 10 years.[67] Thomas Armitage's firm made an average of about 260 deals a week, amounting to £8,257 in 1787.)[68] Armitage's clerk, who had just accepted a brace of two pistols in pawn, became impatient at an intoxicated customer who had entered the busy premises. Without realising the pawned pistols were primed with powder and ball, the clerk fired one at the drunkard to frighten him into leaving the shop.

However the pistol ball struck Mary Rourke, a fruit vendor, who dropped dead instantly. A coroner's inquest ruled accidental death.[69]

In January 1788, a publican's wife in Mercer Street was shot and killed by a servant discharging a pistol,[70] and in July 1790, a washer-woman was shot and killed in Rathmines by a hunter discharging a fowling piece.[71] It is not known what happened in the case of the publican's wife, but the hunter fled the scene of the accident.

Women often resisted such violent attacks on their lives and property. In January 1791, Christopher Thompson, a convict who returned to Dublin after being transported to the Americas about three years earlier, committed his final crime.[72] (In October 1789, Thompson was arrested, but after his release from prison "had been marauding on the public.")[73] At the second lock along the Grand Canal, Thompson robbed a woman with a cocked pistol. After stealing a guinea from her, he spotted two silver buckles on her shoes and demanded them as well. She gave him one buckle to try on for size. He was so delighted with the gleam of silver that he began to polish the buckle, putting his pistol on the bank of the canal. She grabbed the gun and shot him through the head, an act of bravery for which she was rewarded.[74] In addition to her stolen guinea, she was given all the money found in his pocket, amounting to 12 guineas and two bank notes. She was also promised a reward from Co. Dublin "for her determined conduct."[75]

A similar incident had occurred in April 1786. An armed robber named O'Donnell attacked the servant maid of His Grace, the Duke of Rutland, in Phoenix Park while she was riding in a "sumpter" or baggage cart. O'Donnell pressed a loaded pistol to the woman's breast and demanded her money. The maid gave him a guinea, but he was still not satisfied. He put his pistol down to search the cart for more money. She shot him in the head.[76]

The *Hibernian Journal* reported a total of 53 rapes, seven of which resulted in death. In the eight years between 1780 and 1786, 36 rapes were reported. In the following eight years between 1787 and 1795, there were only 17, a reduction of 53 percent. In May 1781, the residents of Mecklenburgh Street placed an advertisement warning women about the dangers of rape near a particular house at which rapists lay in wait. Directed to the high sheriffs, the advertisement said that "neither age nor condition prevents assaults."[77]

In October 1780, Catherine Walsh, a "pedlar" woman, was raped and killed in Slane Road near Clogher Road. A month later, Mr

Gorges Lowther arrested a man named Roger Giveny for the crime, but no report of his trial appeared.[78] In fact, many rapes went unreported, including the rape and murder of a 16-year-old girl in Coleraine Street in January 1778. She was an heiress of "considerable fortune" whose parents decided against reporting the crime to protect the marriage prospects of their other unmarried daughters. The crime only came to light when a similar crime occurred near the same spot 12 years later. In February 1790, the body of a young woman was found in the waste ground to the west front of the Linen Hall, between Coleraine Street and the upper end of Church Street. She too had been raped and murdered.[79]

In the years following the introduction of the police in October 1786, the frequency of rape and violent assaults showed a sharp decline. Evidence that prosecutions for assault increased rapidly after 1786 proves that victims were more willing to seek legal redress. In the eight years between 1780 and 1787, 65 trials were brought on grounds of assault, but in one year, 1788, victims brought 54 trials to court, indicating that the new police encouraged the increase in prosecutions. Rape was a crime that diminished, or appears to have diminished, towards the end of the period, but was a serious problem in the mid-1780s, particularly in the first few years after the introduction of the new police.

Even when rapists were caught, convictions against them were difficult to obtain. According to the newspaper, only 23 trials for rape took place, which accounts for fewer than half of the total number of reported rapes. While a small percentage of rape victims took legal action, only nine defendants in rape trials were convicted and of those only two were hanged, one of them a woman. The lack of convictions in rape trials is made all the more noticeable by comparison with the substantial number of offenders who were hanged for theft. This sheds light on values held by the society of Dublin in the late eighteenth century, clearly showing that property theft was considered far more offensive a crime than rape.

Some rapists avoided convictions by intimidating their victims before trial. In November 1784, four men broke into the house of one Mrs Spear in Temple Street just west of Mountjoy Square and raped her, her maid servant and another woman.[80] Justice of the Peace Francis Graham arrested two of the rapists and committed them to Kilmainham for their trial. Spear and another woman named Mrs

Bray lodged examinations against the men. In December 1784, at the Commission of Oyer and Terminer, Spear and Bray contradicted their earlier examinations, claiming that they had not been raped.[81] Suspecting that Spear and Bray had been "tampered with" by the defendants, the court remanded the prisoners back to prison to stand trial again. The court also indicted the two women for perjury.[82] It is unlikely that the rapists were ever punished.

Rape victims encountered serious obstacles in the courts. In one case a woman was denied a fair trial as a result of a technicality over court jurisdiction. In February 1792, Thomas Hurley and John Kerr, captain and first mate of a passenger ferry, raped Mary Mullen after she boarded their vessel in Dublin. In July, the commission acquitted the two men because the crime had been perpetrated off Ramsgate harbour and thus it fell outside the court's jurisdiction.[83]

In June 1788, William Crane, Mathew Denison and another man raped Elizabeth Knox in James's Street. The three men were arrested and committed to Newgate to stand their trial.[84] Knox, however, did not appear in court to testify against Crane and Denison at the next two sessions of the Commission of Oyer and Terminer and they were therefore released by the court.[85] Knox's refusal to testify against her attackers suggests that the system of justice did not protect victims from intimidation.

Other rape victims were more fortunate. A man servant chased a rapist away from his intended victim in Long Lane in July 1787. His heroism earned him the hand in marriage of the woman whom he had defended.[86] In June 1788, a woman stabbed one of her two attackers through the chest with a knife in the fields between Goldenbridge and Drimnagh.[87] It was no accident that the intended rape victim was armed. Earlier in the same month, a young girl had been raped and stabbed to death directly across the River Liffey in Phoenix Park.[88]

In one rape case, a victim's father urged her to press charges against her alleged attacker in a criminal court. The father, Barnaby Egan, was motivated in part by the prospect of winning sizable damages against the rapist in a civil court. In the summer of 1789, Captain Robert Kindillan had an affair with a local Dublin woman named Elizabeth Egan. Together with a servant of Egan's named Ann Carrol, they stole away to the resort town of Douglas on the Isle of Man. When they returned to Dublin, Barnaby Egan pushed his daughter to press charges both against Kindillan for rape and against Carrol for aiding and abetting. A warrant was issued for the arrest of Kindillan to stand trial at the Commission of Oyer and Terminer in October 1789, but Kindillan disappeared from the scene temporarily. In November, Kindillan surrendered himself to magistrates to stand trial at the Commission of Oyer and Terminer in the following December. At his trial, the jury acquitted him and Carrol.[89] This, however, was not the end of the matter. In the autumn of 1791, Barnaby Egan won £500 in damages from Kindillan at the Court of Exchequer.[90]

Barnaby Egan's determination to defend his daughter's reputation and to punish Kindillan for debasing it illuminates the extent to which society would go to defend a woman's right to a decent marriage. Captain Kindillan had not merely taken advantage of Elizabeth Egan, but had also ruined her marriage prospects. Judging by the amount of damages awarded to Barnaby Egan, the court agreed that his daughter had lost her prospects of finding a good marriage partner in the future. Six years before this event occurred in November 1785, the *Dublin Evening Post* published an instructive poem about courtship, outlining the acceptable patterns of behaviour for young women:

FEMALE COURTSHIP

Two or three looks when your swain wants a kiss,
Two or three noes when he bids you say yes;
Two or three smiles when you utter the no,
Two or three frowns if he offers to go;
Two or three laughs when astray for small chat,
Two or three tears, tho' you can't tell for what;
Two or three letters when vows are begun,
Two or three quarrels before you are done;
Two or three dances to make you jocose;
Two or three hours in a corner sit close;
Two or three starts when he bids you elope,
Two or three glances to imitate hope;
Two or three pauses before you are won,
Two or three swoonings to let him press on;
Two or three sighs when you've wasted your tears,
Two or three hums when the chaplain appears;
Two or three squeezes when the hand's giv'n away,
Two or three coughs when you come to obey;

> Two or three lasses may have by these rhymes,
> Two or three little ones—two or three times.[91]

Kindillan could afford to pay his fine of £500, but other men were less wealthy. In another case, the husband of an alleged victim of rape pressed charges against her alleged attacker in order to push him into total bankruptcy and a debtor's prison. In February 1791 at the Court of Exchequer, John Travers successfully sued Denis McCarthy, his servant, for having "criminal conversation" with his wife Grace Travers (née Lysaght).[92] Damages of £5,000 were awarded against McCarthy, aged between 12 and 15. The court sentenced him to the Four Courts Marshalsea in Bridgefoot Street until the damages were paid. Presumably, this punishment was to prevent McCarthy from coming into contact with Grace Travers again, but in April 1795, Denis McCarthy petitioned the Irish parliament, seeking relief from his debt:

> [T]he Petitioner has been confined in the Four Courts Marshalsea of this Kingdom for upwards of five years, on the Presumption of his having had an improper Connection with his late Mistress the Honourable Grace Travers (otherwise Lysaght) than which nothing in nature could be more improbable, when it is considered that Petitioner was only a poor, abject, illiterate Chaise-boy, and that his Mistress was a Lady of noble Birth, and in high Estimation for her Prudence, Virtue and regular-matronly Conduct of every Respect; that the Petitioner having no Sort of Trade or any Business, save that of Postillion, an Occupation no way adapted for the narrow Limits of a Prison, must have inevitably perished, had it not been for the Humanity of the Gentlemen confined for Debt in the same Prison ... [he] at present unfortunately very young, is doomed to spend the whole of his calamitous Days in a loathsome Prison or pay a Fine of £5,000.[93]

McCarthy's petition was considered by the House of Commons in a bill for the relief of insolvent debtors, which implies that he was released from the Four Courts Marshalsea at that stage.

Not all servants who took liberties with their mistresses suffered to the same extent as McCarthy did. In March 1790, a wealthy family discharged one of their footmen after he fell in love with their daughter.[94] Distraught, the footman wrote a "flaming love letter" to the object of his desire, promising to visit her at home one evening.[95] In response, she warned her father of his impending arrival and, with a group of friends, he waited covertly for the footman's arrival. They surprised him and beat him with a horsewhip.

During the 16-year period, at least 337 cases of assaults were reported, and a considerable number of these involved women and girls. Mary Amyott prosecuted her husband Francis Amyott for assault. Mary was from a poor Dublin family and came to her marriage "without a shilling fortune." She was described as an "extremely handsome" and "beautiful young woman" in contrast to her husband who was described as "a man pretty well stricken in years and well stored with experience of the world." It was her youthful beauty that dominated the court and eventually cost her the case. Her husband was the King's Professor of the French Language at Trinity College, a position he had been elected to at the beginning of December 1790.[96] Trained as a medical doctor, he became a member of the Royal Irish Academy soon after his election to the Professorship at Trinity. Unlike Mary, who found happiness in the comfort of her family, her husband was a publicly demanding individual who courted the attention of a wide audience. In December 1790, he organised an unusual "series of public lectures on the structure and study of the French language" in Dublin.[97] In the course of his active social and professional life, he met and fell in love with Mary. She agreed to marry him, after he threatened to commit suicide if she did not accept his proposal.

In April 1792, no more than a month or two after their wedding, a physical confrontation broke out in their lodgings in Fleet Street. Both received injuries, but Mary pressed charges for assault, alleging she was twice beaten about the head, face, arms and breasts and left out in the cold for two hours with nothing to cover her body. The prosecuting lawyer, Counsellor William Caldbeck, launched a two-pronged attack on the defendant, stressing the moral obligation of society to protect wives from their husbands. Claiming that he was "proud … that the traverser is not an Irishman," Caldbeck accused the defendant of harbouring "savage" customs imported from a foreign country. The counsellor even claimed that Irishmen were "celebrated throughout Europe for their manly attachment to the rights of the fair sex."[98]

If Caldbeck expected the jury to believe this moral imperative, he was badly mistaken. Counsellor William Walker, for the defendant, refuted his arguments and, in so doing, was helped and encouraged by the judge, jury and spectators. Walker first tried to have the case thrown out of court, stating that women who press charges against their husbands were guilty of "perjury" and motivated by "implacable resentment." While this objection was over-ruled, a begrudging Denis George, the Recorder of Dublin, agreed that "it was the general rule of law that a wife cannot be evidence against her husband."

During the course of the trial, a juror taunted Mary about her refusal to have sexual relations with her husband before the attack.

> Q. By Juror. Was not there a great *dryness* between you for some time?
> A. O yes, Sir, a great *dryness*.

In addition, Richard Moncrieffe, an Alderman of Dublin Corporation and a divisional justice of the police, also taunted her:

> Q. By Alderman [Richard] Moncrieffe. Pray, madam, did you sleep with your husband that night?
> A. I did, Sir.
> Q. And did not he make it up with you that night?
> A. No, Sir.
> Alderman M[oncrieffe]. Poh! poh!

In his summing up, the Recorder discredited the prosecution by claiming that "domestic broils between man and wife are more frequently the offspring of caprice and mutual obstinacy than of any just foundation or sufficient cause … In the present instance … the wife had deviated from the injunctions of her husband … had slighted his authority, and resisted his lawful commands." After 75 minutes, the jury returned a verdict of not guilty.

Girls had much to fear from female offenders involved in a wave of kidnapping which took place in Dublin, particularly in the Spring of 1781. Women began to kidnap children to sell as servants to the British colonies, a crime linked to unscrupulous ship masters. A total of 65 children and one tradesman's apprentice were kidnapped, according to the *Hibernian Journal*. Women tricked children with offers of gingerbread cakes. One woman who kidnapped four children was found with gags in her possession.[99] It was reported that a captain of a ship in Dublin harbour offered £30 to a woman for eight kidnapped children.[100] Women who were caught in the act of kidnapping children, like those caught killing infants, were sometimes attacked by the crowds. In one case, a kidnapper was "obliged to be guarded to the gaol to prevent the rage of the populace."

In Dublin, the *Hibernian Journal* reported that female receivers were defendants in 34 of the 57 trials involving stolen property.[101] One female receiver was sentenced to death, but later reprieved, while four more were transported. Women often colluded with men in criminal activity of this nature. In July 1784, the Commission of Oyer and Terminer convicted John Keenan for the robbery of Captain Withers in Liberty Lane. A habitual offender with four previous con victions, Keenan was sentenced to death.[102] On the evening before his hanging, he wrote a letter to his wife suggesting a convenient solution to her impending widowhood: "My dear Polly, I am down at last. I now must die ... my friend, at Harold's Cross, holds a cup, two watches, and six copper-plate papers of mine. I would advise you to marry him, in order to partake of the bit. He will never see you want whilst there is powder and lead."[103] The *Hibernian Journal* did not report whether Polly took up Keenan's advice to marry his friend. Perhaps the hanging of her husband was deterrent enough.

Female receivers were also habitual criminals. In April 1789, Eleanor Scarf, who had returned from transportation before the expiration of her sentence, turned a house in Plunket Street into a fence from which gangs unloaded stolen property. A "notorious old offender", she was well-known to the police who tracked down a suspected robber to her house. On 1 April 1789, John Egan, Robert Fisher and John Whelan robbed Patrick Keefe of his watch, cash, clothes and snuff-box and hit him over the head with a poker while he was walking home in Patrick Street. They dragged him into Limerick Alley, but Fisher prevented the other two from killing him with long knives. After the robbers left, Keefe informed the police of the attack. An hour later at midnight, a deputy constable of police arrested Egan at the corner of Bride's Alley in Bride Street, but the other two escaped. Keefe visited Egan at St. Andrew's guard-house the following morning and Egan told him the names of the two robbers and where they could be found. Fisher and Whelan were arrested in Scarf's house in Plunket

Street (Whelan was married to Rose Scarf, the daughter of Eleanor). At trial, the victim identified his stolen watch and snuff-box, but "would not swear positively to the prisoners' persons." Having listened to the testimony of the arresting deputy police constable, the jury at the Dublin Quarter Sessions acquitted Fisher and Whelan, but convicted Egan who was hanged on Wednesday 22 April 1789.[104] Eleanor Scarf was not arrested following the robbery.[105]

In July 1793, the Commission of Oyer and Terminer convicted Margaret Colligan of receiving stolen goods and sentenced her to transportation.[106] Colligan had been tried in October 1787 for receiving stolen clothes owned by David Bates. At that trial, however, the Commission of Oyer and Terminer acquitted her and an accomplice named Mary Dillon.[107]

An estimated 242 convicted felons were hanged in Dublin between 1780 and 1795, but only 13 of these were female. Two female felons were subjected to particularly horrific executions. In March 1783, the commission convicted Mary Purfield of setting fire to the offices and house of Mr Morgan at Blanchardstown.[108] Purfield, apparently a servant who had harboured a four-year-old grudge against her master, was the only person reported to have been convicted of arson in Dublin during the 16-year period. On Saturday 22 March 1783, the hangman strangled her to death with his hands and flung her body onto a burning pyre at Gallows Hill.[109]

In December 1783, the Commission of Oyer and Terminer convicted Mary Fairfield for stabbing a wet nurse named Mary Funt, née Burne to death. Not much is known about this crime from the newspaper as the circumstances were said to be "too shocking to relate," but it was reported that the court sentenced Fairfield to be burned at the stake.[110] To avoid her fate, she pleaded pregnancy at the December sittings of the commission, and at the following February and July sittings. In respect to the first two pleas, a jury of matrons accepted her story and her execution was respited. At length, the jury decided she was not pregnant and well enough to face her sentence.[111]

On Saturday 21 August 1784, Mary Fairfield was placed in a cart at Newgate prison and led through the streets of Dublin to Stephen's Green. A vast crowd watched the "solemn" procession make its way across town. A newly hired 20-man police guard, by which Dublin Corporation supplemented a moribund parish watch system, surrounded the cart on which the woman rode. The uniformed constables were armed with swords and staves. In addition, a detachment of Lord Drogheda's horsemen kept the "giddy multitude" at bay. On the Green, the hangman strangled her to death with his hands and tossed her body into a fire.[112] By burning the bodies of the two women, the courts inflicted a most humiliating form of collective punishment akin to dissection by surgeons; the families and friends were left only with the charred remains of the corpses, a violation of the traditional rights to wake the bodies in their natural state.

A comparative analysis of punishment indicates that, overall, female felons were less likely to be hanged than male felons. In Dublin, Surrey and London, between five and seven per cent of the felons hanged were female. Capital punishment was thus imposed mainly on the male criminal population in Ireland and England, perhaps due to the frequency and the severity of the crimes committed by male offenders. At Tyburn in London between 1703 and 1772, it was found that 92 women, 17 of them Irish, were executed out of a total of 1,242 people in the 69 years.[113] At Kennington Common in Surrey, it was found that six women were executed out of a total of 104 people in the 16 years be tween 1780 and 1795.[114] In Dublin, 13 women were executed out of a total of 242 hangings between 1780 and 1795.

Apart from the serious crimes of infanticide and suicide, women suffered far more as victims of crime than as perpetrators during the late eighteenth century. Girls were raped and kidnapped, wives were murdered and battered and judges often turned a blind eye to the violence perpetrated against women in their homes. Despite their poor prospects in obtaining convictions against their attackers, many women showed a great deal of imagination and determination in pressing ahead with prosecutions. At the same time, female offenders made a livelihood from crime, by handling stolen goods and organising shop lifting rings. As a rule, women were far more interested in running the black economy in Dublin than in committing violent crimes.

CHAPTER THREE

Industrial Violence

Laws against combinations were passed in Ireland as early as the sixteenth century, but became more numerous and increasingly severe during the late eighteenth century.[1] Combinations are roughly analogous to modern-day strikes, but were far more likely to result in damage to property and injury to limb. Parliament passed the first general law against combinations in 1729,[2] and at least seven more were passed up to 1772.[3] The 1729 Combinations Act, like most subsequent legislation, proved to be "ineffectual, and had been notoriously eluded."[4] Apart from demonstrating how futile the anti-combination laws were, their repeated enactment reflects the unflagging spirit and rising organisational strength of artisans, journeymen and servants.

In 1780, Parliament passed three more anti-combination acts, including a general act which outlawed combinations in all industries and two separate acts which outlawed combinations in the silk and dairy in dustries.[5] The most comprehensive of the three acts has become known as the 1780 Combinations Act.[6] Prof. Maurice O'Connell states that the act meant "nothing less than the destruction of the organized power of skilled labour."[7] Prof. Jesse Clarkson likewise concludes that no act "was ever more thorough in including even the most tenuous connection with the suspected organisation, more elastic in requiring less evidence for conviction, or more supremely indifferent to the objects and motives of offenders."[8] Indeed, the 1780 Combinations Act made virtually all aspects of journeyman activity illegal, including belonging to journeyman organisations, possessing journeyman membership cards, making wage demands and holding meetings of more than seven journeymen for the purpose of combination activity.

The 1780 Combinations Act also extended the death penalty to those convicted of violent attacks on workshops, tools and materials, a penalty that had been on the books as far back as 1757.[9] In 1773, two rope-makers in Cork were convicted and hanged under a combinations law passed in 1763.[10] Most of the clauses in the 1780 Act, such as the one imposing the death penalty, were taken almost verbatim from the pre-existing legislation with only slight modifications.

While the 1780 Act was a specific response to crime in the work place, it was also a reaction to years of mounting violence over the key issue of labour supply. The combinators wanted to reduce the supply of labour in Dublin, the masters to increase the supply. Many of the regulations introduced under the 1780 Act were a direct result of recommendations made in February of that year by some of the 18 merchants and master-tradesmen to the House of Commons Grand Committee for Trade chaired by Sir Lucius O'Brien.[11] Recommendations to the O'Brien Committee also came in the form of petitions submitted by masters before Parliament.[12] The O'Brien Committee was apparently the only inquiry of its kind to examine industrial relations in Dublin in the late eighteenth century.[13]

Giving oral evidence to the committee, Andrew Reynolds and Richard McCormack, both master weavers, recalled how an "extensive combination" had driven women and non-Dublin journeymen out of the weaving industry in Dublin in 1765. Reynolds pointed out that 300 women had once been employed as weavers, but only one remained in employment "and this on account of her grandfather having been a weaver." He also said that the journeyman committees favoured the tactic of "swearing" non-Dublin journeymen out of the trade. Similarly, McCormack said, "all the Munster-men and all the women were at once turned out of the trade [which] ... produced a scarcity [of labour], and established the power of their journeyman committees."[14] In light of their recommendations, the 1780 Combinations Act made it unlawful for journeymen to "prevent any native of any part of this kingdom, or any foreigner, or any woman from exercising any trade, or working at any branch of business."

In his testimony before the O'Brien Committee, Benjamin Houghton, a Quaker merchant and a large cloth manufacturer in the Liberties, blamed the Penal Laws for introducing divisions among masters over the number of apprentices they could hire. According to Houghton, an employer should be free to hire "as many apprentices male or female as he may think fit in any trade within this kingdom, whether such master or apprentice be protestant or papist, any statute, usage, custom, charter, bye law, order, or regulation to the contrary notwithstanding."

On Saturday 3 June 1780, Sir Lucius O'Brien presented the Combinations Bill to the House of Commons.[15] On the same day, the Gordon riots broke out in London, the most serious insurrection in Britain during the eighteenth century. Between 400 and 500 people were killed.[16] Amid mounting tensions in Dublin over the state of affairs in England, several thousand journeymen staged a protest in Phoenix Park on the following Saturday against the Combinations Act Parliament had just passed.[17] A Dublin correspondent for an English newspaper said that "such a numerous meeting at this time, when the metropolis of our sister kingdom is convulsed with dangerous insurrections, was truly alarming."[18] To prevent any disturbances, the Volunteers stayed "on duty in the streets till all fear or riots had passed."[19]

As the economy continued to grow in Dublin, the demand for labour far outstripped the supply.[20] In 1785, Parliament sought to restrict the flow of labour to America by passing a law which made it illegal for ship masters to "seduce" artisans from Ireland.[21] Three years later, two sea captains from the Isle of Wight were charged with seduction. In March 1788, Joseph Harrington and Thomas Philpot, who operated a vessel called the *Baltimore*, were arrested in Dublin and committed to Newgate.[22] In May, the King's Bench found Harrington guilty of attempting to entice a thread maker named John Burlugh to Georgetown, Maryland. (The King's Bench heard only the most serious cases, such as treason.) Harrington was sentenced to one year in gaol and fined £500.[23] Philpot was found guilty of seducing at least two skilled workers to "emigrate with him" and was sentenced to two years in prison and fined £500.[24] Philpot never lived to see his native country again. Within 15 months of his conviction, he was dead of a prison-related illness. (A 1788 parliamentary report exposed Newgate as unfit for human habitation.)[25] Soon after the death of his fellow countryman, Harrington petitioned Dublin Castle for an end to his confinement, whereby his fine of £500 was remitted. The Englishman was pardoned and discharged in August 1789.[26]

In March 1787, Samuel Baird prosecuted 18 journeymen pin-makers for administering illegal oaths to other journeymen in a wage dispute at his workshop. In October, the Commission of Oyer and Terminer convicted the pin-makers: 14 were sentenced to one year in prison and fined £10 and four to two years in prison and fined £20.[27] In July 1788, the journeyman committee representing the imprisoned pin-makers demanded their release from Newgate in a published letter.[28] The letter said that as 18 of Dublin's 60 pin-makers were incarcerated, the remaining 42 could not meet the demand for pins. This imbalance, according to the letter, would result in a "large importation of English pins." The letter appealed to the Lord Mayor of Dublin "to remit the remainder of the confinement and restore them to their afflicted families."

The appeals on behalf of the convicted pin-makers obtained widespread support. In September 1788, Lord Mayor William Alexander granted bail to the 14 pin-makers who had been sentenced to gaol sentences of one year.[29] The other four petitioned Dublin Castle for remittance of their sentences[30] and, in December 1788, the Lord Lieutenant ordered their release although they had served only half of their gaol sentences.[31] The appeals made on behalf of, and the support given to, the pin-makers underline the scarcity in the Dublin labour market and the strength of the working class.

In seeking to reduce the supply of labour, combinators employed at least six tactics. (1) Combinators "swore" non-union labour out of the Dublin work force. (2) They administered secret oaths. (3) They posted anonymous letters containing threats to masters. (4) They organised confrontations at workshops. (5) They resorted to outright physical violence against masters, apprentices and innocent people. (6) They set fire to factories.

The masters also employed a wide variety of tactics to combat these illegal and violent activities. Organised into guilds, they offered large rewards to informers and paid for the prosecutions of combinators. The masters had the support of the city sheriffs, the police, the military and the Volunteers. The struggle between masters and journeymen varied from trade to trade.

TAPE AND GARTER WORKERS: In June 1780, a group of journeymen attacked the homes of three tape and garter masters: James Collison in Dolphin's Barn, Thomas Flint in Cork Street, and Francis Dillon in Bell-view. In the attack, the journeymen broke windows and fired shots at their houses. As a result, the tape and garter masters withdrew their offer of seven shillings per week to those weavers made redundant by the combination.[32] In their withdrawal of redundancy payments, the masters acted on an established practice of not making payments to journeymen who had been made idle as a direct result of combination activity.

SUGAR BAKERS: In May 1780, a journeyman committee sent an anonymous letter to a sugar refinery in Hanbury Lane owned by Mr Galan and Mr Maziere. Seeking to reduce the labour supply, the letter described "what sort of men ought to be employed in the several parts of the business, and threatening the lives of those who should deviate from that order." In fact, a production manager named James Shiel was ordered to quit Dublin because he was "in a rank which the author of said incendiary letter thinks he has attained too soon." In response, the owners offered a reward of £20 for information leading to the arrest and conviction of the authors of the letter.[33] Following up on their threats, however, two combinators followed Shiel from the sugar refinery to the Poddle, where they assaulted him and threatened to strangle him if he did not leave Dublin. This attack provoked outrage amongst master sugar bakers throughout Ireland, including 20 from Dublin, four from Cork, three from Belfast, two from Waterford, one from Derry, one from Ross, one from Newry and one from Dundalk. These masters joined together in offering a reward of £50 for information leading to the arrest and conviction of the authors of the anonymous letter. In April 1781, the same sugar refinery in Hanbury Lane was set alight by a combination committee. Firemen managed to extinguish the blaze before it spread to the mill.[34]

TAILORS: Between October and December 1780, an industrial dispute over wage rates broke out in the weaving industry. The journeymen tailors demanded an increase in wages from 12 shillings to 14 shillings per week.[35] In October, journeymen tailors marched on the house of Alexander Clarke, a master tailor in Chancery Lane who had given testimony to the O'Brien Committee, and broke his windows with stones. Violence flared in Fishamble Street at the end of October when journeymen tailors attacked the house and workshop of Daniel Doyle, a master who had hired a new recruit.[36] They broke into Doyle's house and assaulted him, his wife and a maid servant. They also broke into his workshop, where they assaulted William Keating, the new recruit who had not joined their combination. That same day, the journeymen attacked the home and workshop of James Cullen in Fleet Street. They beat his journeyman "in an unmerciful manner." After the brutal attacks, a surgeon declared that the lives of Doyle and Keating were in danger.[37] In a show of force, both the Dublin and Liberty Volunteers publicly pledged to track down the culprits.[38]

Sheriff Thomas Andrews, accompanied by the two Corps of Volunteers, raided several public houses, arresting John Field and one Conorey as well as 10 other committee members. In the raid they also discovered an arms cache.[39] The master tailors publicly thanked the Volunteers for helping them to combat the disturbances which affected 23 different trades.[40]

SKINNERS: In January 1781, journeymen skinners led an arson attack on a skin-dressing mill in Co. Dublin that had been built "at considerable expense." Thomas Johnson, who owned the new leather tuck-mill, cited losses at £200. A group of master glovers and skinners offered a reward of £50 for information leading to a prosecution and conviction of the arsonists. Dublin Castle offered a reward as well.[41]

CARPENTERS: In February 1781, Sheriff Thomas Andrews, Justice of the Peace William Worthington and a group of Dublin Volunteers raided a public house controlled by journeymen carpenters. The armed raiders seized a chest full of documents, registration books, resolutions and bye-laws.[42] An examination of the captured records brought to light the names of 1,900 journeymen carpenters who had been engaged in combination activity over the past 20 years. After the raid, a reward was offered for information leading to the arrest, prosecution and conviction of both the journeymen carpenters and the publican in whose house they had met. Such publicans were deemed as accessories to crime, "to be punished as those who keep common bawdy-houses." The swift action on the part of the sheriffs and the Volunteers put a temporary halt to the activities of the journeyman committees for a few years. It was not until the summer of 1784 that the combination committees resumed their activities.

The turbulent events in that summer were preceded by a decline in the influence of the Volunteers and an unwillingness on their part to combat combinations. Five years earlier on 4 November 1779, James Napper Tandy, one of the most active Volunteers and a radical politician inside the lower house of Dublin Corporation, staged a large protest outside the House of Commons in support of "free trade." This incident annoyed some of the more conservative elements in the Volunteers, producing friction within the leadership.[43] The underlying tensions within the movement gave way to an open rift in the spring of 1780, when the Duke of Leinster resigned from the Dublin

Volunteers.[44] The organisation continued to stage colourful parades and patriotic demonstrations in the Phoenix Park during the last few years of the American War of Independence. After that war ended, however, interest in the Volunteers waned.

At an annual review of the Volunteers in the Phoenix Park in June 1784, only 972 members marched in the parade, down from 2,400 a year earlier.[45] Without the conservative check imposed by the early Volunteers, industrial violence returned to the streets of Dublin and in the spring and summer of 1784, the journeyman committees organised another round of violent attacks which threatened the stability of in dustrial relations. the violence was sparked by the failure of Parliament to pass a "moderate" bill to protect jobs.[46]

On Saturday 19 June 1784, 100 journeymen armed with pistols and swords marched down Chancery Lane to the house of Alexander Clarke, the same master tailor who had given testimony before the O'Brien Committee. After 10 men forcibly broke into his home, the crowd frog-marched Clarke "almost naked" to the Tenter Fields in Marrowbone Lane. Here they removed the remainder of his clothes and covered his body in tar. Just as they were about to pour a sack of feathers onto his tarred body, Sheriff Benjamin Smith arrived with a party of soldiers and rescued him from the mob.[47] A few days after the attack, Dublin Castle issued a proclamation, offering £500 for in formation leading to the arrest and conviction of those responsible.[48] At the same time, Clarke and the Corporation of Tailors offered a reward of £110.[49] Clarke maintained his innocence with regard to importing and selling foreign cloth, claiming that he sold Irish-made cloth only.

Despite the offers of reward, the journeyman committees widened their attacks to include those working at lower wages than the standard they had set, those working in branches of manufacture to which they were not originally trained and those who had come to Dublin from the countryside. On Saturday 26 June 1784, a tailor named Boyle was snatched from his house in Usher's Court, taken to the Tenter Fields, stripped of his clothing and tarred and feathered.[50] In this condition, Boyle was led in procession through the Liberties until a detachment of soldiers rescued him. He refused to lodge examinations against any committee members afterwards, perhaps for fear of further violence.

In July, a mob hijacked a cargo of spring looms on their way to a factory in Co. Wicklow, burning them in Weaver's Square.[51] A month later, a mob abducted James Crombie, a partner in a thread factory in Dundalk, from his office in Church Street. They tarred and feathered him in the open corn market at Purcel's Court.[52] In the aftermath, Crombie's business partners published an advertisement stating that the attack represented a serious blow in their efforts to establish a large-scale industrial factory. Archibald Wright, the major partner, said the Dundalk-based firm plowed back £20,000 per year into the Irish economy and employed over 1,500 workers per day.[53] The attacks in Dublin, however, continued unabated. On Friday morning 12 August 1784, one Corbett, "an extensive dealer," was tarred and feathered, beaten with a cat of nine tails and wounded on the head with a pistol.[54]

Initial efforts to obtain convictions against unruly journeymen met with failure. In August, the Dublin Quarter Sessions acquitted a man charged with rioting.[55] This acquittal had the effect of encouraging more hard-line elements to step up their attacks. Thomas Orde, Chief Secretary to the Lord Lieutenant in Dublin Castle, predicted that the actions of the journeyman committees would destroy Ireland's nascent industrial base, "ruin the credit of the metropolis, [and] deter every man possessed of capital … from residing here."[56] Orde assigned three reasons why more arrests were not made: the speed with which the journeyman committees carried out their attacks, the people's fear of these committees and the abhorrence of informers within the committees.[57]

On Monday 22 August 1784, events finally turned against the journeyman committees when the Dublin Quarter Sessions convicted Patrick Dignam for a tarring and feathering offence, the first conviction for such a crime. At his trial, a defence witness testified that the arresting officer had an ulterior motive, namely to collect the £500 that Dublin Castle had offered as a reward.[58] After considering the evidence, the jury rejected this and returned a guilty verdict. Dignam was sentenced to be whipped from the Tholsel through some of the most densely populated streets in the Liberties—Nicholas, Patrick, Francis and High Streets—on that Wednesday.[59] A large detachment of soldiers and a group of magistrates attended the spectacle, which went badly wrong.[60] In Francis Street, soldiers opened fire on stone-throwing crowds, killing a wool-comber. The dead man, who was armed with a sword, had attempted to rescue Dignam from the military guard.[61] A few days later, a massive funeral procession for the wool-comber took place in the Liberties. This sobering event marked the end of the tarring and feathering campaign and a summer of lawlessness, violence and anarchy.

The boom of the 1780s, however, came to a halt by 1790, a year in which an estimated 300 silk and broad-cloth weavers emigrated from Dublin.[62] The decrease in the demand for labour produced tensions amongst the journeyman committees and the calm which had reigned in the Liberties came to an end. In October 1790, Baron Hamilton, one of the presiding judges of the Commission of Oyer and Terminer, offered the Dublin grand jury an apology for having been too lenient with combinators. Hamilton said that levels of violence arising from combinations had reached a "dangerous height."[63] His statement reflects the overall change in industrial relations in that year, when the economy was no longer suffering from a labour shortage.

In 1789, a gang called the Liberty Light Horsemen took over the leadership of the committee representing the journeymen tailors. Operating from a public house in Michael's Lane, the gang first came to public attention on Easter Monday 13 April 1789, when a general meeting of over 100 journeymen tailors erupted into a riot with the police.[64] In a riot outside a public house owned by Thomas Quinn in Michael's Lane, a policeman named Walter Anderson and a tailor named Moran were killed.[65] The killings resulted in a bitter trial, but not a single policeman could identify any of the six defendants. In July 1789, the Commission of Oyer and Terminer acquitted Richard Patten of the murder of Anderson and five other men for being present, aiding and abetting Patten in the murder.[66] In a second trial for the same murder in October 1789, the Commission of Oyer and Terminer acquitted another defendant for want of evidence.[67]

This incident was just the beginning of a campaign of violence. In June 1790, a committee of deal sawyers organised a violent industrial dispute over demands for a wage increase.[68] Aiming to bring production to a complete halt in Dublin, the journeyman committee forcibly broke into several deal yards, assaulted non-union apprentices, broke windows and threatened "destruction to the premises."[69] In an attack on Patrick Wall's deal yard in Spitalfields, the committee assaulted several non-union men and fired a weapon at Wall's wife.[70] Wall pressed charges against John Read and Thomas McDermott, who were members of the Liberty Light Horsemen.[71] On 3 July 1790, the Commission of Oyer and Terminer convicted the two men under the 1784 Houghing Act, which incorporated the same punishments set out in the 1778 Chalking Act, but with an additional penalty whereby convicted felons were executed within two or three days of their trials.[72] Read and McDermott were hanged at the front of Newgate prison on Wednesday 7 July.[73] Their bodies were removed to the College of Surgeons for dissection.[74] The quick hangings and follow-up dissections minimised the possibility of martyrdom and social disorder.[75]

In May/June 1790, linen weavers banded together to oppose the introduction of gigg mills and fought running street battles with the silk weavers who operated the gigg mills.[76] Gigg mills contained advanced industrial machinery employed by the principal clothing manufacturers for the production of woollen garments. It was estimated that a horse and a single man operating a gigg mill could put 12 men out of work.[77] George Nixon, who had invested in gigg mills at his woollen clothing factory (supplying to the military) as early as 1780, testified before the O'Brien Committee that weavers had gone on strike against the introduction of gigg mills at his plant.[78]

On Monday 31 May 1790, a group of aggrieved linen weavers attacked a silk weaver named Crowder at the door of his workshop in the Black Pitts. Armed with swords, they severed the thumb and finger from his right hand.[79] Afterwards, a pitched battle in Marrowbone Lane between linen weavers and silk weavers left one man dead.[80] Worse was to follow. On 5 June 1790, a group of linen weavers broke into the home of a silk weaver and, discovering his wife Alice Fitzgerald alone, Michael Sullivan, a linen weaver, raped her. He then dragged her down a two-pair of stairs and beat her about the body.[81] This outrage was followed by a riot in Marrowbone Lane, leading to the death of William Barlow, a worsted weaver, on 24 June 1790.[82]

On Tuesday 6 July 1790, the Kilmainham Quarter Sessions convicted a man named Sky under the Houghing Act for maiming Crowder.[83] On Thursday 8 July, Sky was hanged at Gallows Green, Kilmainham. Sky declared his innocence at the hanging, saying that he had not been in the clash with Crowder. At the same time, the Commission of Oyer and Terminer convicted Michael Sullivan for raping Alice Fitzgerald. Sullivan was hanged together with a common criminal named Thomas Coleby at the front of Newgate prison on Saturday 24 July 1790.[84] All four journeymen—Read, McDermott,

Sky, and Sullivan—were hanged within the same calendar month, three within 24 hours of each other. No longer constrained in their sentencing policy by labour shortages, the Dublin courts had indeed taken a tougher line against convicted journeymen.

The increased severity of punishments did not deter journeymen tailors from participating in vicious murders and brutal assaults against non-union labour. On 20 January 1792, a group of journeymen tailors led by Thomas Whelan attacked a non-union tailor named James Lightholder. At the Commission of Oyer and Terminer in the following July, the badly injured Lightholder came forward to prosecute Whelan. The wounded tailor described the tactics of his assailants thus:

> Lightholder swore to his having on said morning gone towards the house of his employer, Mr Leet, a tailor on the Merchant's quay, about half past seven in the morning, when he was waylayed by the prisoner and several others; and on his endeavouring to escape, was pursued by them, and turning the corner of Winetavern-street, the prisoner gave him a blow with a large naked sword, which knocked him down, and inflicted a large wound on the right side of his head through his hat. That when he was down, he was instantly surrounded by the prisoner and eight or nine others, and received two other desperate wounds; one on the left side of his head, and the other on his left wrist which nearly amputated his hand, and which, though healed, had totally disabled that hand.[85]

On the same day that Lightholder was attacked, Whelan's gang murdered a non-union tailor named Michael Hanlon in Cope Street, inflicting a fatal wound to his skull with a heavy sword. Like many victims of such attacks, Lightholder and Hanlon had been working for lower wages than the union standard. At the trial, three master woollen drapers provided good character references for the defendant. Despite an eye-witness account of Whelan's assault on Lightholder, the Commission of Oyer and Terminer acquitted Whelan for the Lightholder assault and for the Hanlon murder.

The acquittal of Whelan seemed to encourage more violence. In October 1792, the Liberty Light Horsemen attacked the house of John Dry, a master clothier who lived in Weaver's Square, and ransacked his drying loft.[86] In response a party of police, joined by a detachment of soldiers, arrested Charles Wall, John Thomas, Frederick Connor and Patrick Kilmurry at a public house in Cork Street. In November 1792, the Kilmainham Quarter Sessions convicted Wall, the principal leader of the Horsemen, and sentenced him to transportation. His co-defendants were sentenced to be whipped three times from Cork Street to Weaver's Square and back again and to serve six months in prison.[87] A riot erupted outside the Kilmainham court house when the sentences were announced, but a military detachment restored order.

In 1784, Parliament passed legislation which established the death penalty for robbing the mails. The 1784 Postal Act stands out in this period as one of the harshest pieces of legislation ever enacted against working people convicted of theft.[88] Between 1784 and 1795, postal workers were brought to court on four occasions and accused of robbing the mails. Three of these trials resulted in the hangings of four people. Even before the 1784 Postal Act was passed, however, the postal authorities took a tough stance against their own work force. In May 1782, it was reported that a letter carrier named Crinnion had been hanged (prior to 1780) and that a postal clerk named Knox had been sentenced to hang but was respited on condition that he transport himself out of Europe for the rest of his life.[89]

Alexander Maclivery, a boy who carried the express between Dublin and Drogheda, was the first postal worker to be hanged under the Postal Act of 1784. In November 1785, Maclivery was arrested on charges of stealing lottery tickets out of a letter with the intention of negotiating them.[90] He was committed to Newgate to face trial at the King's Bench—his second trial for this offence. (He had been acquitted and released on bail at his first trial before the Commission of Oyer and Terminer.)[91] After Maclivery's initial release, Justice Francis Graham discovered stolen mail at the boy's stable in Drogheda. Maclivery had sworn examinations against two innocent men, but these charges were dropped upon his arrest. The King's Bench convicted the postal boy,[92] who was executed at the front of Newgate prison on Saturday 18 March 1786.[93]

In April 1792, Thomas Styles Walsh, a letter carrier, stole two notes worth about £60 from the mail, passing them to Thomas Walsh, his father.[94] (In July 1787, the Commission of Oyer and Terminer acquitted one Thomas Walsh of a robbery, but it is not known if they are one and the same person. A co-defendant in this case named Richard Troy was convicted and hanged on Saturday 28 July 1787.)[95] In October 1792, the jury at the Commission of Oyer and Terminer deliberated for four hours before finding the father and son guilty. The judge sentenced them to death, but Counsellor George J. Browne moved for an arrest of judgement on the grounds that the Commission could sentence only felons convicted under statutes that Parliament had passed before 1729, the year in which Parliament had, in fact, created the Commission of Oyer and Terminer.[96] According to Browne's logic, the Commission had no legal authority to sentence his clients because they had been found guilty under a statute which Parliament had passed 55 years after the creation of the Commission.[97] By challenging the legality of a large number of trade-specific statutes, such as the 1784 Postal Act which carried the death penalty, Browne managed to stop the death sentences. On 10 December 1792, however, Lord Clonmel, the Lord Chief Justice of the King's Bench, overruled Browne's motion.[98] The Walshes, father and son, were hanged on Saturday 15 December 1792.

This hanging was followed within seven months by a hanging of another postal worker. In June 1793, the Commission of Oyer and Terminer convicted Patrick Hayden, a letter carrier, for illegally opening letters and removing bank notes worth £30.[99] After the court sentenced him to death, the people living near Newgate prison in Green Street voiced their concerns to the city sheriff about public order disturbances on previous hanging days. The local residents said that they "could neither get into or out of their houses, nor could any person have access to them, let their business be ever so urgent, for four or five hours."[100] In compliance with their wishes, Hayden was executed at the unusual time of 8:45 a.m. (most hangings occurred at high noon) at the front of Newgate prison on Saturday 20 July 1793. This was done to avoid a public spectacle and not disrupt traffic on the normally congested market day. Sheriff Henry Hutton received thanks from the neighbourhood for his attention to its wishes.[101]

Between 1784 and 1795, four highwaymen were also convicted under the 1784 Postal Act and hanged.[102] While this number equals that of postal workers who were hanged (including the father of one), the number of highway robbers who eluded detection was far greater. At least 15 mail robberies by highwaymen took place in Dublin during this 12-year period, but only a handful were detected. All known thefts by postal workers were detected. In short, postal workers stood a far greater chance of being hanged for criminal activity than high-waymen. Undoubtedly, the absence of journeyman committees representing postal workers encouraged the Post Office to exercise the full might of the law against its work force.

In July 1792, Thomas Casey and William Trevor, two journeymen shoemakers, were indicted under the 1780 Act because they attempted to obtain an illegal wage increase of 40 per cent from Samuel Dixon, a master shoemaker on Ormond Quay.[103] This was more than double the wage increase awarded to the journeymen tailors by the Dublin Quarter Sessions in 1789. Dixon was unsuccessful in obtaining convictions against the two men, but events turned in his favour two years later. In December 1794, Dixon successfully prosecuted John McArdell, a journeyman shoemaker, for seeking to negotiate an illegal wage increase. The Commission of Oyer and Terminer sentenced McArdell to gaol for six months.[104]

In June 1792, the *Hibernian Journal* published a satirical essay called the "Shoeboy's Address to the Citizens." 1792 was a year of hardship and industrial unrest in the Liberties. Shorter working hours, lower wages, higher prices and increased taxation made conditions for ordinary working people more austere than before. In this commentary on life in Dublin, two shoe-polishers named Madden and Rooney explain why they have increased the price for shining a pair of shoes to two marks. The text, in which words were spelled as they were pronounced (the words "pig," "hog" and "make" refer to a coin called a mark), is a rare example of colloquial English spoken by working people in late eighteenth-century Dublin:

TO DE PEOPLE

We, de Shuboys of de city, made a resolution not to clean shues less dan a pare a coppers de pare. We usd to get a make a hundred yeers ago, when we could live on a couple of pigs in de week; now dat we cant get so much as a rotten egg widout payin for it, and when dere is not a trade in de city dat did not get their wages razd, why shouldt wee? If dere be any of our trade dat does not stick up to de rules of our body, weel colt him. Dere is a great many people may wonder at us for raizing our price, but are we not as good as any oder trade? Havent we as good a right to it as de painters? Dont we handle de brush as well as dem? But de say we did not serve a time to it; but we find our own stuff, dat de do not. We expect dere is not one dat has de smallest drop ove gentleman's blood in him will refuse us our price, especially when de noe how hard it is to get tings. You wont get a pair of eggs now less dan tree makes. If you go in now to call for a glass, deil charge you a pair of coppers, when we remember to get a full naggin for it. Dese dam police has risd everyting on us. You wont get a decent bed now less dan a teaster a week, when we remember three of us to have a bed in de Liberty for a pig. Dere is anoder ting; dere is such a damn parcel of bricklayers and plaisterers, dat it is de Devil to paint deir shoes for dem; it takes almost a hole egg to give dem any sort ove a polish; but de Devil resave the bricklayr or plaisterers shues weel do less dan tree coppers de pare aveter dis, for dey may take notice ove it. Dey say we are a parcel of vagabonds, but de lie; dere is nere a tradesman in de city wears a cleaner shirt ove a Sunday dan we do. We are a parcel of decent fellows, and can pay for our naggin as well as demselves; and dere souls to de gallows, why should dey refuse to give us our price, when dey get deir own. But I will tell you how one ove dem was gong to sconce Nickey, de red shueb[o]y, dat servd his time to Cheny Eye, at de corner of Anglesea-street: when Nickey gave de last polish to his crabshells, de fellow handed over a make. Dis wont do, says Nickey: Why soa, says de oder? Why, bekase you must hand over a pare ove dem, says Nickey. Id see your soul to de gallows first, says the fellow. Why, den, says Nickey you must fight me for it; you see he had blood in him. Nickey stript ove in have a second; and in less dan a pare ove minutes closd his day-lights, and dats de way weell serve all such fellows, if de dont behave demselves, do de Chancellor may take deir part. So, Mr Printer, we will be much obligd to ye to let de people noe, dat de may not be vext with us for any ting we do aveter dis. Signed by Dicky Madden, at de old established corner of Anglesea-street; And by Ohi Rooney, at de constable corner of Christ Church-lane, for all de rest ove our trade.[105]

Overall, journeymen shoemakers faced an uphill battle to obtain wage increases. Inflation was driving up the cost of living and, indeed, the journeymen argued that the cost of living was so high that they could no longer support themselves and their families without obtaining a large wage increase.[106] In May 1794, an estimated 50 master shoe-makers offered a £50 reward for the prosecution and conviction of journeymen shoemakers involved in industrial disputes.[107] In July 1794, John Dooley, a master shoemaker in South Great George's Street, arrested four journeymen shoemakers at Higginson's Ale House in High Street. Union books, papers and cards were seized in the raid, a similar tactic employed against the journeymen carpenters 13 years earlier. The four journeymen shoemakers were charged as members of the "Superior Council," which oversaw the activities of an illegal journeyman committee, "the Crispin Union," which repre-sented shoemakers.[108] The Commission of Oyer and Terminer con-victed them on charges of having sought to increase wages illegally. They were sentenced to 12 months in gaol and placed on bail for three years.[109]

Dooley had also been the victim of a minor burglary four years earlier. In October 1790, his shop in South Great George's Street was burgled, but William Shea, the chief inspector of the Dublin police, arrested the hapless burglar, James Murphy, with a pair of stolen boots on his feet. At his trial, it was established that Murphy had forcibly removed a set of locked window shutters attached to Dooley's shop and had pushed an innocent boy through a window to steal footwear valued at £30.[110] Convicted by the Commission of Oyer and Terminer, Murphy was hanged on Saturday 30 October 1790.[111]

In 1791, the journeymen carpenters won a large wage increase in their daily pay packet—from 3s. to 3s. 6d., an increase of 14 per cent. (Between 1761 and 1792, wages paid to carpenters increased by 75 per cent.)[112] The 1791 wage rise apparently annoyed the building masters, who banded together to draft a new combination bill which would impose drastic measures against organised labour.[113] In March 1792, the Recorder of the Dublin Quarter Sessions, Denis George, presented the bill of the master builders to Parliament. George claimed that combinations had increased in strength and numbers since the jour-neymen carpenters had organised their committee in 1761. According to him, the journeymen carpenters had pushed wages from ten shil-lings per week to a guinea per week between 1761 and 1792, an increase of over 110 per cent. The builders also claimed that the journeyman committees had limited them to a certain number of apprentices and that in "almost every trade the masters experienced the same hard-ships." [114]

In an amended form, the bill passed through the House of Commons. But it met opposition in the House of Lords.[115] John Fitzgibbon, the Chancellor of the Exchequer, said that the bill represented "a system of oppression and injustice" and should have been called "a bill for the encouragement of outlaweries and highway robberies." He feared that it would encourage industrial violence on building sites in Dublin and elsewhere. Fitzgibbon's stand against the combination bill was followed by demonstrations in the summer of 1792. Thousands of journeymen carpenters demonstrated their anger at the bill in marches and rallies in the Liberties and at Phoenix Park, concerning not only this issue but also the threat to jobs from imported goods.[116] The bill failed to pass the House of Lords, marking a clear victory for the journeyman committees.

In summary, the 1780 Combinations Act proved to be as ineffective a deterrent to combinations as any previous legislation. It is debatable whether Parliament helped the masters or hindered them from going about their business as all the anti-combination laws came to nothing. The absence of proper legislation encouraged journeyman committees to develop their own strategies for winning industrial disputes, by leading well-organised and violent struggles against the masters. When the economic recovery of the 1780s gave way to the sharp downturn of the 1790s, industrial conflict became even more frequent and bloody.

The journeyman committees were the true survivors of late eighteenth-century Dublin, outlasting the Volunteers, the new police and Parliament itself. Despite their weaknesses, these committees survived to tell their proud story where others with far greater resources had failed. With their strength in numbers, their spirit for combinations, their organisational skills and even their predilection for violent behaviour, these rudimentary working-class organisations dug the footings for the powerful trade unions of the twentieth century.[117]

CHAPTER FOUR

Murder at Large

In the 16 years between 1780 and 1795, the *Hibernian Journal* reported 189 murders, approximately 12 per year. Prosecutions of murderers during this period, however, resulted in only 21 hangings (17 men and 4 women). In fact, of the 199 convicted felons known to have been hanged in Dublin at this time, murderers accounted for a mere 11 per cent of the total hanged. Many factors accounted for this apparent failure to bring more of these violent criminals to justice. Private prosecutions were an expensive business, particularly for those surviving relatives who were too poor to pay the cost of legal fees. Even when murderers were brought to court, convictions were often difficult to obtain. Juries were unwilling to convict on the basis of circumstantial evidence and key witnesses were often unwilling to come forward.

It is likely that the introduction of the new police in 1786 began to alter collective mentalities. The new police often deterred violent offenders and encouraged more prosecutions for murder. In the eight years between 1780 and 1787, the *Hibernian Journal* reported 116 murders. In the following eight years, however, the same newspaper reported 73 murders, which represents a significant decrease of 37 per cent. Prosecutions for murder, however, increased in nearly inverse proportion. In the first half of the period, 38 prosecutions for murder were heard in Dublin courts, but in the latter half there were 50, an increase of 32 per cent.

If measured by the number of murders, levels of violence in Dublin were exceedingly high in 1780. In this year alone, the *Hibernian Journal* reported 26 murders—over two murders per month. Only four murderers were prosecuted in 1780, underlining the degree to which perpetrators of violence went undetected and unpunished in this year. In February 1780, two unknown gunmen shot Dr John Moore in the thigh in Dorset Street.[1] Neighbours came to his rescue, but the killers escaped. Dr Moore died of his wounds, giving rise to a gloomy report which said that "murder in this city has become so common, that it has lost all its horrors; every day teems with new instances of the most horrid barbarity."[2] It does not appear that Moore's killers were ever caught because two months later Dublin Castle was still offering a £50 reward for information leading to the arrest and conviction of the attackers.[3]

In 1780 alone, defendants in three of the four prosecutions for murder were watchmen or guards, suggesting either that only the most visible cases of homicide were detected or that policemen may have been scapegoats for a public demanding justice. Although sentences of death were imposed on all three policemen, no hangings were carried out, according to the newspapers.

After the Gordon riots in June 1780, it was feared that prisoners who had broken out of London's Newgate prison would flee to Dublin to avoid re-committal to their former lodgings.[4] This fear was compounded in the wake of second prison breakout in London in just as many years. The escape from the prison hulks at Woolwich in London in 1782 prompted the Lord Mayor of Dublin to open lines of communication between Dublin and Bow Street magistrates to apprehend "those offenders and atrocious villains who fly from justice to either city."[5] Two months later, a list of 117 prisoners who had escaped from prisons in London was drawn up by London magistrates.[6]

Apart from releasing convicted felons onto the streets of Dublin, the Gordon riots contributed towards a general breakdown in law and order. Immediately after the riots, four soldiers burgled the Liffey Street Chapel.[7] Within six months of the riots, at least three Catholic clergymen were attacked: Rev. Mr Barnabas O'Farell, who had large paving stones thrown at him in Britain Street in July 1780, Rev. Mr Boylan, who was attacked in Anglesea Street in October and died of his wounds in the following month, and Rev. Mr Conolly, who was wounded by gunshot in Ranelagh Road on Christmas Day.[8] The picture that emerges of criminality in Dublin, therefore, is a complex interplay between pre-existing social relations which led to criminal opportunism and exogenous factors such as war, insurrection and religious conflict. A fast-growing city, Dublin drew together this violent mixture.

Almost all murders outside of the household had a motive, with the exceptions proving the rule.[9] The gang that murdered Rev. Boylan in Anglesea Street had no apparent motive. The fact that his murder occurred five months after the Gordon riots in London suggests that the gunmen were motivated by sectarian reasons. Rev. Boylan was not robbed and robbery was usually the principal motive in non-household killings. Doctors were particularly at risk of attack as they were often visiting patients at their homes at all hours of the day and night. The murder of Dr Moore in Dorset Street was followed eight months later by the robbery of Dr Francis Montgomery in nearby Mabbot Street. Having just visited a patient, Dr Montgomery was robbed of his hat, shoe and knee buckles and surgical instruments.[10] His attackers wore aprons and carried long knives, which made him suspect they were local butcher boys.

Murders within the extended household and the family were, understandably, easier to trace than random murders. In December 1780, a coroner's inquest was held in the case of a man murdered in a lodging house near the upper Coombe. The returned verdict was of murder by person(s) unknown. The inquest heard evidence that the deceased, who had a heavy drink problem, returned to his lodgings intoxicated. He lived in a "poor lodging room" with six other tenants, who all gave testimony at the inquest. The inquest heard that his landlady confronted him at the door, demanding his back rent—which he had spent on alcohol. A struggle broke out and the man sustained a concussion on the right temple. None of the witnesses, however, saw the landlady deliver the fatal blow. Although testimony at the coroner's inquest implicated the landlady in the murder of her tenant, examinations were not lodged against her.[11]

A jury presiding at a coroner's inquest had the power to return verdicts in the event of homicide. If the jury's verdict was wilful murder, examinations were often lodged with a magistrate against those suspected of the crime. Thus, to protect the integrity of the coroner's verdict, any tampering with the composition of the coroner's jury was cause for concern. In December 1780, Mr Simpson, who kept a china shop in Essex Street, was murdered at a public house on Essex Quay. Mr Farrel, the owner of the public house, claimed that Simpson had slipped and fallen into a cellar in front of the public house. Farrel and a group of others carried Simpson's body to his home on a bier. Suspicions about Simpson's death arose, however, and a coroner's inquest was established. When Farrel heard about it, he sought to obtain a place on the coroner's jury, but the chief coroner turned his request down. "Composed of persons of credit," the jury at the inquest returned a verdict of murder, after which examinations were lodged against the publican. Meanwhile Farrel left town and, when a sheriff failed to find him at home, he arrested his wife and maid servant and committed them to Newgate.[12] The fact that his wife and servant were taken to be accomplices in the murder of Simpson suggests that members of a publican's household could face prosecution following crimes or disturbances committed on the premises.

In 1781, the *Hibernian Journal* reported a total of 19 murders, down 27 percent on the year before. Only one of the total of four prosecutions for murder that year resulted in a conviction and, in that case, the court settled on a verdict of manslaughter.[13] The case involved a dispute between the crews of two coal vessels, in which one man died of wounds inflicted by a handpike.[14] High levels of violence were typical among working people in Dublin, but the docks seemed to have more than their fair share of brutality.

In 1785, the number of murders jumped to 26—a return to the level of 1780 and a sharp increase over the four murders reported in the *Hibernian Journal* the previous year. In the month of August alone, five murders received widespread attention: a boy was killed in a sword fight, a soldier was bayoneted to death, a man murdered his mother with a razor, a labourer murdered a skilled stonecutter with a bayonet, and a watchman murdered the son of the keeper of a cock pit in Essex Street with a blunderbuss. By September it was said that "simple robbery, where no violence or cruelty is used, may be reckoned almost a virtue."[15]

In August 1785, William Fullarton, a watchman for St. Thomas parish, arrested James Elliot as he climbed into the window of his lover's house in Mabbot Street. The son of the cock pit keeper in Essex Street, Elliot managed to escape the grasp of Fullarton, but was shot in the back by his blunderbuss.[16] A coroner's inquest returned a verdict of wilful murder and examinations were lodged against Fullarton for murder.[17] On 27 February 1786, the Commission of Oyer and Terminer ruled that the killing of Elliot was a "justifiable homicide." The jury found Fullarton guilty of manslaughter.[18] No details of the terms of his punishment were reported, but it is likely he was only sentenced to prison for six months and burned in the hand.

In the same month that Elliot was murdered, a family dispute led to the death of a mother and the hanging of her son. Intoxicated at the time of the incident, James Ennis slashed his mother to death and badly cut his father with a razor blade at their home in Angel Alley.[19]

He had come home to eat, but his mother refused him a meal.[20] She then ordered her husband, a barber by profession, to give him a sound beating. In the ensuing brawl, Ennis pulled the razor from his pocket and cut his father in the arms, thighs and body. When his mother stepped into the fray, Ennis slashed her once across the left arm, cutting her arteries and veins. With blood spurting from her wounds, she went for treatment at an apothecary's shop in High Street, but the apothecary refused to administer first-aid. A surgeon and a clergyman arrived at the Ennis house, but such was the loss of blood that she died three hours after the attack.

Once word of her murder got out, a wave of anger swept the Liberties. An angry multitude of people seized Ennis, but a sheriff rescued him from the crowd, conveying him to Newgate prison, where he was remanded until his trial. Surprisingly, members of the Ennis family rallied round James or at least sought to prevent his prosecution. Samuel Gamble, a linen-draper in High Street, determined to bring Ennis to trial, paid for the costs of his prosecution. Some prosecution witnesses were forced to take out "articles of peace" against family relations of Ennis, who tried in vain to stop them from giving testimony.[21] Family obstruction of the prosecution failed in the face of an overwhelming sense of public outrage at the murder of one family member by another. A jury found Ennis guilty and the judge at the Commission of Oyer and Terminer sentenced him to hang.[22] On Saturday 15 October 1785, Ennis was hanged in front of Newgate prison, attended by a large crowd of people.[23]

If quarrelling among family members degenerated into deadly brawls, disputes among neighbours could also turn vicious. It is suggested by the evidence that residents in local communities continuously turned against each other over minor non life-threatening incidents. In March 1789, after a day's work, a brewery worker relieved himself at the steps of a cellar in Dirty Lane. Unbeknownst to John O'Hoolahan, he was urinating on a man and wife who lived at the bottom of the stairs.[24] Woken from his sleep, Anthony Dempsey surfaced from his open cellar to ask O'Hoolahan not to urinate on him. Intoxicated, O'Hoolahan "bade him ask his a__e," upon which Dempsey delivered O'Hoolahan a devastating blow on the temple. He died almost instantly. A coroner's inquest returned a verdict of wilful murder.[25] In July 1789, after a jury found Dempsey guilty, the Commission of Oyer and Terminer sentenced him to be hanged, quartered and beheaded.[26] Counsel for Dempsey, however, successfully pleaded an arrest of judgement, arguing that their client did not show a "premeditated design of effecting the death of the deceased." Dempsey's case then went before the King's Bench, which apparently reduced his conviction from murder to manslaughter.[27] Dempsey's crime underscores the unassailable—that poor living conditions contributed in no small measure to high levels of violence.

In 1790, the number of murders reported in the *Hibernian Journal* surged upwards to 19 from 11 the previous year, giving rise to lurid imaginings on the part of the middle classes. On Monday 4 October 1790, the body of a bricklayer was brought before a sexton at St. Kevin's church for burial, but after "overhearing some suspicious conversation" the sexton suspected that the deceased had been murdered. Before burying Hugh Donnelly, he called upon a magistrate to summon a jury to investigate the circumstances surrounding his death. It transpired that on Thursday 31 September 1790, Donnelly had spent the night at a funeral wake. On Friday, a chairman had taken Donnelly home from the wake "violently afflicted with a colic." To cure himself, Donnelly drank nothing but salt and water until he died "in extreme agony" on Saturday. Whether Donnelly died of dehydration or an illness contracted at the wake was never determined, but surgeon Smith did report that no marks of violence were found on his body nor were signs of poisoning evident. The suspicions of the sexton were thus disproved by the inquest jury, which returned a verdict of natural death.[28]

Evidence drawn from the *Hibernian Journal* indicates that the murder rate declined considerably with 33 murders being reported between 1791 and 1795—only 17 percent of the total number between 1780 and 1795. This decline suggests that the police managed to bring the level of murder under control. Over the same period, however, 30 prosecutions for murder occurred—34 percent of the total number of such prosecutions between 1780 and 1795. This increase would seem to suggest that the process of detection had also improved.

Guns were used in 51 murders and unlawful killings. Weapons included muskets and hunting rifles, but the gun employed in the majority of murders was the pistol, the preferred weapon of professional criminals and duellers. According to the newspaper, the 87 duels or so that occurred in Dublin during this period resulted in the deaths of nine men and injuries to many more. While the chances of being killed in a duel were only about one in ten, the chances of being seriously injured were much higher.

None of the four prosecutions for murder initiated as a result of fatal duels resulted in murder convictions. In April 1782, Mr Samuel Forster Jr., who lived in North Earl Street, shot Mr J. Anderson through the head, near the left eye, in a duel at the North Lotts. Anderson died two days later.[29] In October of that year, Forster appeared before the Commission of Oyer and Terminer charged with murder. He successfully argued that the death of Anderson was a justifiable homicide and, as a result, the court reduced the charge of murder to manslaughter. Moreover, the judge released Forster on bail in recognition of his "distinguished" behaviour in court.[30] In January 1787, Counsellor Dominick Trant shot Sir John Conway Colthurst in the chest at a duel near Bray. Colthurst died of his injuries.[31] (Trant was shot twice in the chest, but a heavy coat protected him from injury.)[32] Trant was charged with murder but, in the following July, the Commission of Oyer and Terminer acquitted him.[33] In February 1792, Roderick O'Connor killed Henry Kerr in a duel on the same North Lotts.[34] At the Commission of Oyer and Terminer in the following July, O'Connor was likewise admitted to bail after his trial was postponed. He was acquitted at the next Commission.[35]

In July 1790, William Whaley, an officer in the military and a member of a well-known Dublin family, shot Counsellor Dennis Kelly in a duel at Stephen's Green.[36] The death of Kelly, who was survived by his wife and small children, is noteworthy for two reasons. First, Kelly took the unusual step of making out a will just before the duel, showing that he recognised the possibility that the duel might result in his death. Second, the *Hibernian Journal* published two long poems, written by Ann Kelly, his wife, in September 1790.[37]

In her first poem, Ann Kelly explained why Whaley intended to kill her husband. Before the duel, a dispute erupted over some money that Whaley owed to Kelly. In the heat of the moment, Kelly produced a horsewhip and whipped his debtor around a room. His wife, however, found poetic justice in Whaley's whipping:

> He who Hibernia's sacred fame
> From infamy once wrung,
> The horse-whip'd Twist,—to tell, O shame
> Had round thy carcase sung.

So neat he whip'd, so smacking sweet,—
    In truth I this may write,
No phaeton beats with whip in street,
    Could smack with more delight.

E'en by the handle of thy face
    He led thee a sad dance;
And round a room—oh sad disgrace!
    For fun he made thee prance.

In truth to say a man you met,
    Both able, Sir, and willing,
To pay with whip a lawful debt,
    Contracted with a villain.

The reputation of the Whaley family as "hell-raisers" went back a
generation. Richard Chapell Whaley, William's father, was a magistrate and "a notorious priest-hunter," who built a palatial house at No.
86 Stephen's Green South. Thomas Whaley, William's brother, de-
voted much of his time to gambling at Daly's Club and, in 1788, went
on a much-publicised trip to Jerusalem on a wager. His mounting
debts from gambling eventually ruined his finances and he left Dublin
permanently before his death in November 1800.[38] Ann Kelly, while
acknowledging the "noble" reputation of the Whaley family, spared
no words to conceal her contempt for William's behaviour:

Ah! then you great, you noble crew,
    What gun is it to take
A life away—and more pursue,
    While honour is at stake?

Honour!—the bloody trump can found,
    A breath too often used,
And sink into a depth profound,
    A soul through life abus'd.

But O! thou bleeding piece of clay,
    How hard was thy sad doom?
Thou little thought another day
    Shou'd lose thy manly bloom.

In her second poem, Ann Kelly struck a chord of pessimism and lamentation. It was with apparent difficulty that she came to terms with her loss and grief:

> O life! What are thou but a breath,
>   That which a moment gave;
> But 'twist the doating nurse and death,
>   The cradle and the grave.

Putting words into action, Ann Kelly prosecuted Whaley for murder. Due to the non-appearance of key witnesses in court, the first trial at the Commission of Oyer and Terminer was postponed in October 1790 and Whaley was discharged after he had entered into a recognisance of £4,000 and two sureties of £2,000 each.[39] At the next Commission in December, Anne Kelly did not appear in court and Whaley was acquitted for want of prosecution.[40]

Ann Kelly's public cry of outrage was in marked contrast to the soft approach of the courts towards duellers. She was not alone, however, as public opinion also turned against duelling. After a lengthy historical analysis, the *Hibernian Journal* concluded that duelling was "a mongrel compounded of romantic bravery, Gothic barbarism, and diabolical anti-christianity."[41] The apparent contradiction between the public perception towards duelling and the legal perception anticipated later changes in the law, whereby the frequency of duelling declined dramatically in the nineteenth century.

As well as being the favoured weapons of duellers, pistols were also employed by members of Dublin's criminal fraternity. One of the most well-known murders in Dublin involved a gang of thieves and burglars armed with pistols. In January 1790, a shipload of returned convicts, earlier expelled from Newfoundland, arrived in Dublin. Shortly thereafter, a report surfaced of a robbery committed by two of their number. John Cunningham and one Ellis were accused of robbing Mr Robinson, a cotton-printer, of his watch and money at Beggar's Bush.[42] (At his hanging for a different crime over two years later, Cunningham denied any involvement in the Robinson robbery.[43] In his dying statement, he also revealed that he had robbed the Earl of Clanwilliam in October 1791, a crime for which Police Inspector William Shea had arrested William Dalton, a returned convict who had been transported to the West Indies in November 1789.)[44]

In July 1790, Cunningham escaped from Newgate along with 40 others, but Shea arrested him a month later.[45] That October, the Dublin Quarter Sessions convicted Cunningham of assaulting Shea, sentenced him to gaol for six months and ordered him to find security for his good behaviour.[46] Along with two other men, Cunningham was also convicted that same month by the Commission of Oyer and Terminer for the burglary of John Kealy's house in Bride's Alley, but the conviction was reduced to a lesser offence.[47] After Cunningham completed his six-month prison sentence, he left Ireland temporarily and travelled to England, where he robbed a man at Prescott, Lancashire, in August 1791. (At his hanging, he also said that an innocent man had been hanged for this crime.)

Cunningham returned to Dublin soon after the Prescott robbery to join up with George Robinson, the leader of a gang in the Liberties which was committing crimes—including murder and highway robbery—over a wide area of Dublin. In March 1792, Shea took charge of a police effort to bring the gang to justice, working closely with Police Commissioner William James. Apart from Cunningham, the gang was composed of George Robinson, the principal leader and son of a carpenter, William Norton, the only Protestant of unknown occupation, Charles Brooks, a former sailor, John Conran, an informer and former shoemaker, and several other small-time thieves. Between December 1791 and March 1792, the gang committed several crimes, including the attempted burglary of a shop in Upper Ormond Quay, the robbery of a woman at Goldenbridge, the robbery of George Sturgeon in Marlborough Street and the robbery of two men named Blair and Magee.[48] They also attempted to burgle the house of Benjamin Lyneal in Dolphin's Barn on three occasions, the later one resulting in Lyneal's death from a gunshot wound to the chest.

Robinson's gang had been thieving in the Dolphin's Barn area of Dublin since February 1790, when residents were said to be fleeing the area.[49] In February 1792, the gang stepped up its activities with the arrival of Cunningham. On 1 February, Dalton, the returned transport, was arrested for attempting to burgle Blair's premises by picking the lock. Dalton was not charged with any crime, perhaps because he provided the police with information. Cunningham, Brooks and Robinson were later charged with the burglary of Blair's house and an unspecified offence against Magee. A gold watch belonging to either Blair or Magee was found on Robinson's person.

On 10 March, the gang robbed a woman of her money at Golden bridge after she pleaded with them that "she had nothing left to buy bread for her children."[50] It is unlikely they stole much in this theft. On the following night, the gang moved their operations from Dolphin's Barn to the north-east quadrant of the city, where they robbed George Sturgeon, a wealthy resident of Summer Hill. Sturgeon was relieved of his double-cased gold watch, capped and jewelled, a silver-mounted Moroccan leather pocket-book containing a promissory note for £36 and half a guinea. Sturgeon found the two empty cases of his watch at a pawnbroker's, but the works had been taken out. His robbery may have been planned well in advance. In January 1784, Matthew Seery, a former servant at Sturgeon's house in Gloucester Street, robbed him of silver and cloth.[51] Sturgeon's advertisement for the arrest of Seery may very well have drawn attention to his wealth.

On Friday night 16 March 1792, the Robinson gang robbed the house of Benjamin Lyneal in Cork Street. They had gone to the Lyneal house on two previous occasions to rob it, but observed on one occasion that the "brass rapper had been taken in, and concluded that the family were in bed."[52] A far greater deterrent, but one which was dismissed, was the likelihood that neighbours of the Lyneals, who were mostly weavers, would come to their defence in the event of a robbery. In fact, one gang member who refused to take part in the burglary described the weavers as "people of resolution."[53] To allay the growing fears of his gang, Robinson boasted that "we're strong enough to drive all Dolphin's Barn before us."[54]

Robinson, Norton, Brooks, Cunningham and Conran armed themselves with stolen pistols and swords and, without attracting any notice, made their way to the front door of the house. Inside, Lyneal, his two daughters and a friend named Mr Crane were playing cards. Outside, Robinson disguised his voice to trick the maid servant into opening the door. A commotion ensued when the door opened. Hearing the noise, Lyneal and Crane rushed to the foyer. Lyneal grabbed Conran's pistol, but it went off and discharged a lead bullet into his chest. Lyneal died instantly. Meanwhile, Crane was overpowered by Brooks, who wielded a sword. Crane would have been killed, but miraculously survived when the sword broke into two pieces after it was thrust into his chest.

The scabbard to the sword was found by a policeman in a garden opposite. Robinson dropped his gun in the hallway and part of Norton's pistol fell in the street outside. An observant policeman found the trigger guard. The gang then attempted to rob a public house, but three of them were arrested, one with a pistol barrel in his possession. The pistol barrel matched Norton's pistol guard and thus became a part of the evidence against Norton and the entire gang.

William Shea put pressure on Conran to become an informer, apparently not suspecting that it was Conran who had fired the fatal shot. He conveyed Conran to a cell in the debtor's side of Newgate prison, where "the rats used to run over" him.[55] This arrangement did not please Conran, but was only changed when Police Commissioner James secured a confession from him in return for a room at the Marshalsea, a separate debtor's prison. On the basis of his confession, police arrested the remaining two gang members and conveyed them to Newgate to await their trial.

At the Commission of Oyer and Terminer on 18 July 1792, events did not go according to plan. Conran testified against the other four, but Counsellor Leonard MacNally discredited his testimony: "What degree of credit is due to the evidence of a man, who, after himself being guilty of the whole catalogue of human crime, comes here to swear against other men, with a view to save his own neck and secure a reward."[56] The four were first acquitted of the robbery of Sturgeon and then were tried for the murder of Lyneal. At the end of the second trial, a juror was seized with an epileptic fit. In the confusion, Brooks attempted to escape, but Shea stopped him.[57] Despite immediate medical attention to the juror from Dr Teeling, Judge William Downes discharged the jury and postponed the case to the following Commission of Oyer and Terminer in October 1792. Counsellor William Caldbeck objected, on behalf of the prosecution. The prisoners, however, were conveyed back to Newgate to stand their second trial.

While in Newgate, the four men were conveyed to the Kilmainham Quarter Sessions to stand trial for the robbery of the woman at Goldenbridge. Ominously, the judge at the Kilmainham court was Counsellor William Caldbeck, the same lawyer who had prosecuted them at the Commission of Oyer and Terminer in July. He sat in as *locum tenens* for Robert Day, the acting chairman of the Kilmainham Quarter Sessions, for the August sessions.[58] It is not clear whether Conran testified against the four men, but the weight of evidence and the adverse publicity surrounding the earlier trial would have been sufficient. The jury returned a guilty verdict and, not surprisingly, Caldbeck sentenced them to hang at Kilmainham Commons on Wednesday 12 September 1792.

Caldbeck wore two different hats (albeit in two courts) to obtain a conviction against the Robinson gang, one as a prosecutor and the other as a judge. This questionable stratagem drew the attention of Dublin Castle. The Lord Lieutenant demanded a report of the Kilmainham trial from Caldbeck and, in the meantime, temporarily respited the hangings of the four men. The Lord Lieutenant was satisfied with Caldbeck's report and the hangings were scheduled for Saturday 15 September. Thousands of people from Dublin and the surrounding counties turned up for the public spectacle. Rev. Mr Gamble of the Church of Ireland and the chaplain of Newgate attended Norton while Rev. Mr McKernan of the Roman Catholic Church attended Robinson, Brooks and Cunningham.

One after the other, each of the four condemned prisoners was made to confess to their various crimes in Ireland and England, for many of which several innocent men had been convicted and hanged. In addition, each made detailed statements which established beyond a reasonable doubt that Conran had fired the fatal shot which killed Benjamin Lynear Cunningham said that Conran "could not help firing, as the gentleman who struggled with him held a death grip of the pistol he held."[59] (Two weeks after the hanging, John Conran was arrested for a robbery, but the Dublin Quarter Sessions discharged him at the order of Dublin Castle.)[60]

The weapons settled upon in many other homicides ranged across a wide spectrum. Rifles, a common sight in the countryside, caused a number of fatalities in the suburbs of Dublin. In July 1794, John Farrell was indicted for the murder of Frank Farrell (no relation). Both 15-years-olds were working on a building site near the house of Dean Coote at Stillorgan Park when John fired a shotgun and hit the back of Frank, who died at Mercer's hospital two days later. At the Commission of Oyer and Terminer, one Mr Cody, master of the deceased, testified that John did not intend to shoot Frank, but "that he was only exercising as a volunteer." Apparently this convinced the jury, who acquitted the defendant.[61]

In 56 homicides, the means of death was by sharp instruments, including long knives, daggers, dirks, swords, and handpikes. Bayonets accounted for at least ten fatalities. Many deaths were caused by sharp instruments not designed as weapons but as tools. Butchers', curriers', and shoemakers' tools often found their way into the hands of killers; hatchets, slaughtering axes, barber razors, bill hooks, and tailoring scissors became weapons of destruction.[62]

On 1 July 1793, Henry Grogan, a retired shoemaker, quarrelled violently with his wife. Taking up one of the knives he designed for his trade, Grogan chased his wife out of their upstairs lodgings into a tobacco shop in Watling Street. Wielding his knife, Grogan pulled it on a female customer who got in the way, slashing her across the face and breasts. Grogan then stabbed James Gordon, the owner of the shop, in the heart after he tried to protect his customers. Gordon died instantly. Afterwards, Grogan "wiped the bloody knife in his coat, threw it away, and went up to his room to bed."[63]

According to the evidence, Grogan was the first prisoner in Dublin to be indicted under the 1791 Murder Act.[64] Offenders convicted under the act were punished in the same manner as those convicted under the 1784 Houghing Act. On Friday 5 July 1793, the Commission of Oyer and Terminer found Grogan guilty of murder and he was hanged at the front of Newgate prison on the following Monday. Afterwards, his body was conveyed to "Surgeons-hall for dissection, where his unhappy widow, though he attempted to murder her, attended, to beg the body for interment."[65] Blunt instruments, including instruments designed as tools of a trade, were used in approximately 26 homicides. Deaths were caused by such diverse weapons as the stock ends of muskets, hooked poles carried by watchmen, hangars, bludgeons, cudgels, oaken sticks, soldering irons, hammers, shovels, pokers, chisels and lapstones. The occasional household item could be brought into action as well, including pewter quarts and large keys.

In May 1791, the same William Whaley who had killed Counsellor Kelly in a duel less than a year earlier beat a coachman named James Purcell to death with a wooden cudgel in Denzil Street.[66] On the night of 18 May, he hired a coach to take him from the Rotunda to his lodgings in Denzil Street. He paid Purcell 1s. 7dh., but took the money back and went inside his house when the coach man "required to see if the money was good or not." Purcell shouted up to his window and rapped at his door for the correct fare and, in short order, got water thrown onto him and a beating with a large knotted cudgel. Whaley called the police, who were about to arrest Purcell when he drove off

Table 2: *Apparent Method of Killing*

SI	Sharp instrument		DR	Drowning
BI	Blunt instrument		PO	Poisoning
HK	Hitting, kicking, etc.		VE	Vehicular
SA	Strangulation or asphyxiation		OT	Other
SH	Shooting		NK	Not known
BU	Burning		TT	Total

Year	SI	BI	HK	SA	SH	BU	DR	PO	VE	OT	NK	TT
1780	6	3	2	2	3	0	2	0	0	0	18	36
1781	3	7	2	2	1	0	3	0	4	0	10	32
1782	1	1	1	1	2	0	4	0	0	0	3	13
1783	2	0	1	2	2	0	5	1	2	0	4	19
1784	1	0	1	0	2	0	5	0	0	0	6	15
1785	9	2	1	3	5	1	2	0	1	1	10	35
1786	3	1	2	2	2	0	4	0	0	2	7	23
1787	3	2	3	0	7	0	2	0	0	0	5	22
1788	5	0	3	5	2	0	5	2	0	1	8	31
1789	7	2	1	4	6	1	2	1	2	0	7	33
1790	2	2	6	3	4	0	5	1	0	1	23	47
1791	4	3	2	0	2	0	1	1	0	0	3	16
1792	2	3	1	2	4	0	0	0	0	2	5	19
1793	2	0	3	1	5	0	2	0	0	1	3	17
1794	2	0	0	0	2	0	6	0	0	0	1	11
1795	4	0	0	0	4	0	6	0	1	0	6	21
Total	56	26	29	27	53	2	54	6	10	8	119	390

(Source: *Hibernian Journal*, 1780–95.)

in his coach to his home in New Street. Purcell worked the following day, but he was dead within the week. A coroner examined the body and returned a verdict of wilful murder.

Whaley's trial was not heard until the following October, five months after the death of Purcell. Curiously, the judge at the Commission of Oyer and Terminer had sworn in a county jury to hear the case and return the verdict. One would have expected a city jury to be sworn in as the crime was committed within the city. It is not known why this occurred, unless a city jury was considered more sympathetic to the prosecution's case. At the trial, Clement Archer, a surgeon employed by the new police, directly contradicted the coroner's report, which stated that Whaley had murdered Purcell "by giving him several mortal strokes, kicks and bruises on the head, neck, breast, belly, and sides." Archer, who examined the body at the request of the coroner, claimed that Purcell could have died from "very bad putrid fevers in the neighbourhood" or even by the "great number of waist-coats" he wore. Purcell's brother and several other witnesses testified against the defendant, but none of them could undo the damage inflicted on the prosecution's case by the police surgeon. The jury took only three minutes to reach a verdict of not guilty and Whaley was acquitted of murder a second time in just as many years.[67]

While this case exemplifies the risks facing all taxi drivers in late eighteenth-century Dublin, the fact that Purcell's death at the hand of a fare happened less than a month after the murder of another taxi driver illustrates the copycat nature of the crime. In the early hours of Thursday morning 21 April 1791, a chairman named John Gordon was mortally wounded in Great Britain Street. He died at his home in Smithfield on the following day.[68] The incident began when Gordon and his partner, John Callaghan, picked up a female fare in Hanbury Lane. The woman was accompanied by Alexander Nesbitt, William Tyrell and a man named Wise. When they set down the fare at Kearney's Public House in Great Britain Street near the corner of Denmark Street, a dispute broke out over the payment of the chair hire. Tyrell and the woman had already gone into Kearney's, leaving Nesbitt and Wise to sort out the problem with the chairmen. Nesbitt gave them two shillings and a noggin of brandy, but this did not satisfy the fare and a violent brawl broke out. The consequences were fatal: Gordon was stabbed in the back, just below the shoulder, with a long bayonet. Nesbitt and Wise attempted to run away, but a lamplighter named Denis Parkinson seized the two men and brought them to a police guardhouse. Nesbitt was committed to Newgate prison, but Wise managed to escape from police custody. A coroner who examined the body of Gordon bound Parkinson over in a recognisance of £100 to prosecute against Nesbitt.

In July 1791, at the Commission of Oyer and Terminer, the testimony of the prosecution witnesses went conclusively against the defendant.[69] The dying deposition of Gordon was read in court and Callaghan and Parkinson both testified that Nesbitt had stabbed Gordon in the back. On behalf on the defendant, several witnesses, including the owner of Kearney's Public House, testified that one of the chairmen had knocked

Nesbitt down and kicked him. A passer-by to the incident testified that it was Wise who had stabbed Gordon and not Nesbitt. After considering the evidence for two hours, the jury brought in a verdict of guilty. Since the murder took place two weeks before Parliament passed the 1791 Murder Act, Nesbitt was not indicted under it and the Lord Lieutenant respited his hanging on several occasions.[70] The whereabouts of Wise, the man alleged to have committed the murder, remained a mystery and Nesbitt was quietly hanged at the front of Newgate prison on Wednesday 2 November 1791.[71]

The causes of homicide were as varied as they were frequent. About 30 people died from hitting and kicking, 27 of asphyxiation and strangulation and at least 10 in vehicular incidents caused by careless horsemen and carriage drivers. In 1781, four people in Dublin were killed by careless drivers, including a man who was run over by a chaise carrying the servants of the Lord Lieutenant. In compensation, the Lord Lieutenant offered to make payments to his wife and family.[72] Six people were poisoned to death, one by an industrial solution. In September 1791, a boy who worked at a button factory on Merchants Quay poisoned another boy by offering him a glass of spirits which turned out to be a highly dangerous acid, possibly sulphuric acid. The victim "expired in the utmost agonies."[73]

Many deaths were caused by riots which got out of control, including a riot in north Co. Dublin which led to the loss of two lives. In 1787, the small village of Finglas Bridge played host to the traditional St. Stephen's day celebration on 26 December and unwittingly became the scene of an ugly confrontation which left two people dead and many others injured. A group of journeymen butchers from the city went to Finglas to beat a bull with dogs but, failing to find an animal for their sport and much in liquor, they became violent on their way back to Dublin. At Finglas Bridge, the butchers chased townspeople into their houses and cabins, but the wife of Nicholas McCann did not make her escape in time. With the butchers in hot pursuit, she managed to reach the house of James McClean where her husband was. As soon as McClean opened the door to admit her, the gang burst into the house. What followed is not clear but it seems that David Bobbitt, one of the journeymen butchers, stabbed McClean with a bayonet and, in the struggle which ensued, Bobbitt himself was killed with a bill hook. The other ruffians ran out of McClean's house to wards the bridge pursued by McClean, McCann, Thomas McNamee and others. When the gang regrouped on the bridge, a violent confrontation broke out. Thomas Leggatt was later found dead from a sword wound. Afterwards, McClean and a number of others were taken to Meath Hospital, but Justice of the Peace Robert Wilson transferred McClean to Kilmainham gaol to stand trial for murdering Leggatt. Surgeon Rooney continued to treat McClean for his wounds at Kilmainham.[74]

In July 1788, the Commission of Oyer and Terminer acquitted Nicholas McCann of the murder of David Bobbitt.[75] At the same sessions, the Commission put McClean and McCann on trial for the murder of Thomas Leggatt. William Shaw testified that he saw McClean stab Leggatt with a bayonet. A jury acquitted McCann, but sentenced McClean to hang.[76] He was later reprieved and sentenced to transportation. With justice seen to be served in the case of Leggatt, the butchers wanted the same in the case of Bobbitt. In August 1788, examinations were lodged against Thomas McNamee for the murder of Bobbitt.[77] In October 1788, the Commission of Oyer and Terminer heard the trial, but it came too late for many residents from Finglas Bridge to give testimony; having waited till late in the afternoon, they had returned to their homes in the mistaken belief that the trial would take place on the following day.

On the same day, nine other trials were heard before McNamee's, including three murders, one attempted murder and several robberies and burglaries. No doubt the rapid pace of many criminal trials would have tired out less experienced witnesses, particularly those from the countryside and, by the time McNamee's trial was heard, only two character witnesses remained to give testimony. A country magistrate named Smith and a property owner named Bayly declared an interest in preserving law and order in north Co. Dublin but, despite their testimony, the Commission of Oyer and Terminer found McNamee (who was under 18) guilty of the murder of David Bobbitt, sentencing him to hang on 8 November 1788.[78] Following the conviction, McNamee wrote a long petition to the Lord Lieutenant, pleading a royal pardon.[79] Although sketchy reports of the riot appeared in newspapers, McNamee's petition remains the only detailed description of the episode and its aftermath.[80] At the same time, a letter to the Lord Lieutenant appeared in the *Hibernian Journal*, outlining the merits of McNamee's defence.[81] At the last minute, his hanging was respited for two weeks.[82] In December, a year following the riot, McNamee was finally granted a pardon.[83]

Violent riots were a feature of the annual bullfight on St. Stephen's Day 1789. A group of men, perhaps some of the same ones who had been to Finglas Bridge, were successful in their purchase of a bull. But they were less fortuitous in their selection of a site in which to hold the bullfight. They organised the contest behind a high stone wall in a vacant field near the new Custom House. Certain people opposed to the cruelty of the sport asked Sheriff James Vance to interrupt the contest but, aware of the potential for violence and ill with a cold, Vance was reluctant to proceed against the large crowd of men and boys assembled in the makeshift ring. Police Divisional Justice John Carleton, however, insisted that the city sheriff do his duty and, in the end, both Carleton and Vance advanced to the scene followed by a column of soldiers.[84]

When they arrived at the bottom of Abbey Street, the armed detachment marched directly through the gate into the enclosure and called a halt to the bullfight. The crowds, however, failed to disperse peacefully and, impatient with their stubbornness, Vance arrested eight onlookers. The quick arrests had the opposite effect from that anticipated by Vance. Instead of submitting to his authority, angry spectators pelted the soldiers with stones and oyster-shells as they poured out of the ring and into the streets. In retaliation, Vance ordered his men to open fire on the unarmed crowds. One man was immediately killed opposite the Custom House. A military detachment then chased a group of panic-stricken men up Abbey Street, where more volleys rang out. Three more unarmed men were shot dead. In all, four men were killed: James Mahassey, Patrick Keegan, Farrel Reddy and an unnamed man.[85]

On 27 December 1789, Alderman Henry Howison held a coroner's inquest at an infirmary in Jervis Street. Howison exonerated the soldiers, stating that they were acting under the orders of Vance and Carleton. In February 1790, the King's Bench heard the trial of Sheriff Vance, charged with the murder of Reddy. Family and friends of the deceased had no money to obtain proper legal representation, but they were able to organise a fund-raising meeting at St. Mary's parish hall. £50 was collected to obtain the legal services of Counsellor Archibald Hamilton Rowan, whose total bill came to £130. In his autobiography, Rowan said that firing on unarmed men was "a most diabolical exercise of power."[86] The jury, however, after deliberating for only one minute, acquitted Vance of murder.[87]

In late eighteenth-century Dublin, violent assaults were a daily feature of ordinary life. The number of assaults reported in the *Hibernian Journal* ranged in the hundreds. Assaults would often cause mortal injuries but, if not, they would invariably leave their victims with serious bodily injuries.

Servants and apprentices were occasionally targets of abuse and it was unlikely that legal redress would follow. Only if finances were made available from outside sources were servants able to press charges against their attackers. On 29 April 1792, Edward Wingfield Dowse and Robert Darlington violently assaulted Henry Neill, a defenceless servant. Both were wealthy property owners, one an agent of Lord Powerscourt and the other a fox-hunter. In December 1791, Neill's master, a Mr Patrickson, had ordered him to stand guard over a rabbit warren "with directions to shoot all dogs he should see." Neill did as he was told and shot one of Darlington's dogs. Four months later, Darlington and Dowse attacked Neill in front of a drinking house on the Scalp. Dowse hit him with the butt end of his whip, inflicting irreparable damage to one of his eyes. For over two weeks, surgeon Andrew Cranston attended Neill, but he lost permanent sight in the eye. In respect to the suffering caused to his servant, it is likely that Mr Patrickson paid for the cost of Neill's prosecution. At the trial, William Caldbeck, the prosecuting counsellor, said that the law provided "for the equal protection of every order of subject, and which warranted not the rich to tyrannize wantonly over the poor."[88] The two men were sentenced to two weeks in gaol and fined one mark each. They paid only £50 to Neill in compensation for the loss of his eye.

Violence against ordinary people, like violence against servants, seemed to be less tolerated in the courts by the mid-1790s. One case in particular would have brought this message home to the polite society of Dublin. On 22 September 1793, several members of the wealthy Egglesoe family travelled to Booterstown to spend the day at the home of one Mr Boyle. They were accompanied by a clergyman and a friend. Peter Egglesoe and his son Henry Egglesoe were prominent cabinet-makers and upholsters in Dublin. During dinner, James Ryan, the friend who accompanied the Egglesoes, sang some indecent songs to the party. No one complained about his rude behaviour at the time.

On the trip back to Dublin, however, the party split into two groups and Ryan was put into the same coach as the Egglesoe women. They were followed back to Dublin by the Egglesoe men and Rev. Mr Byrne in a four-wheel chaise. All went well until Ryan began to bother the women. He took "some indecent familiarities" and "behaved otherwise indecorously and troublesomely" towards Mrs Peter Egglesoe. In fact, Ryan put his legs under her petticoats. This unwanted attention caused her much distress and anger. As soon as the party arrived in College Green, Mrs Egglesoe complained to her son and husband about Ryan's disrespectful behaviour in the coach. She may have come to regret her decision for within a few minutes Ryan was laying in the street nearly dead of his injuries.

Henry Egglesoe, her son, immediately pulled Ryan out of the carriage, threw him onto the ground and mercilessly kicked and beat him. Ryan's legs sustained the brunt of the attack; one leg was smashed and broken by a blow from a cudgel. During the vicious assault, Peter Egglesoe and Rev. Mr Byrne looked on approvingly and did nothing to stop the son's fury. For the next three months, Ryan could barely move and remained in "very dangerous" condition. For a full year after the incident, he was unable to walk without crutches and extreme pain. As a result of his injuries, Ryan lost his job and an income of £30 per year.

Ryan, however, managed to raise the funds necessary to bring the Egglesoes to justice. In December 1793, the Commission of Oyer and Terminer found Henry Egglesoe guilty of assault, but acquitted Peter Egglesoe and Rev. Mr Byrne of aiding and abetting the attack.[89] Egglesoe's sentence was not reported, but it is estimated that he was sentenced to two weeks in gaol and fined one mark. Nine months following this conviction in the criminal court, Ryan sued Henry and Peter Egglesoe at the Court of Exchequer for £500 in damages.[90] After hearing the evidence, the court ruled that "the offence ... could not justify so violent an assault." Ryan was awarded £100 in damages, which was a large settlement by contemporary standards. By responding as they did, the courts expressed their determination to curb the violent appetites of the polite society.

This important change in the attitude of the courts towards gratuitous violence, however, did not represent a fundamental shift in thinking or a liberalisation of overall sentencing patterns. The severity with which the courts viewed property theft and the horrific punishments meted out to petty thieves remained an integral feature of Dublin society for a long time to come. Less than two weeks after the Egglesoes were publicly humiliated at the Court of Exchequer, they were back in court again. Peter Egglesoe launched a prosecution against a petty thief named Ann Foy for the theft of a chair valued at 10 shillings. Compared to the damage and injury sustained by Ryan, the theft of an item worth 10 shillings would amount to very little indeed, but this was not how the courts viewed matters. For this trivial theft, the Dublin Quarter Sessions sentenced Ann Foy to transportation for seven years.[91]

The thief was conveyed to Newgate prison but, as it was not known when the next convict ship would set sail to Australia, she was released to relieve overcrowding in prison. In the following May, however, her luck ran out. The Kilmainham Quarter Sessions convicted Foy, alias Ann Fay, and an accomplice named Catherine Byrne for breaking into a house and stealing goods worth just over four shillings. Foy was again sentenced to transportation.[92] This time, she was put on board the *Marquis Cornwallis*, which set off from Cork to Botany Bay in August 1795.[93]

According to the *Hibernian Journal*, the level of violence as measured by the number of assaults fell sharply over the 16-year period. In the eight years between 1780 and 1787, the newspaper reported 238 assaults. In the eight years between 1788 and 1795, however, the same newspaper reported only 99 assaults, a reduction of 58 percent. In contrast, the newspaper reported a steep increase in the instances of litigation for assault. In the first half of the period, the *Hibernian Journal* reported 65 prosecutions for assault, but in the last half of the period, the same newspaper reported 341 prosecutions for assault, an increase of 425 percent. To explain by example, six masters were put on trial for assault between 1780 and 1795, but five of these were tried in the 1790s. This increase in the number of prosecutions at the end of the period indicates that, with the introduction of the new police, Dublin became a far more litigious society.

Despite the great increase in litigation, the courts remained sympathetic to the wealthier members of society. Thomas Ward beat his apprentice Andrew Carty, aged 12, for two days, beginning on St. Stephen's day 1793. At one point Ward almost killed Carty with a sword. Surgeon Rivers, who treated Carty for several days following the attack, described his condition as "extremely ill." As a result, Carty pressed charges of assault against his master. In July 1794, the Commission of Oyer and Terminer heard the testimony of Carty as well as corroborative testimony from James Carty, his father.[94] The jury found Ward guilty and the judge sentenced him to six months in gaol.[95] Ward successfully pleaded a royal pardon at the following Commission of Oyer and Terminer on 30 October 1794. Having only served three months of his sentence, Ward was discharged immediately out of court.[96]

In summary, the great number of violent attacks in Dublin can be linked to the city's vast trade in firearms. Blunderbusses, fowling pieces and particularly pistols could be legally purchased new from factories and gunsmiths' shops or bought second-hand from pawn-brokers. In addition, receivers of stolen goods supplied the criminal fraternity with a wide range of firearms. Furthermore, a vast array of industrial tools and metal or heavy wooden implements were em-ployed for violent ends. Virtually everyone in Dublin carried some sort of weapon on their person, be it gun, stick, cudgel or metal instrument.

If the murder rate seems exceptionally high, one must consider that victims died from injuries that would not be considered life-threaten-ing today. Surgeons and anatomists took the view that dissections on the bodies of hanged felons helped to improve methods of repairing and restoring broken bones and tissues. Victims of gunshot wounds, however, rarely survived the operating tables. Wounds inflicted by other weapons were more likely to be healed. Nevertheless, victims of beating and stabbing in the late eighteenth century were far more likely to die than victims of similar assaults in the late twentieth century. This difference in survival rates rules out a direct comparison between present homicide rates and homicide rates in the late eight-eenth century.

What is certain about Dublin during this period is that death was a daily experience, far more public than it is now. In fact, the *Hibernian Journal* once called on parish directors in Dublin to build more mor-tuaries to challenge the otherwise callous behaviour of some of their parishioners in the presence of death. No voice, however, called out for legislation banning weapons. Dublin had still to wait for humani-tarian, enlightened and evangelical influences to make casual violence and consequential death seem less acceptable.

CHAPTER FIVE

Property Theft

In the 16 years between 1780 and 1795, the *Hibernian Journal* reported 3,628 property thefts and 1,263 court cases involving property theft. Nine years of peace (1784–1792) prevailed in this period, as well as seven years of war (1780–1784, 1793–1795). An analysis of the reported court cases reveals that the average number of indictments was 40 in war and 109 in peace—a similar pattern to that found in Staffordshire.[1] The majority of property offences were street robberies; the newspaper reported 1,883 robberies and 670 court cases involving robbery. 62 per cent (1,168 reports) of the incidents of robbery were reported in the six years between 1784 and 1789.

Determined to bring property theft to a halt, the new police arrested hundreds of petty thieves in their first three months of operation from October to December 1786. The new police kept the pressure on the criminal fraternity for the next six years. Indeed, over 64 per cent (434 trials) of all of the trials for robbery were reported in the six years between 1787 and 1792. The presence of the police encouraged victims of robbery to prosecute. In many trials, victims could rely on the evidence supplied by policemen to obtain convictions.

In the 16 years between 1780 and 1795, there were 199 verified hangings in Dublin for crimes committed in the city and county (the 43 unverified hangings have not been included in table 3) and of these, 165 were convicted of robbery, burglary, horse theft and a wide variety of other property offences. This number represents 83 per cent of the total hanged and shows that more convicted robbers and burglars were hanged than other types of felon. Of the 199 people who were executed, only 34 had not been convicted of property offences. 68 men and 2 women were hanged for robbery and 64 men and one woman were hanged for burglary, together representing 68 per cent of the total number of people hanged.

The courts apparently viewed capital punishment as an appropriate deterrent to property theft. Transportation, however, was the most frequently imposed penalty for this particular crime. From the trials

Table 3: Crime and Punishment
Transportation and Verified Executions
Dublin, 1780–1795

Types of crime tried in Dublin courts		MH	Dublin men hanged
MT	Dublin men transported	WH	Dublin women hanged
WT	Dublin women transported	HA	Total hanged
TR	Total transported		

Types of Crime	MT	WT	TR	MH	WH	HA
Murder	2	0	2	17	4	21
Theft of lead, other metal	18	0	18	0	0	0
Street, Highway robbery	149	56	205	68	2	70
Horse theft	1	0	1	2	0	2
Theft of sheep and cattle	4	0	4	6	0	6
Theft from bleach-greens	4	0	4	11	1	12
Theft from ships	1	0	1	0	0	0
Shop-lifting	10	11	21	0	0	0
Pick-pockets	4	1	5	0	0	0
Mail theft	1	1	2	8	0	8
Burglary	38	8	46	64	1	65
Rape	0	0	0	1	1	2
Theft by trick	6	0	6	0	0	0
Receiving stolen goods	0	4	4	0	0	0
Embezzlement	4	2	6	1	0	1
Uttering forged notes	1	0	1	1	0	1
Assault	1	0	1	1	0	1
Industrial violence	1	0	1	3	0	3
Arson	0	0	0	0	1	1
Vagrancy	13	5	18	0	0	0
Others	53	11	64	0	0	0
Not known	40	1	41	6	0	6
Total	351	100	451	189	10	199

(Source: Transportation Count, *Hibernian Journal*; Hanged Count, *Hibernian Journal*, *Walker's Hibernian Magazine, Dublin Evening Post, Freeman's Journal*, Prisoners' petitions and cases.)

reported in the *Hibernian Journal*, the courts sentenced a total of 451 convicted prisoners to transportation, 317 of whom were convicted of property offences. As this represents 70 per cent of the total, it again shows the severity with which the courts viewed crimes against private property.

According to the *Hibernian Journal*, the largest proportion of offenders sentenced to transportation had been convicted of robbery:

149 men and 56 women, or 45 per cent of the total transported. These figures are also borne out in the hanged count, which indicate that 35 per cent of those hanged were convicted of robbery. However, a much smaller proportion of offenders sentenced to transportation were burglars: only 38 men and eight women out of the total of 451, or only 10 per cent. In contrast, 32 percent of the total hanged were convicted of burglary. The greater willingness of the courts to sentence convicted burglars to death rather than to transportation shows the severity with which society viewed this type of crime.

In absolute terms 159 more robbers were transported than burglars, but this is so merely because there were 464 more prosecutions for robbery than for burglary. This throws up two interesting points: that more incidents of robbery occurred in Dublin than burglaries and that robbers were easier to detect and easier to prosecute than burglars. However, given the greater number of prosecutions for robbery, one would expect to find a greater number of robbers hanged than burglars. This is not the case; nearly the same number of robbers and burglars were hanged. One may therefore conclude that the courts considered burglary, which includes break-ins of houses, warehouses and shops, to be the most serious of all property offences.

Between 1780 and 1795, the three Dublin courts heard 206 trials involving burglary. These trials comprised 16 per cent of the 1,262 court cases involving property theft. Burglars often worked in gangs and in a substantial number of cases, several burglars were sentenced to death for the same crime. As a result of 45 separate prosecutions for burglary, 65 people were convicted and hanged. Amongst these 45 trials there were 11 prosecutions for burglary in which the courts sentenced two convicted felons to death, resulting in 22 hangings. Likewise, in another four prosecutions for burglary, the courts sentenced three or more burglars to death, resulting in 13 hangings. Burglars also worked alone and, in 29 prosecutions for burglary, the courts passed a capital sentence for each prosecution.

In May 1786, Patrick Leonard planned to rob the Treasury building in the lower yard at Dublin Castle, but a soldier at Newgate, in whom he had earlier confided, informed the authorities of his plot and Leonard was arrested.[2] In February 1790, a man nearly succeeded in breaking into an office in the Treasury, but an observant sentinel revented the burglary. The soldier chased the thief off the grounds, not knowing that he had nearly succeeded in breaking the door open to the office, as the acting treasurer Mr Standish discovered in the morning. Mr Standish's office contained 4,000 new guineas.[3] In both cases, soldiers foiled the plans of lone burglars, suggesting that gangs did not plan jobs where tight security measures were in place.

Gangs were more likely to plan burglaries of the homes and villas of wealthy people, particularly along the "gold coast," which ran from Merrion Square to Blackrock. The unlucky fate of one victim exemplifies the general picture. In December 1787, Samuel Sproule's house in Merrion Square was burgled and badly vandalised.[4] A wealthy architect, Sproule moved away from the green square soon after the burglary to a villa at Ballinclea Heights above Killiney Bay.[5] On Thursday 27 November 1794, at one o'clock in the morning, two armed burglars broke into Sproule's house through an unfastened kitchen window, subdued two men lying in a room opposite the kitchen and burst into Sproule's bedroom.

Sproule put up a stout resistance against them, but seriously injured his hands in wresting two of their swords from them. Beaten into submission, Sproule could do nothing as the jewel thieves took virtually all he owned, including a collection of highly prized art objects, several red carnelian pieces (including one quartz of a double head of Socrates and Homer), some expensive silver pieces (including a large silver trowel engraved on one side with the front of the Newry Linen Hall and on the other with a ship in full sail), a capped and jewelled silver and gold watch made by George Chalmers of Dublin, two cases of pistols and many articles of clothing. The variety, quality and amount of property stolen indicate that the prowlers knew what to look for in such a house.

In the aftermath, Justice of the Peace William Beckford, who directed the Blackrock Felons Association, offered a reward of £30 for information leading to the prosecution and conviction of the gang. In a published advertisement, Sproule gave detailed descriptions of the stolen property, along with descriptions of the two robbers, putting every reputable pawnbroker in Ireland on the alert. If this concerted campaign to recover the goods had been foreseen by the culprits, they would no doubt have sold the stolen property abroad. In the advertisement, Sproule was careful to point out physical differences between the two men. One was "young, smooth faced, and handsome, slender and middle sized, wore a round hat, and had his own dark hair, a lightish brown coat." In contrast, the other was "ill looking, [had] a round short nose, and small eyes, [was] low set, and middle aged, with a torn frize loose coat, seemingly a labourer, or quarry-man; when he went away, his coat, hands, and face, were covered with blood." In other words, while the first burglar looked on, the second one did the dirty work, suggesting that the first employed the second for the break-in. The evidence indicates that contractual relationships were a common feature amongst members of criminal gangs in this period, a feature which had strengths and weaknesses depending on one's point of view. Informers were known to betray their fellow thieves when victims such as Sproule offered them enough money to make it worth their while.

On 21 September 1787, five armed men burgled the house of James Frood in Claremont, near Glasnevin, stealing some watches and plate.[6] A neighbour managed to apprehend some members of the gang and those who were caught were taken to Kilmainham prison to stand trial. The ringleader, Hugh McGowran alias the Morning Star, managed to escape and his description was released by the *Hue and Cry*, the police gazette.[7] On 2 October 1787, George Roe, the keeper of Newgate, and Walsh, his deputy gaoler, arrested McGowran, who had a previous record stretching back at least three years. McGowran was a sophisticated burglar known to make his own weapons. In November 1784, after breaking into a house near Greenhills, McGowran dropped a hand-made gun consisting of "four rifle barrels, capable of discharging eight balls alternatively" and able to fit into his breeches pocket. It also had a tomahawk at the end of it.[8] McGowran looted over a wide area. In September 1786, Justice Francis Graham arrested him for a robbery in Co. Wicklow, but apparently no charges were pressed against him on this occasion.[9]

In November 1787, the Commission of Oyer and Terminer convicted McGowran of the Frood burglary in Claremont, but the jury reduced the value of the goods stolen to 4s. 9d., which was three pence below the capital value of a burglary.[10] Thus the judge did not sentence McGowran to death, but instead sentenced him to transportation. His innocence in the Frood burglary was attested to by two convicted burglars—Thomas Robinson and John Conlan—just before they were hanged on 22 December 1787. Convicted for the burglary of Peter Callage's house in Bonnybrook, Co. Dublin on 9 November 1787, they said that McGowran had nothing to do with the Frood burglary.[11] This was typical of the manner in which condemned convicts exonerated other members of the criminal fraternity, showing that loyalty often prevailed over treachery.

The Callage burglary in November 1787 spawned a great deal of publicity and fear about crime in Co. Dublin. Following the burglary, 45 people jointly issued a paid advertisement offering a reward of £100 for the burglars. Many of the sponsors were well-known figures in Dublin, such as Lord Charlemont.[12] In July 1788, the Kilmainham Quarter Sessions sentenced another man named James Maughan to death for the Callage burglary, but his sentence was not carried out according to the *Hibernian Journal*.[13] The last trial involving the Callage burglary took place at the Kilmainham Quarter Sessions in October 1788. Joseph MacDaniel, a servant to Callage, was sentenced to transportation for his role in the crime.[14] MacDaniel had been sentenced to death along with Robinson and Conlan, but he avoided the gallows by turning King's evidence.[15] He apparently supplied enough information to bring not only Conlan and Robinson to the gallows for the Callage burglary, but also two other people for the same crime.

Three prisoners still awaited trial for the Frood burglary. In January 1788, the Kilmainham Quarter Sessions sentenced John Maguire, his brother Terence Maguire and Charles Gallagher to death.[16] At the same Kilmainham Quarter Sessions, Charles Dignam was convicted for the Callage burglary and he and his mother were also convicted for the burglary of John Booth's house on Kilmainham Road, from which they stole £14 in cash and clothes. The two were sentenced to death.[17] Also at this same Kilmainham court sitting, John Kelly was convicted for the burglary of Patrick Gracy's house near Mulhuddart, Co. Dublin in early December 1787. Kelly, too, was sentenced to death.[18] On Saturday 26 January 1788, Kilmainham Commons saw the hangings of five men and one woman, including two brothers and a mother and her son. It was the largest public hanging spectacle on Kilmainham Commons since it had become the site for hangings in the previous April.[19]

The first hanging on Kilmainham Commons took place on Saturday 28 April 1787. William Hackett, John Maguire, Caleb Fitzpatrick, and Daniel Flinn were hanged on the newly erected gallows near the Grand Canal bridge.[20] (Hangings had stopped at Gallows Hill to make room for construction of the existing Kilmainham gaol in April 1787.)[21] Hackett, Maguire and Fitzpatrick were convicted at the Kilmainham

Quarter Sessions for breaking into Peter Keefe's house at Cardiffs Bridge. They were sentenced to death and hanged within four days. In offering an explanation for the swift end to their lives, the newspaper reported that "from the number of burglaries and robberies committed within these few weeks Serjeant John Toler found it highly necessary to make a speedy example of the above criminals."[22]

Two years after starting to patrol the streets of Dublin, the police were successful in solving a burglary which left a woman near to death. On the evening of 3 November 1788, James Wade, his brother John Wade and a gang of men burgled the house of Warden Flood in Summer Hill. The burglary went badly wrong. A pregnant servant named Jane Brady was slightly injured, but a woman named Mrs Kelly was critically injured. John Wade, a postillion, called on Jane Brady, who was in her servant quarters in the Warden house. At first, he appeared friendly enough to her, offering her a shilling and some punch. A few minutes later, however, James Wade, a journeyman paver, and several other men burst into the room:

> One of them instantly seized Mrs Kelly by the breast, demanded with horrid execrations to know where her money was; they threw Mrs Kelly on the floor, and threw the prosecutrix over her, and one of the villains held them both forcibly down in that position, at the same time keeping his hand on the prosecutrix's mouth, while the rest of the gang plundered two trunks and a box filled with wearing apparel, linen, and other articles, all which, together with the 29 guineas, they carried away. They also beat and abused the women in a very violent manner, particularly Mrs Kelly, who from the blows given her, and the injury she received by the prosecutrix being held down upon her as she was in an advanced state of pregnancy, now lies so dangerously ill, that her life is despaired of. When the villains had completed their robbery and drank the punch which the prisoner brought in, they made off, but first fastened the door.[23]

After the burglary, the gang fled across the river towards the Liberties, but a policeman foiled their escape. Observing two men with a large bundle between eight and nine o'clock in the evening, Martin Davis, the policeman, challenged the brothers. Not satisfied with their reply, Davis arrested James Wade in High Street with the bundle, while the other brother escaped to his lodgings in Church Street. Meanwhile, James Wilson, chief constable of the Rotunda division, two policemen and John Gorey, a relation of Jane Brady, all went to the lodgings of John Wade in Church Street to question him about his whereabouts that evening. Not satisfied with his answers, they arrested Wade and conveyed him to the office of police Divisional Justice Thomas Emerson, who committed both brothers to prison to stand trial for burglary at the Dublin Quarter Sessions. After listening to the evidence, the jury deliberated for 15 minutes and returned a verdict of guilty. Sentenced to death, the Wade brothers were hanged on Saturday 10 January 1789.

In the 16-year period, the three Dublin courts heard 669 trials for street robbery, representing over 50 per cent of the 1,262 court cases involving property theft. In 52 prosecutions for robbery, the courts convicted and sentenced 70 people to death. In such cases when more than one defendant appeared in the dock for the same robbery, juries exercised considerable discretion in their verdicts. Likewise, judges exercised flexibility in sentencing. On 22 April 1788, five robbers ambushed William Dwyer, a former fencing master, on Donnybrook Road, took his coat and hat and cut him badly. Once the alarm was raised, a detachment of police horsemen chased the robbers to a brothel in Smock Alley, where they arrested four of them—Patrick Reilly, Thomas Sheridan, Richard Murphy and one Kelly.[24] Kelly became an informer to avoid prosecution, although a policeman discredited his testimony at the trial. In July 1788, at the Commission of Oyer and Terminer, a jury convicted Reilly and Sheridan, but acquitted Murphy.[25] The judge then sentenced both Reilly and Sheridan to the gallows, but Sheridan's sentence was later respited. In the end, Reilly was hanged at the front of Newgate prison on Saturday 12 July 1788.

Most robbers selected their targets for opportunistic reasons. In May 1780, William Corkman, a mealman and factor, was robbed of £400 in pound notes by three men in Church Street.[26] This was an exceptionally lucrative robbery considering that principals in firms did not often carry large sums of money on their person when going about their business. Most robberies were on a much smaller scale. Servants, often obliged to carry money on behalf of their masters, were a frequent target of robberies. In April 1782, three footpads robbed a servant of 13 guineas, a watch, a pair of shoe buckles, a coat and waistcoat near the end of the Circular Road at Ballsbridge.[27] For the servant, these belongings represented his entire savings for two years.

While most thieves were motivated by making quick riches, certain ruffians made a point to settle long-standing disputes in blood. Perhaps as a result of his anti-combination activities, Benjamin Houghton was singled out by the criminal fraternity. In April 1782, he was robbed of £70 and a gold watch and assaulted by a gang of five men who left him to die of knife and sword wounds in Cork Street.[28] Alderman James Horan and a detachment of Volunteers arrested four men: John Wall, alias "Jack the Smasher," John Murdock (or Mordaunt), James Rooney, aged 15, and Barnaby Ledwith, aged 13. The Commission of Oyer and Terminer tried the gang for the assault and robbery in July 1782. They were all convicted and sentenced to hang.[29] Rooney and Ledwith had their sentences remitted due to their youth, but Wall and Murdock were hanged at Stephen's Green on Saturday 20 July 1782.

Robbers stole a dizzying array of saleable items. They were motivated by greed as well as by need, wanting things just to keep up with the changing fashions. A flourishing black market followed in the footsteps of a rapidly expanding consumer society. In October 1785, the *Hibernian Journal* published a poem in which the female author delights in the materialism of the age:

MODERN GALLANTRY

Two or three sweets, and two or three
   dears;
Two or three sighs, and two or three tears.
Two or three ogles, and two or three bows;
Two or three lies, and two or three vows.
Two or three love letters, writ all in rhymes;
Two or three presents, for two or three times.
Two or three baubles, from Bailey and Lowes;
Two or three sweet bags, to put in her cloaths.
Two or three trinkets, from Jeffreys and Jones;
Two or three pearls, and a few precious stones.
Two or three times led from the play;
Two or three soft things said by the way.
Two or three squeezes, and two or three *kisses*;
Will buy half the Wives, and most of
   the *Misses*.[30]

The *Hibernian Journal* reported thefts of over 400 watches and over 80 shoe and knee buckles. Watch makers did a brisk trade in Dublin. In 1791, 48 watch makers owned shops in Dublin, indicating a strong demand for watches.[31] Bernard Delahoyde, a watch maker at 81 Dame Street, sold "cheap gold, silver and gilt watches" which he promised to keep "in order for 2s. 2d. per year, accidents excepted."[32] Despite the proliferation of cheap watches, many watches were extremely valuable and treasured by their owners. In reports of watch thefts, the *Hibernian Journal* occasionally reported the name of the maker and the place where the watch was made.

Victims of watch theft often paid for advertisements giving details of their stolen watches to alert the owners of pawnshops and the reading public as to the precise characteristics of their stolen property. In March 1787, one Lewis was robbed in Moss Street of his pinchbeck watch, marked no. 391, made by Vane, a watch-maker in Liverpool.[33] A month later, one O'Connor was robbed in Thomas Street of his silver watch, marked no. 35, made by Black of Dublin.[34] At Christmas time in 1792, Rev. Mr Broderick, a Catholic priest from the Adam and Eve chapel, was robbed at the "town's arch" of a watch, marked no. 58, made by John Knox of Belfast.[35] A watch found in the possession of two thieves in Leixlip not only gave the maker's name—John Drake, London—but also gave the name of the jeweller who last cleaned the watch—Dunning and Ash, of Strabane, Co. Tyrone.[36]

On 14 August 1787, William May, a writing master, stole a gold watch from the house of Sir Frederick Flood, pledging it at the house of Thomas Armitage in Skinner's Row, the largest pawnbroker in Dublin. In October 1787, the Commission of Oyer and Terminer convicted May, but reduced the value of the watch to below five shillings to prevent the death sentence from being imposed.[37] In July 1788, he appeared again before the Commission of Oyer and Terminer, pleading his majesty's pardon on the condition that he transport himself out of Ireland.[38] In some editions of the *Hibernian Journal*, however, a mistake occurred in the latter report of the pardon, giving the name of Frederick May, instead of William May. The newspaper corrected the mistake in subsequent edition that same day.[39]

The mistake proved to be a serious blunder: Frederick May was a watch-maker at 138 Capel Street and his reputation obviously suffered as a result of the misleading court report linking him to the watch theft.[40] In October 1788, he himself prosecuted Michael Delany at the

Commission of Oyer and Terminer for obtaining a silver watch from him under false pretences, which led to the sentencing of Delany to transportation.[41] If the defence had been able to call May's character into question, his prosecution of Delany would have been at risk and May's status in the community and his prospects would have been seriously undermined, making him an easy target for every thief in town.

Items of personal clothing were also favoured by thieves. Hats seem to have been the favourite target; over 125 hats were reported stolen, according to the *Hibernian Journal*. Judging from the prints by James Malton, most people in Dublin wore hats in the late eighteenth century.[42] In June 1782, Mr Stafford, a linen-draper who lived in Back Lane, recovered his stolen hat from the hatter who made it after the robber attempted to dispose of it at the same shop where it was bought.[43] Like watches, hats were often marked by their owners to aid in the process of detection. In July 1782, James Byrne was robbed in Vicar Street of two guineas, both his shoe and knee buckles and his hat.[44] In the case of the hat, however, the robber offered Byrne a stolen hat for the one he was about to steal. This was not an act of kindness. Byrne discovered that the name Thompson had been written at the bottom of the exchanged hat which, if found on the robber, would have linked him to the crime. This episode sheds light on the fear robbers had of being traced via marked hats or watches.

Silk, "the fabric of power and class command," was stolen only occasionally, according to the *Hibernian Journal*.[45] Seven silk coats and one pair of silk stockings were stolen. Only three wigs were stolen, again suggesting that the rich travelled with due caution for the thieving classes. Female robbers were involved in over 70 robberies in which clothing was the only kind of item reported stolen.

Victims of clothing robbery were frequently small children or older people. On Christmas Day 1782, an elderly Catholic priest was robbed of the clothes on his person.[46] Clothes were stolen from children in 30 cases. Most children suffered the indignity as best they could, but sometimes even they fought back. In October 1788, an eight-year-old victim nearly poked a woman's eye out with his toy castle-top as she attempted to steal his shirt-sleeve buttons set in gold.[47] Robbers who stole from children ran the risk of being punished by angry mobs and, on eight occasions, such thieves were set upon. In February 1780, a woman caught stripping an infant in St. Patrick's Close was dragged through "the kennel" and pelted with stones.[48]

In the 16 years, the *Hibernian Journal* reported 17 bleach-green thefts, involving a wide variety of cloth: five thefts of linen and one theft each of calico, muslin, superfine, broad-cloth, sheeting and dowlas. Bleach-greens were often located on the south side of the River Liffey. Workers carried large quantities of fabric from the looms in the Liberties to huge fields along the river beginning at Island Bridge. Once hundreds of fabric sheets had been attached onto the tops of tall wooden posts, the field would come to resemble a multi-coloured tent city. It would also have attracted the unwanted attention of intruders.[49]

Those caught stealing cloth from open bleach-greens were almost certain to hang or be transported. According to the *Hibernian Journal*, there were 12 prosecutions for bleach-green theft which resulted in 11 men and one woman being hanged and four men being transported. All the felons hanged and all but one of the convicts transported were convicted at the Kilmainham Quarter Sessions, confirmation that the locations of most bleach greens were in Co. Dublin. In November 1789, the Kilmainham Quarter Sessions sentenced a father and son named Hastler to death for robbing a bleach green. The father, aged 60, was hanged in front of Kilmainham prison on 11 November 1789, but the son was reprieved from death and sentenced to transportation.[50] The son's age (which was not given) was probably the deciding factor in extending him mercy since hanging members of the same family was considered acceptable.

As an indication of the high value of finished and printed cloth, the courts sentenced several convicted bleach-green robbers to death. In July 1791, Michael Dooley, Thomas Hughes and Joseph Dungan swam across the River Liffey to rob Jacob Sisson's bleach yard. To make the robbery worthwhile, the gang first threw pieces of calico to the other side of the Liffey and then towed a second batch of printed cloth behind them while they swam.[51] This gave the police enough time to arrest Dungan, a young boy, near the scene. Dungan provided the police with information which led to the arrest of Dooley in Francis Street.

In September 1791, the Kilmainham Quarter Sessions sentenced Dooley to death. He was hanged at Kilmainham Commons on Saturday 1 October 1791.[52] In December 1791, the Kilmainham Quarter Sessions sentenced Hughes to death, but his sentence was apparently never carried out.[53] Two years later, the Kilmainham Quarter Sessions convicted Richard Farrell, Thomas Plunkett and Thomas Archbold, for robbing a bleach green in Glasnevin. The three were hanged at Kilmainham Commons on Saturday 3 August 1793.[54] Police Inspector William Shea arrested Michael Dooley and the three men who had robbed the Glasnevin drying yards.

Robbers sank to the lowest depths imaginable in order to steal items of value. Robbing graveyards for their lead coffins was just such a crime. Grave robbers sold the lead coffins to receivers of stolen goods who, in turn, found buyers for the expensive metal. In September 1783, the *Hibernian Journal* reported the tragic case of a man who bought a slab of lead from a female receiver. When he noticed that the slab bore an inscription from his wife's coffin, he was shocked. He had buried his wife seven years earlier. The receiver, who kept a cellar in Castle Street, was committed to Newgate to stand trial. In prison, she denounced the grave digger of St. Mary's churchyard as the culprit who had sold her the coffin.[55]

The graveyard near the Royal Kilmainham Hospital was often the scene of robberies. In April 1780, a similar story emerged of a man who interrupted grave robbers at work:

> A few nights ago, returning from Island-bridge, by the Circular Road, I met four Men armed, coming out of the Burying-ground in the Royal Hospital-fields; at first I was much alarmed, thinking they were Robbers, but as I advanced I saw a Coach, and three dead Bodies lying close by it on the Road. I was chilled with Horror at such Depredations on the Dead, particularly as some of my Friends were interred there; however, I thought it prudent to set Spurs to my Horse, without asking Questions. Next morning I returned to the Burying-ground, and brought with me a Man with a Spade, to examine the Grave where my Wife was lately buried; but, alas! my Wife was gone—her Coffin, and Grave-cloaths in it, were safe. I went over the Ground, and was struck with a Scene of Horror beyond Conception: I found Legs, Arms, Skulls, and Pieces of dead Bodies scattered over the Ground, the Prey of Swine and Dogs.[56]

If grave robbers were detected in a cemetery, they could face the wrath of mourners. In December 1784, a robber named Moran dug up two coffins from the graveyard near the Royal Kilmainham Hospital, but was unable to shift the heavy objects from the cemetery in time. Two men, who happened to be visiting the grounds, seized Moran and dragged him to the River Liffey. They stripped the grave robber of his clothes and ducked him into the ice-cold waters. Moran was left to dry in Phoenix Park.[57]

Co. Dublin was the scene of a far more frequent type of property theft, albeit less infamous. The *Hibernian Journal* reported 39 prosecutions arising from destruction or theft of farm animals. Six cattle and sheep rustlers were hanged and four were transported. In February 1784, the hide of a stolen cow was recovered under Hazelhatch bridge on the western fringes of Co. Dublin, but the motive in this case was said to be hunger alone.[58] In April 1785, a sheep farmer in Kilcock named Mr Fraine shot dead a linen-weaver named Cosgrave who was caught in the act of stealing his sheep.[59]

On 25 January 1786, Peter Rigney was executed at Kilmainham for stealing fat from stolen sheep on the lands of Ballynadrin.[60] Again in May 1787, rustlers stole 17 sheep from the Palmerstown estate of John Hely Hutchinson, provost of Trinity College. The carcasses turned up at a market in Dublin soon after the animals went missing,[61] but at trial the Commission of Oyer and Terminer did not have enough evidence to convict William Cooper for the sheep theft.[62] In 1795, the Kilmainham Quarter Sessions convicted and sentenced to death three brothers and a brother-in-law for rustling cattle. In the end, only two brothers named Connelly were hanged on Wednesday 25 April 1795.[63]

The *Hibernian Journal* reported 26 horse thefts and 17 trials for horse theft. Two men were hanged and one man was transported for stealing horses. Nine horse thefts were reported in 1787, suggesting that a gang of horse thieves was at work. In January 1787, a thief rode off with a horse from a horse-hire shop in Cook Street, whose owner then placed an advertisement in the *Hue and Cry* offering a reward. As a result of the advertisement, the Lord Mayor of Kilkenny spotted the horse in his town.[64] In the wake of the publicity surrounding the theft, many questions were answered about the practices of horse thieves. Dublin horse thieves were known to steal horses in fields on the outskirts of Dublin at night and then ride to provincial towns where they would commit house burglaries and highway robberies. In the morning, the thieves returned the horses to their former fields, "fatigued and jaded."[65]

The *Hibernian Journal* reported 23 mail thefts, the majority of which

involved thefts of mail-bags on their way to and from the north of
Ireland. The *Hibernian Journal* reported 14 prosecutions for mail theft,
resulting in the hangings of three letter carriers and five robbers, all
males, in seven separate trials. A further two trials resulted in transportation for a man and a woman. The crime was considered serious
enough to warrant severe penalties. For this reason, mail snatchers
went to great lengths to avoid detection. In January 1781, mail thieves
who robbed the post in Wales disappeared to avoid arrest. When the
robbers were detected in Dublin, John Lees, secretary to the Irish Post
Office, arrested them in College Green and transmitted them back to
England for trial.[66]

On 2 January 1784, three men robbed a postal boy carrying the
entire Munster mail, consisting of 31 postal bags, near Chapelizod on
the Naas Road.[67] In response, the Post Office offered a reward of £100
and Dublin Castle promised a free pardon for informers. An Englishman presented himself at Dublin Castle and offered to provide information about the recent postal theft in exchange for a favour by the
Lord Lieutenant on his behalf.[68] Charles Lawrence Barrow, who apparently was of Jewish origin, had been convicted for an unknown
offence at London's Old Bailey court in February 1783. Originally
sentenced to transportation to the Americas for seven years, Barrow
was offered a pardon in July of that year on condition that he transport
himself out of Britain for seven years.[69] Barrow caught the first boat to
Dublin where he found company to his liking. (How many others
were offered conditional pardons allowing them to emigrate to Ireland
is not known, but such offers would have expired when Britain began
transportation to Australia in 1786. Britain, in essence, opened a door
of opportunity between 1783 and 1786, enabling a section of its convicted criminal fraternity to transport themselves to Ireland for seven
years. It may indeed partly explain why crime rates went up in the
mid-1780s and down in the early 1790s). Barrow provided the Post
Office with enough information to have six men arrested. Lord
Northington, the Lord Lieutenant, then wrote a letter to Whitehall
with a request that Barrow be given a free pardon. Apparently, Barrow
was granted the pardon because his testimony convicted two of the six
men. In November 1784, the Commission of Oyer and Terminer
convicted James Farran, a former smuggler, of the mail theft.[70] He was
hanged at Gallows Hill on Saturday 6 November 1784.

In December 1784, the Commission of Oyer and Terminer convicted Byrne, aged 25, for the same mail theft and sentenced him to hang on 29 December 1784.[71] In the days before the scheduled hanging, a wave of anger against the prosecution of Byrne swept Dublin. Letters in the *Hibernian Journal* castigated Barrow for being a "felon Jew" and accused him of being motivated by a racial hatred against Christians.[72] In the end, the Duke of Rutland, the new Lord Lieutenant, respited Byrne's death sentence.[73] This episode highlights the problem of obtaining convictions based on the testimony of convicted criminals, which seemed to lack credibility with the public. In addition, the event sheds light on a vein of anti-Semitic prejudice in Dublin.

Like watch thefts, mail robberies were often reported in the news papers via paid advertisements, which not only offered rewards but also advised bankers to watch out for stolen bank notes. In September 1787, a gang purloined the mail bags destined for the North at the Eight-Mile Stone on the Balbriggan Road. The Post Office offered a reward of £200 for the culprits. In addition, bankers John Finlay and Company warned bankers in a paid advertisement to stop payment on a set of 50 stolen bank notes worth £10 each.[74] It was this advertisement that was seen by a banker in Liverpool who in turn sent a letter to a mercantile house in Dublin stating that 14 of the stolen bank notes had been deposited at his bank. Finlay sent a detective to Liverpool to obtain more information about the individual who deposited the notes. It was learned in Liverpool that the man in question had just sailed to Dublin. Based on a detailed description of the man, Finlay's man returned to Dublin and traced one Charles Echlin to Essex Street, where he was found in possession of five of the stolen notes and 52 guineas in cash. Police Divisional Justice John Exshaw placed Echlin under arrest and committed him to Newgate in November 1787.[75] In February 1788, the King's Bench sentenced Echlin to death. He was hanged at Kilmainham Commons on 27 February.[76] This is a striking instance of the high level of co-operation and speedy communication between banks on either side of the Irish Sea.

In the period under study, the *Hibernian Journal* reported 108 shop-lifting offences and 42 trials, landing 11 female convicts and 10 male convicts on board transportation vessels. Surprisingly, no one was hanged for stealing goods from shops. All those transported were convicted at the Dublin Quarter Sessions as the offences took place in the city. The merchants and shopkeepers of Dublin were particularly vulnerable to shoplifters. In December 1785, a light-fingered woman kept a shopkeeper busy for some time at a haberdasher's shop in Grafton Street. The thief stole the lace on the counter without once moving her two hands—they were crossed over her heart. As she was about to leave, the shopkeeper observed that one valuable piece of lace had gone missing. He discovered that the shoplifter "was possessed of a third hand, of ... animation and dexterity." One of her exposed hands was a prop covered with a glove to correspond with its fellow on her chest.[77]

In 1792, Denis George, the Recorder of Dublin, sentenced five female shop-lifters and three male shop-lifters to transportation—40 per cent of the total number of shop-lifters transported, according to the *Hibernian Journal*. In October 1792, at the Dublin Quarter Sessions, George sentenced two women to transportation for "intending to shop-lift."[78] In the first trial, George said "if it appeared there was an intent to steal, [it] was as ... if the thief had carried them [the stolen goods] effectually off the premises."[79] George's interpretation of the law was endorsed by Mathew West, one of the shopkeepers, who complained that previously the law did not grant shopkeepers the right to arrest thieves before they had sneaked the goods outside the doors of the shops.[80]

The *Hibernian Journal* reported 81 instances of coining operations and 20 trials. Wild estimates circulated that 800 coiners were "actually employed in coining and vending money in this city."[81] Coining provided a link between robbery and the economy, as coiners depended on stolen plate and silver to carry out their activities. In March 1782, one Mr Lyster's house in Abbey Street was burgled of plate, which turned up as melted silver at a coiner's house on Ellis Quay a month later.[82] On 31 April 1782, Justice Francis Graham and Mr Lyster, accompanied by a party of men, raided the assembly plant where they found over 300 ounces of melted silver. They also found base metal in imitation of shillings, together with tools to make coins.[83] Moreover, they unearthed a "hieroglyphic or caballistic [*sic*] manuscript" which contained directions for coining. The book of crime also contained instructions for robbing and breaking into houses. Working according to established guide-lines, coiners knew how to co-operate with house-breakers in order to acquire precious stolen metal to make bad coin look authentic.

In October 1786, the new police raided John Clarke's coining works in Dirty Lane. Found was "an amazing quantity of counterfeit guineas, half-guineas, shillings, sixpences, and halfpence."[84] An industrious man, Clarke had "amassed £800" in a short time as a coiner. He openly sold halfpence, shillings and sixpences on the streets of Dublin, but managed his gold and silver counterfeit coins through an agent operating in Smithfield Market.[85] In October 1786, at the Commission of Oyer and Terminer, Clarke was found guilty of two misdemeanours and sentenced to a whipping and three months in Newgate.[86] At his whipping from Newgate to Dirty Lane, the local community turned up in force to show their support for the coiner. Obviously, Clarke had performed a valuable service to the community by providing residents with much needed coin at reduced rates.[87]

In summary, the Dublin courts viewed the gallows as the most effective deterrent to property offences in Dublin. Those convicted of offences such as robbery, burglary, bleach-green theft and theft from the mails faced a greater risk of being hanged than ever before. Some of those who were hanged were convicted under parliamentary statutes that had been on the books for a long time, but many were hanged under a number of recent statutes which created new death penalties. The 1784 Postal Act, for example, was passed at a time when reports of property thefts were increasing dramatically and put the authorities in a position to obtain capital convictions against those convicted of robbing the mails. In Parliament, few countervailing influences were at work to prevent such acts from reaching the Irish *Statute Book*. Thus, Parliament acted as the great protector of the propertied classes from all types of property thieves.

CHAPTER SIX

The Parish Watch

During most of the eighteenth century, the streets of Dublin were patrolled by a parish watch. Each of the 21 parishes in Dublin employed their own watchmen to man a guard house during the night. The parishes, however, were unable to raise the funds necessary to maintain a proper watch, and hence the city was poorly patrolled. According to the author of a pamphlet critical of the parish watch, Dublin was faced with a serious crime problem in 1765:

> The extraordinary distresses which have fallen upon this city, during the course of the two last winters, have been felt very sensible by the inhabitants: they arose to such a degree, as made the internal commerce of the city languish: the higher sort were attacked in their carriages, plundered and abused, and put in fear and danger of their lives. The trader, after the close of day, was afraid to stir out of his house, on the necessary matters of his calling; the shop-keeper with reluctance, kept his shop open: the journeyman, in dread, carried home his work, to receive payment due for his week's labour: old men, young women, servants, and children, were alike the prey of these rapacious villains.[1]

Calls were made on Parliament to reform the parish watch system, but its complete overhaul had to wait until 1786.

In 1778, Parliament passed a Police Act, which contained some tough new measures, such as granting the right of watchmen to seize, search and break into the houses of suspected robbers. By 1784, the combined strength of the parish watch was 463 watchmen in the winter months and 368 in the summer months.[2] Despite their strength in numbers, the parish watch system suffered from a lack of trained professionals. In addressing this failing, critics of the parish watch looked to Britain and other countries for new ideas. The *Hibernian Journal* proposed that a version of the watch system of Edinburgh be considered for Dublin "in place of the present watch, against whom complaints are daily making."[3] While this proposal did not substantiate its criticisms, it went on to estimate that if 60 watchmen were hired for each of the five wards, the total cost to the city would amount to £10,092 per year. (Ironically, when the new police were introduced in 1786, the costs were nearly double this estimate.)

During the American War of Independence, the parish watch was assisted by the Volunteers. Normally the military would have offered their services, but the war reduced the standing army at the garrison. The *Hibernian Journal* reported 28 incidents in which the Dublin Volunteers were actively engaged in maintaining law and order between September 1780 and October 1781, a period when, in fact, Parliament was prorogued.[4] It was a period when public unrest was not acceptable for reasons of national security.

An incident in Co. Dublin shows how patriotic the Volunteers were and from what social classes they were drawn. In April 1781, a near mutiny broke out amongst 80 recruits who had just enlisted in the military. Captain Featherston, their recruiting officer, was unable to march them beyond Lucan. The new recruits disobeyed his orders to march to Dublin's North Wall, where a vessel was waiting for them. Captain Featherston called on the Dublin Volunteers to provide assistance. Featherston was himself a member of the Dublin Volunteers. Sir Patrick King led a detachment of Dublin Volunteers from the city to Lucan and escorted the recruits to a vessel bound for England.[5]

During this period, the parish watch suffered some serious setbacks. Four watchmen were killed and six assaulted in 1780. Two of these were actually killed by other watchmen.[6] Anger against the watch was sparked over a shooting in April 1780 when William Deane, an owner of a field near Eccles Street, asked the parish watch to stop football players from playing on his property. Force was thought necessary because the men regularly played on his field on Sundays. On the first Sunday in April, the football players came to the field as usual, but the watchmen prevented play. A group of players then began shouting "abusive language and throwing stones" at several of the watchmen.

John Eagan, one of the watchman, opened fire on the crowd with his blunderbuss and killed Richard Coleman, a baker's apprentice. After the shooting, Justice Francis Graham arrested Eagan, and Alderman Thomas Emerson committed him to Newgate to await trial. On the following Monday, a coroner's inquest deliberated over the death and returned a verdict of wilful murder.[7] In July 1780, at the Commission of Oyer and Terminer, Eagan was convicted and sentenced to be executed on 11 November 1780.[8] As no further details were reported, it is unlikely that the death sentence was carried out. In fact, the football players in question had acted in violation of a long-standing Sabbatarian law prohibiting the playing of football on Sundays.[9]

The decision not to execute Eagan apparently angered some members of the community. Two watchmen of St. Bride's parish were murdered soon afterwards. In November 1780, Sheriffs Patrick Bride and Thomas Andrews arrested Thomas Heany, who was charged with the murder of one of the watchmen.[10] Another watchman, William Mooney, of St. Bride's parish, was found murdered with a deep wound to his head in Holles Street in December 1780.[11]

It was within this climate of fear that the Volunteers apparently drew up their plans to patrol parts of the city, especially after Alderman James Horan, a firm believer in law and order, joined the Liberty Volunteers in October 1780.[12] First the Volunteers divided up the city wards, with the Liberty Volunteers taking responsibility for the Liberty ward and the Dublin, Goldsmiths, Merchants and Independent Dublin corps taking responsibility for policing the other wards. The Volunteers took over some of the vestry rooms of various parishes to plan their police patrols, including those of Saints Werburgh's, Andrew's, Michan's and Mary's parishes. In their first major campaign since the Phoenix Park demonstration in June 1780, the Volunteers "apprehended upwards of 100 robbers or other disorderly fellows who had no visible way of livelihood" in October, just one month after Parliament was prorogued.[13] The Volunteers also closed down a number of brothels or "night-houses," where "servants and such fellows pick up an odd night's lodging for three-pence a night."[14] According to a writer for the *Hibernian Journal*, who had consulted a Newgate prison register in the first week of January 1781, the Volunteers lodged 80 vagabonds in Newgate within their first three months of operation.[15]

The Volunteers proceeded in military-like fashion to patrol the city. They signed on a night duty-roster "so that when we consider their numbers, it will probably not come to each gentleman's turn to be out two nights in the whole winter."[16] They also took critical note of the performance of the parish watch. In their "perambulations" round the parishes of Saints Mary's, Thomas's, Michan's and Paul's in December 1780, a group of Independent Dublin Volunteers "found a deficiency in the number of watchmen in each parish ... several [were] drunk."

They were also critical of watchmen leaving their stands before five o'clock in the morning.[17] In short, the Volunteers were the first to complain vigorously about Dublin's watch system while solving organisational problems in the patrolling of the city.

After their initial successes, the Volunteer patrols found it necessary to bring forward their starting hours of work due to the number of robberies being committed in the early evening. They also found it necessary to reduce the flow of information regarding the movements of their patrols.[18] In addition, the Volunteers obtained information at the bar of the Royal Exchange Coffee House, where well-heeled informers could pass on information about disorderly houses and provide descriptions of thieves.[19]

According to the *Hibernian Journal*, the Volunteers were reported to have organised arrests on 19 different occasions in their first winter of activity, from October 1780 to March 1781. The seemingly low number of arrests probably conceals the true (but unreported) extent of their activity in preventing crime and disorderly conduct. On at least three occasions in that winter of industrial discontent, the Loyal Union and the Liberty Volunteers arrested journeymen.[20] Morale within the parish watch continued to sink and St. Mary's parish advertised for more "able bodied watchmen" in October 1781.[21] Despite the failure of the parish watch, the Volunteers inspired others to follow their example. Sheriffs and justices of the peace, who had the legal power to commit offenders to prison, often accompanied the Volunteers on their patrols. These included Aldermen Henry Hart and James Horan, Justices of the Peace William Beckford, Francis Graham and Robert Wilson, as well as Michael Toole, the undergaoler of Newgate, and several city sheriffs.

Because of the poor state of the parish watch, local civic leaders with links to the Volunteers formed associations for the prevention of crime at the parish level. In the early 1780s, almost half of the parishes in Dublin city—Saints Paul's, Ann's, Mark's, Mary's, Thomas's, John's, Audeon's and Michan's—raised funds through private subscriptions to finance their own patrols or parish associations.[22] The first parish association was apparently founded by a Dublin Volunteer with considerable experience. In August 1781, Thomas Moore led a party of Dublin Volunteers to prevent a dozen wreckers from stealing a cargo of wine and brandy from a Swedish vessel that had run aground on the North Bull island during a storm.[23] A month later, he established the

Association for the Preservation of the Peace in Essex Street.[24]

A local shopkeeper, Moore owned a cheese warehouse at 44 Essex Street which stocked a wide range of goods, including cheeses, porter, hams, teas, fish and hemp sacks.[25] In his spare time, he organised patrols to protect the private interests of the shopkeepers and residents in Essex Street. His main targets were prostitutes, vagabonds, petty thieves and night-houses—the same targets as the Volunteers. In September 1781, Moore and his association raided two night houses in Essex Street. A number of people were arrested and committed to the House of Industry and Newgate prison.[26]

In October 1781, under pressure to expand his activities, Moore employed three "respectable housekeepers" in Essex Street to serve as the association's civil officers and assistants "in order to keep a patrol each night, [and] to avoid having too much stress on any one member of the association."[27] Its impact was immediate: "formerly one of the most riotous and dangerous streets in this city," Essex Street began "to wear an aspect of tranquillity for many years unknown."[28] Essex Street had a reputation to maintain because the shopkeepers in the area depended on the buzz of activity around the old Custom House for much of their trade. They were annoyed at the decision to build a new Custom House, even though "by the middle of the century the mercantile centre had begun to shift down river."[29] On Wednesday 8 August 1781, John Beresford (or Mr George Semple, according to the *Hibernian Journal*) laid the first stone of the new Custom House, but the violent opposition from some of the merchants was so strong that the stone was laid in secret.[30] James Napper Tandy led a "rabble … armed with adzes [sharp tools], saws, shovels" and attempted to bring construction of the new Custom House to a halt in September 1781. James Gandon, the architect, received anonymous letters threatening his life.[31]

In November 1781, the old Custom House was engulfed in flames, which Thomas Moore and his supporters extinguished. In recognising him for his bravery, the Revenue Commissioners awarded Moore a silver cup worth £40 which contained an inscription expressing their gratitude for saving the old building from a certain destruction.[32] Putting out the fire was a fitting reminder of his long years of service to the Temple Bar community. In the last ten months of his life, Moore directed most of his attention to making Essex Street safe for residents, merchants and the many visitors to the area. Between October 1781 and July 1782, Moore and the association arrested criminals operating in the area on eight occasions for crimes including robbery, prostitution, assault and disorderly conduct. His work began to attract the notice of those in the city who wanted to clean up Dublin and give it an image more in accordance with its splendid architecture and growing international reputation.

In November 1781, Moore's association arrested a prostitute who robbed a Dutch sailor and committed her to the House of Industry.[33] The House of Industry was to a certain extent a prison for vagabonds and prostitutes rather than, as the name might suggest, a factory. It publicly thanked Moore for his efforts to drive out prostitution in the Temple Bar area just as it had paid tribute to the Quaker merchant, Benjamin Houghton, who was a founding member of the House of Industry. Such was his spirit that Houghton introduced a force of beadles to round up sturdy vagabonds at his own cost in November 1772.[34]

In July 1782, Moore died and was buried at St. Mark's church. The Dublin Volunteers and the Essex Street association attended his body to the grave, the latter group wearing scarves and hat bands.[35] The Essex Street association and the local parish watch seemed to fall into a state of apathy after his death. Interestingly, in October 1782, three months after the death of Moore, the Essex Street association did resume activities, but only three arrests were reported that winter. St. Andrew's parish, which included Essex Street, was the only parish not to comply with a parliamentary investigation on the state of the parish watch two years later.[36]

In June 1784, the new Lord Lieutenant, the Duke of Rutland, concerned at the rising tide of violence in the city, ordered an inquiry into the "state of the police."[37] Rutland's Chief Secretary, Thomas Orde, oversaw the investigation, asking the clerks of every parish and the Seneschal of the Liberty to draw up a report about the watch system between March 1782 and March 1784. St. Andrew's parish did not submit a report.[38]

In October 1781, a second association—the St. Mary's association—was organised.[39] According to the *Hibernian Journal*, it boasted a membership of 237 people. The newspaper also reported that St. Mary's employed 14 peace officers with powers of arrest to accompany the parish association on nightly patrols.[40] Thus, St. Mary's parish had more men patrolling the streets than any other parish. In response to

Orde's investigation, Henry Howison and Francis Armstrong, the church wardens of St. Mary's in 1784, reported that the parish employed 60 watchmen in the winter months and 50 in the summer months from 1782 to 1783—the most watchmen employed by any parish.[41] The two wardens, however, may have exaggerated the number of watchmen employed by St. Mary's parish because on 25 March 1784, Richard Gladwill, who summarised the reports for Orde's investigation, said that "the number of men employed in some parishes, imagined [*sic*] over-rated."[42]

Information about the social composition of the executive of St. Mary's association reveals that it was middle class in background. Richard Dobson and Mary Dobson, tea-merchants and grocers at 38 Capel Street, along with Benjamin Tilly, wine merchant at 29 Abbey Street, were on the executive committee of the association.[43] Unfortunately, shortly after becoming a member of the executive, Richard Dobson died as a result of the collapse of the upper floor of the Music Hall in Fishamble Street on 6 February 1782. His wife carried on the Capel Street business with a firm hand, which may partly explain why St. Mary's association also continued to be active after the death of her husband.

In a few incidents, peace officers and parish watchmen were known to clash, but there is no evidence to indicate that senior inspectors of the watch were generally opposed to their counterparts in the associations.[44] The wages paid to members of associations are not known, but the evidence suggests that it was volunteer work (in the literal sense) and unpaid. Nevertheless it seems that some members of the associations went on to become full-time watchmen, given the difference in the number of watchmen employed by those parishes who formed associations and those who did not. In Thomas Orde's report, there were a total of 463 watchmen in the 17 parishes for the winter months of 1783 and 1784, an average of 27 watchmen per parish. The average number of watchmen in the winter months for the eight parishes who formed associations was 35 in 1784, while the average number of watchmen for the nine parishes who did not form associations was 20, a difference of 75 percent.[45]

Wages paid to watchmen varied according to the parish. St. Catherine's paid 12 watchmen just over 4 pence a night each (£4 9s. per year) during the summer months and paid six pence a night each (£6 5s. per year) during the winter months.[46] St. James's parish paid their eight watchmen a flat rate of £7 per year.[47] St. Mary's paid 50 watchmen who worked the whole year a wage of £8 5s. St. Ann's paid its 24 watchmen the highest wages—£14 4s. per year.[48] When the police were introduced in 1786, they earned an annual income of £18 5s., which is over £4 higher than the earnings of the highest-paid watchmen, a difference of nearly 30 per cent.[49]

Only a few associations, particularly those in the suburbs such as Blackrock, Ranelagh and Harold's Cross, continued to function up to the mid-1790s. For most, the active years were 1781–82, during which time the *Hibernian Journal* reported 45 operations involving such associations. At least 14 different associations were known to exist in Dublin city and county, including five at the street level—Essex Street, Fishamble Street, upper Dorset Street, Meath Street and Upper Coombe—and Stoneybatter. The *Hibernian Journal* made only six references to arrests carried out by the associations over the entire city in 1783.[50] Without the support of the Volunteers, who "were broken as a political power," the associations themselves were weakened.[51]

A felons association in Mortlake, Surrey survived for ten years before it went into decline in the 1790s. Compared with other felons associations in London, the Mortlake association was short-lived. London's longer-lasting felons associations concentrated their protective activities entirely on their paid-up list of subscribers, a policy which made better use of their limited resources. The Mortlake association, however, extended its policing activities to all residents of Mortlake regardless of whether they contributed to the association and, in the end, could no longer afford to provide such "wide-ranging help."[52] Likewise, the demise of the parish felons associations in Dublin was due to their over-ambitious plans to patrol large areas of the city and not to the declining political fortunes of Dublin's Volunteers. The Dublin associations had neither the resources nor the inclination to take over the policing functions from the parish watch. As a result, the felons associations in the city were unable to live up to the expectations of thousands of parishioners promised relief from crime.

In November 1782, St. Mary's association published a statement of purpose, declaring that it was "formed for apprehending robbers, taking up night walkers, rioters and strollers." [53] In December 1782, it sent a patrol to ward off a large gang of robbers and housebreakers threatening Summerhill, Richmond, and the North Strand—an area to the north-east of its parish boundaries at Rutland Square. As St.

Mary's parish did not extend beyond Rutland Square, the association was not within its remit to patrol a section of St. Thomas parish. In the event, no arrests were reported and, in fact, the Richmond and the newly formed Summerhill associations of St. Thomas parish publicly thanked St. Mary's association for its quick response.[54]

If St. Mary's association over-stepped its bounds geographically, it may have also overstepped its bounds legally. In December 1782, a "country gentleman" prosecuted St. Mary's association "for having taken him in the street at an unseasonable hour of the night, and confining him in the watch-house until the next morning." While the association was acquitted by a jury, legal fees in the case may have been substantial.[55] In January 1783, St. Mary's association called one of its last meetings to "settle accounts" and to "preserve arms and ac-coutrements."[56] The association did make one more reported arrest in conjunction with St. Thomas's association in September 1783.[57]

The demise of St. Mary's parish association may be partly explained by its political views which, like the Volunteers', were patriotic. In December 1781, St. Mary's association threatened to withdraw its pro-tection from warehouses and shops owned by merchants in the parish who engaged in trade to Portugal. The association alleged that a conspiracy was underfoot to restrict exports to that country from Ireland. By refusing to provide protection to some of Dublin's Portu-guese traders, the felons association was hoping to obtain some sort of guarantee of a "fair and equal trade for our manufacturers to that kingdom."[58] Clearly this action had little to do with their stated aims of preventing crime. Some merchants may have even suspected St. Mary's association of being an unwelcome meddler in their crucial import/export trade, especially given the large demand for Portuguese wine in Dublin.

While some associations wound up their affairs during the early 1780s, others had just begun theirs. On 9 December 1782, the Blackrock Felons Association was established in response to a double set of robberies on the Blackrock Road on the night of 4 December 1782. In the most serious incident, James Moore Davis, a pawnbroker in Dublin, was shot and seriously wounded when the carriage in which he was travelling with three people was ambushed by a gang armed with pistols. The party was robbed of seven guineas and silver.[59] In another less serious incident on the same night, John Irwin was robbed of about six guineas near Ballsbridge, also on the Blackrock Road.

Highway robbery and burglary were serious problems in south Co. Dublin perhaps because by December the parish watch and the newly formed parish associations had driven many gangs into the suburbs, to suburban neighbourhoods without associations, "where the inhabitants were too lazy or too fearful to protect themselves."[60] By the time their association was formed, Blackrock had "become notorious for robbers."[61]

On 9 December 1782, the first general meeting of the Blackrock Felons Association took place, with William Ogilvie in the chair. 41 people adopted a plan for "apprehending, prosecuting and convicting all persons guilty of housebreaking, highway robbery, felony or trespass, in or about Black Rock, Booterstown, Merrion, Stillorgan, Kilmacud, Newtown, Monkstown, Dunleary, Bullock [Harbour], Dalkey, Cabinteely and the county adjoining." Thus the association made claims to protect a vast area, including 12 different communities as far as the Co. Wicklow border. Would the £46 12s. 9d. raised at the first meeting be enough? Not for the plans that were eventually put into place. Within a month, 12 more names were added to the list, bringing the membership of the association to 53 and, more importantly, bringing total subscriptions to £60 5s. 9d., as each member of the association paid an annual membership fee of one guinea. Money was deposited in La Touche's bank, two partners of which played an active role in the association. Many wealthy people and members of the nobility supported the association, including Viscount Ranelagh, Lady Arabella Denny, Lady Lisle, the Countess of Brandon and the Recorder of Dublin. This base of support distinguished the Blackrock association from city associations, which relied more heavily on merchants and shopkeepers in the community. This difference may explain why the Blackrock association lasted longer and why it was able to build a police station in Blackrock.

The association's first order of business was to arrest those responsible for the shooting and wounding of Davis on the Blackrock Road. Its initial fund-raising efforts were to provide enough money for once-off payments to constables. The association also set out a list of rewards in its preamble. It promised to pay 20 guineas for information that resulted in the arrest and capital conviction of highway robbers, burglars and felons. Five guineas was promised for information leading to the arrest and conviction of petty thieves, tree cutters and hedge mowers. It also promised to pay for costs incurred by prosecutors, including legal fees, and compensation for constables and assistants for appearing in court. In addition, some of the money raised from subscribers would go towards the cost of placing criminal advertisements in newspapers. At the first general meeting, it was decided to delay plans to establish a police force in Blackrock until more subscribers to the association could be recruited to fund the force.[62] In short, the association aimed to provide better protection for the suburban villas and the busy arterial roads in south County Dublin.

At the first working committee meeting of the association, a proposal to employ six constables on a fixed salary was debated and rejected.[63] (The issue came up again a few years later.) The building of a "proper lock-up" was discussed at a later meeting, with plans and estimates to be submitted in the near future. Pressures on finance, however, continued to work against the establishment of a paid police force and the building of a police station. It was not until September 1784 that peace officers received weekly wages.[64] By this time, the association had recruited at least two peace officers and provided them with 12 hangars (truncheons).[65] In January 1785, a case of pistols costing 16s. 3d was also provided to peace officers.[66] Arming officers with deadly weapons was not unusual—the Summerhill association armed its constables at this time. No other association, however, appears to have established a police station, largely because the parish associations worked from existing parish facilities.[67]

In May 1785, more than two years after the idea was originally brought up at committee level, the building of a lock-up was given the go-ahead.[68] Details of a rental agreement between the association and one of its members were faithfully recorded in the minutes. As a result, the house in Blackrock owned by William Ogilvie was to be converted into living quarters for constables and into a small gaol. Ogilvie charged the association an annual rent of one guinea, with the association expected to pay for any expenses on alterations.[69] In October 1785, bricklayers were employed to fit up a room on a lower floor in which prisoners were to be confined. The house developed into a fully operational small police station shortly after 1785.

The Blackrock Felons Association continued to strengthen their organisational structure and pursue their goal of stopping crime. Justice William Beckford played a leading role in this. Beckford had already acquired a reputation as an active magistrate before the formation of the Blackrock Felons Association. Dublin county had serious problems with gangs of burglars and in Milltown on February 1780, Beckford arrested Simon Doyle, a member of the gang that had burgled a Kilgobbin farmer named Farrel of £400.[70] Doyle became an informer, providing enough information to enable Justice Robert Wilson to arrest another burglar named Lee.[71] In January 1781, Beckford arrested Edward Brady and Peter Murphy for their part in the armed burglary of a cabin in Kilmacud owned by Owen Mitchell.[72] Mitchell and his wife were badly injured in the burglary, which resulted in the loss of their box of rent money and all of their clothing. Although Brady was apparently released, Beckford committed Murphy to Kilmainham gaol. The Commission of Oyer and Terminer convicted him and sentenced him to death. Peter Murphy was hanged at Stephen's Green on Saturday 17 March 1781.[73]

In September 1781, Beckford made one of his most important arrests when he became indirectly involved in a drive against a Dublin-based gang specialising in stolen bank notes. In early September 1781, Florence McCarthy, a boy aged 15, robbed Stephen Gordon, an iron-monger, in Dame Street of £370 in bank notes.[74] A messenger, who was a member of McCarthy's gang, took the stolen money to a banker in Clonmel for payment.[75] Notified of the illegal transaction, Sheriff Patrick Bride and a party of Volunteers arrested the messenger at Ranelagh on his return from Clonmel and committed him to Newgate. In a co-ordinated effort, Beckford also arrested Nicholas Mulhall at Donnybrook and charged him with being an accomplice of Florence McCarthy in the robbery of Gordon.[76] A stolen silver watch, a steel chain and three seals—the products of other robberies—were found on Mulhall's person.

In addition, Beckford and several Dublin Volunteers arrested Daniel McDonagh and Elizabeth Mulhall and charged them with receiving the notes that McCarthy had stolen from Gordon.[77] McCarthy was found guilty at the Commission of Oyer and Terminer in October 1781, but was spared the fatal noose because the jury recommended him as an object of mercy due to his youth. McDonagh and Elizabeth Mulhall were acquitted.[78] Nicholas Mulhall was acquitted at the following Commission of Oyer and Terminer in December 1781.[79] Upon Mulhall's acquittal and subsequent release from gaol, the gang planned another crime, but this time in another city.

In January 1782, one Mr Connor, probably a clerk or cashier with the large banking house of Warren and Company of Cork, was robbed of

£2,700, one of the largest robberies in this period (indicating also that bank clerks carried around great sums of money). An advertised reward of £500 (not reported in the *Hibernian Journal* until 31 May 1782) may have served its intended purpose because a huge operation was mounted to arrest those responsible for the Warren robbery. While William Beckford himself was not directly involved in this second operation, his earlier arrests of Elizabeth and Nicholas Mulhall probably contributed to its successful outcome. After news of the Cork robbery reached Dublin, the Volunteers, three associations, a parish watch, a Dublin sheriff and a Newgate under-gaoler all joined forces to arrest the culprits. In January 1782, James Donnelly, a leading member of the gang, was arrested in Dublin in possession of £600 in stolen notes.[80] Donnelly was committed to Newgate, but £2,100 in stolen notes were still missing.

Soon after Donnelly's arrest, a bag-man for the gang passed a stolen note for payment to a bank in Dublin. After the illegal transaction, a bank clerk followed the bag-man to a house in Poolbeg Street. Information obtained by the clerk was soon relayed to Sheriff James Campbell and Newgate's Michael Toole, both of whom arrested one Brady and committed him to gaol.[81] Later in the same evening, the St. Mark's association arrested Thomas McDaniel, another member of the gang, on George's Quay. McDaniel was temporarily committed to a watch-house of St. Mark's parish. The only blunder in an otherwise smooth operation was McDaniel's escape from the custody of the parish watch. St. Mark's parish wardmote court investigated the conduct of a deputy constable and a corporal on duty at the time and dismissed them, warning of "further punishment as the law directs."[82]

Less than a month later, with most of the money still missing, the whereabouts of Nicholas Mulhall, the organiser of the gang, were discovered. In a well-planned raid on 11 February 1781, Sheriff Campbell, Toole and both St. Mary's and St. Thomas's associations participated in a joint operation against Mulhall, who was armed with pistols at his lodgings in Lower Abbey Street.[83] In a search, Toole found £1,936 in stolen bank notes on Mulhall's person, leaving only £164 not accounted for from the total £2,700 stolen. According to *Walker's Hibernian Magazine*, a detachment of Highlanders then arrested one Fleming, another member of the gang, in Abbot Street.[84] The combined operation was a huge success.

In both robberies of stolen notes—from Gordon in Dublin and

Connor in Cork—the Dublin-based gang was composed of seven men and a woman. Its members clearly performed distinct functions, including picking pockets, receiving stolen notes and passing stolen notes for payment at cities other than where the notes were stolen. No familial connection has been established between the receiver Elizabeth Mulhall and the gang leader Nicholas Mulhall, but the coincidence of name does suggests a relationship.

Ranged against the gang were parish associations, sheriffs, gaolers, magistrates and even the military. As a result of the earlier blunder, St. Mark's parish launched an immediate investigation of its own affairs, indicating the seriousness with which it took its policing duty. The reward of £500 offered for the robbers concentrated many minds. Ironically, the only bitterness about the operation came when the monetary reward was not paid to Toole, who apparently did more than anyone else to arrest the culprits. Toole was only paid a "paltry sum" because not all of the stolen money was returned to Warren; a "trifle" went missing. Along with the Dublin high sheriffs, Toole was commended for attending at the trial of Donnelly and Mulhall in Cork.[85] The Cork assizes convicted the two men and an arrest of judgement against their sentences failed. On 15 April 1782, Donnelly and Mulhall, neither of whom delivered a dying declaration, were hanged at Gallows Green in Cork.[86]

Obtaining guilty verdicts was an important consideration for all law and order forces operating in Dublin. At meetings of the Blackrock association, often scheduled to coincide with the court sessions, both past and upcoming court cases were discussed. At the second meeting of the association, it was decided to pay the expenses for the prosecution of a court case that had been heard at the Commission of Oyer and Terminer on the previous day, even though the outcome was unsuccessful.[87] In December 1782, the Commission acquitted William Delaney, part of the same gang that robbed Davis, for the robbery of John Irwin of Co. Leitrim on the Blackrock Road on 4 December 1782. The testimony of Irwin was not strong enough for the jury to convict.[88] To prosecute the case had cost the association a total of £8 3s. 7d., including the most expensive item—legal fees of £4 11s. to Counsellor William Caldbeck and to an attorney named Peters.[89] The second most expensive item was the fee paid to Irwin himself—£2 16s. 11d. for "his steady conduct" during the trial.

In January 1783, William Beckford gave evidence in court against three men accused of burglary. The case concerned the burglary of surgeon George Daunt's house in Harold's Cross in September 1781.[90] Although Daunt had employed counsel to carry on with the prosecution, he did not give evidence himself at the trial. Hence, Beckford's testimony was decisive in winning the case. In January 1783, the Kilmainham Quarter Sessions convicted James Kennedy, Patrick Farrell and Daniel Gaynor of burglary and sentenced the men to death. They were hanged at Gallows Hill on Saturday 18 January 1783. The gaoler of Kilmainham built a drop platform modelled on the same gallows from which Lord Ferrers was hanged at Tyburn, London on 5 May 1760.[91] Before their deaths, the three men confessed to a murder in Co. Meath in September 1781.[92]

Meanwhile, the Blackrock Felons Association continued to pursue the gang that robbed Davis on the Blackrock Road in December 1782. One of the robbers, James Egan, escaped from Newgate shortly after his initial arrest in December 1782.[93] Egan fled to Limerick, where he was arrested by Michael Toole, who travelled to Limerick to identify him in February 1783.[94] He was then transmitted from Limerick to Dublin to face trial.[95] Egan was a member of a large gang, which included John Short, aged 13, who was arrested in Kevin Street soon after Egan had been transmitted back to Dublin in March 1783.[96] In July 1783, the Commission of Oyer and Terminer heard the trial of Egan and Short, both indicted for the Davis robbery on Blackrock Road seven months earlier. Convicted, the two men were hanged before a enormous crowd of spectators in front of Newgate on Saturday 9 August 1783.[97]

In September 1784, a small item in the *Hibernian Journal* caught the eye of the Blackrock Felons Association. An unnamed person alleged that William Beckford was a "trading" justice of the peace, suggesting that he had accepted bribes in return for favours. No more details were provided concerning the allegations, but this initiated a scandal which nearly succeeded in destroying Beckford's reputation.[98] With the association heavily committed to their leader, his trial at the Court of Exchequer in the following year must have been a considerable embarrassment to their subscribers. Beckford was tried, convicted and fined £100 by the court for "improper execution" of his job. He claimed that the conviction was "obtained by perjury and connivance."[99] Humiliated, he went to Bristol to recover his "health." The Blackrock Felons Association, however, called him back and paid his fine of £100.[100] In the end, he returned to Blackrock and once again took charge of the felons association until its dissolution in 1797.

During the early 1780s, Dublin was concerned about improving its image abroad and strengthening its existing law enforcement agencies, particularly the offices of Lord Mayor and sheriff. In September 1782, Nathaniel Warren was elected to serve a one-year term of office.[101] (He became the first police commissioner under the new city police four years later.) Warren sought to prevent the Dublin meat industry from falsifying the weight of meat it shipped abroad, "which if suffered might ruin the exportation of barrelled pork from this kingdom." He discovered that Irish exporters were not bleeding pig carcasses before shipment abroad, thus illegally increasing their weight from ten to fifteen pounds each. Accompanied by Sheriffs John Carleton and Samuel Reed, Warren raided several slaughter-houses to break-up the illegal operation.[102]

Warren also led a successful campaign to prevent stray pigs ranging through the streets of Dublin and eating rubbish. On more than one occasion, he sent "a great number of pigs and some roots" to the House of Industry.[103] Sheriffs Patrick Bride and Thomas Andrews (1780/81) and Sheriff Ambrose Leet (1784/85) were particularly active during this period. According to the *Hibernian Journal*, Leet made about 30 arrests in his term of office. (He later became the comptroller of the new city police.) Sheriffs Bride and Andrews—the only sheriffs who actually worked together on a consistent basis—made about 20 arrests between them. Leet concentrated his efforts in the Liberties, making eight arrests in this area. He directed much of his attention to coiners and receivers of stolen property, making six arrests for each of these crimes.

While 1780 was a bad year for the parish watchmen, the situation improved dramatically over the following years. It still remained a high-risk occupation, particularly in the violent year of 1784. On 26 March 1784, a gang robbed a countryman in Church Street. In response, St. Michan's parish watch arrested George Cruise and conveyed him to their watch-house on Inn's Quay. The rest of the gang attempted to set Cruise free by firing into the watch-house. In the attack, a watchman sustained a bullet wound and died. The gang ran off without Cruise, but returned to reclaim a large pistol which one of them had dropped. On the following morning, Philip Duffy and Michael Hughes were arrested for the murder.[104]

Cruise, Duffy and Hughes were tried at the Commission of Oyer and Terminer in July 1784, convicted and sentenced to hang.[105] Duffy was hanged at Gallows Hill on Wednesday 21 July, apparently charged as the person who fired the fatal shot. Before hanging, Duffy said that neither Cruise nor Hughes had shot the watchman. On 23 July, Cruise and Hughes wrote a quick petition to the Lord Lieutenant pleading for mercy. They enclosed statements by Sheriff Benjamin Smith, who attended Duffy on the gallows.[106] The petition either reached the Duke of Rutland too late or else he rejected it out of hand. On Saturday 24 July 1784, Cruise and Hughes were hanged, not at Kilmainham but at the front of Newgate.[107] On the same day, three convicted thieves were hanged at Gallows Hill for a robbery at Island Bridge.[111] The sheer number of hangings is proof that the Dublin courts had embarked on a severe policy of sentencing more felons to death than ever before.

The increasing number of executions in Dublin at this time (22 hangings in 1784 and 33 hangings in 1785), however, were cause for concern. In October 1785, a letter that implicitly criticised the harsh sentencing patterns of the Dublin courts appeared in the *Hibernian Journal*. Written by an anonymous author named CATO, the critical essay was entitled "Thoughts on the frequency of our Executions." The letter argued that the problem of crime was embedded in society and could not be solved by the machine in the gallows:

> It is evident, that a state receives no benefit from the death of offenders, while offenders continue to operate to as great a degree as if no punishment was annexed; to talk of lopping rotten and corrupted members, when the diseases of the body remain, is both idle and cruel. The poor souls we are perpetually executing, the number of whom increases every sessions, are incapable of reasoning as we reason, or acting as we act; they feel themselves miserable through poverty and hunger, and liable, by a regular course of nature, to continue in a long life of misery; they are taught to believe that death ends that misery; they are most of them men of hardiness or great courage, and prefer a short life attended with present advantage, and instant enjoyment, to a life of slavery or oppression; and the example of their superiors stimulate them not a little to the pursuit of those pleasures, which must end in ignominy and death; for in the moment of natural impulse, few men examine its propriety, but especially the

ignorant, who never can, in the vortex of passion, carry consideration one instant beyond the present time, and have not the
most distant idea of consequence of contingency.[109]

This public criticism at the severity of the Dublin courts was apparently taken seriously as the number of hangings declined steadily after
1785.

In summary, the Volunteers rejuvenated the parish watch system
through the building of parish and street associations for the prevention of crime in 1780. Volunteers such as Thomas Moore helped to
build the parish associations throughout the city. Parliament even
passed legislation empowering the residents of Rutland Square to raise
a subscription which would finance a private police force to deter
crime in the area. Under the act, passed in 1784, those residents
agreeing to pay taxes for their own private police were absolved from
contributing to the general Dublin watch tax.[110] The enthusiasm for
raising associations seemed to diminish as the Volunteers went into
decline in 1783. The exception to the rule was the Blackrock Felons
Association, which had the support of the wealthy residents in south
Co. Dublin.

In the summer of 1784, after the Duke of Rutland had settled into
his Viceroyalty, the government seized the initiative on ways to im
prove the policing of Dublin. On 22 June 1784, the privy council met
to consider how to slow down the increase in violence and crime.[111]At
the following privy council meeting, Rutland instructed Thomas Orde
to carry out a full-scale inquiry into the state of the parish watch.[112] It
did not take long for Orde to come to a conclusion. In August 1784, he
decided that the watch in Dublin had to be replaced.[113] Crime and
punishment had overtaken the meagre parish watch. As a first step,
Orde established an embryonic police force. In conjunction with the
Castle, Dublin Corporation hired an independent force of 20 constables to shore up the existing parish watch system.[114] They were paid
£20 each per year, well above the wages earned by their counterparts in
the parish watch.[115]

By February 1785, most of the parishes had submitted the necessary
information to Orde in his investigation of the watch. He found that
the cost of running the watch was £4,667 for the year ending 25 March
1784; a figure that by contemporary standards was very low.[116] Under
pressure to put the policing of Dublin on a sound footing, Thomas

Orde developed a plan to organise a far more efficient, centrally organised and better paid police force. Whether this would succeed would be a great test for Orde and Dublin Castle.

CHAPTER SEVEN

The New Police

On Friday 29 September 1786, the first modern police force in Ireland began patrolling the streets of Dublin. Overnight the city was occupied by an army of uniformed men: 40 petty constables mounted on uniformed horses and 400 policemen armed with muskets charged with bayonets.[1] Seeking to establish their superiority over the old, discredited parish watch, the new police arrested hundreds. of criminals in their first weekend. The parish watch, which had served Dublin since 1714, was disbanded in 1786 because violence in Dublin had reached catastrophic proportions. Between 1780 and 1786, the *Hibernian Journal* reported 173 homicides, including 107 murders, 27 suicides, 10 cases of manslaughter, 11 infanticides, three deaths from duelling, and 15 other fatalities, an average of 25 violent deaths per year.

The Dublin courts also increased the severity of punishment meted out to offenders, particularly after the American War of Independence in 1783. In November 1784, Ireland resumed transportation to the Americas even though England had discontinued the practice eight months earlier.[2] The three Dublin courts transported 226 convicts to the Americas in 1784 and 1785 and, in the same two years, approximately 55 felons were executed in Dublin, including the two women who were burned at the stake.

Thus it was not surprising that the 1786 Police Act passed through both houses of the Irish Parliament within 49 days.[3] This speed is particularly noteworthy as the British Parliament failed to pass a similar police bill for London in the preceding year.[4] The most important aspect of the act was that it introduced centralisation to the policing of a city with 21 parishes and the Liberties.

Dublin was divided into a four-part square with the River Liffey running through the middle. A central police headquarters was established at 8 William Street to the south of the river and police stations were established in each of the four quadrants.[5] Three police commissioners, one of whom was to take up permanent residence at 8 William Street, were to run the new police headquarters. Nathaniel

Warren, a strong-willed individual, was the first and only commissioner to reside in the residence.[6]

Warren had been in close consultation with Thomas Orde, Chief
Secretary at Dublin Castle, over the drafting of the police bill since the
decision was first taken to review the existing parish watch system in
the summer of 1784.[7] As a police commissioner, he controlled the
operations of the force with a degree of independence unknown to any
previous parochial authority. He had four divisional justices beneath
him, 19 guard houses and 400 policemen and had control over a huge
jurisdiction contained by the North and South Circular Roads surrounding Dublin.

The Police Act of 1786 was a far-reaching statute that covered many
aspects of local government. It empowered the commissioners to raise
the police tax on houses and tenements from 1s. to 1s. 6d. in the pound,
an increase of 50 per cent. It also empowered them to license, regulate
and control a bewildering array of small businesses and trades, to
publish a weekly list of wanted felons in the *Hue and Cry* and to visit
and inspect the gaols. Under a unique provision in the act, the Lord
Lieutenant had the authority to transport convicts to the Americas on
as many as four transport vessels per year. Thus transportation to the
Americas continued unabated from Dublin until 1789, even though
London had stopped transportation to the Americas in 1784.[8] Compared to the previous 1778 Police Act, which was contained within
three pages in the Irish Statute Book, the 1786 Act contained so many
new rules and regulations that it required 28 pages.

The 1786 Act generated opposition from certain Whigs in Parliament led by Henry Grattan and a group of radical representatives in
Dublin Corporation led by James Napper Tandy. Both groups united
to form a single faction which was opposed to the loss of parochial
control over the policing of the city. The faction claimed that Dublin
Castle had usurped power from the parishes. The 1786 Police Act also
generated hostility from householders in Dublin, who were asked to
pay higher taxes to finance the new police. Under the legislation, thousands of small business people, hawkers, porters, and penny boys were
required to pay license fees. Henry Grattan, the prominent Whig MP
for Dublin city, put it in a nutshell when he said that the act represented
"a new constitution for the city of Dublin."[9]

The start-up costs of the new police force were high even by
contemporary standards. Nathaniel Warren had an annual income of

£500 and his two commissioners, William James and John Rose, had an annual income of £300 each. The four divisional justices—Richard Moncrieffe, Henry Hart, Thomas Emerson, and John Exshaw—each had an annual income of £200.[10] With two clerks each, the combined annual salary of their clerical staff came to £500. John Sankey, the police secretary, had an annual income of £200 and his three clerks had a combined annual income of £240. Ambrose Leet, the chief accountant, had an annual income of £100.[11] In total, £2,690 was paid annually to 11 clerks, four divisional justices, three commissioners, an accountant and a secretary. The amount of money was of such enormous proportions that it defied the contemporary imagination.

Apart from the cost of bureaucracy, the incomes of the police constables and policemen were high in comparison with the incomes of the former parish watchmen. Oliver Carleton, the high constable of the police, had an annual income of £100, the four chief constables an annual income of £60 each, the forty petty constables £30 each, the forty watch constables £25 each and the 400 policemen £18 5s. each.[12] In sum, the combined annual income of the 85 ranking constables and 400 policemen amounted to £9,840.[13] Previously, the wages paid to the watchmen of Dublin had been paltry. Just two years earlier, the combined annual income of the parish watch system had been only £3,767, which was spread unevenly among 463 watchmen, 25 inspectors and 17 part-time clerks. In total, Dublin Castle had the power of nomination over 505 armed men whose combined annual income was £12,530. In addition, the police spent about £5,330 on incidental expenses, such as publishing the *Hue and Cry*, which cost £352 in its first year of operation.[14] Such expenses pushed the total cost of the new police to £17,861 in its first 12 months of operation.[15]

Who was going to foot this enormous start-up bill? The act stipulated that city householders would pay. They were asked to submit to the higher police taxes within 10 days of demand or be subject to distress payments (seizure of assets).[16] To collect the new police tax, 13 house-tax collectors were appointed, some of whom had to be accompanied by parties of police. Resentment grew sharply against the bullying tactics employed by the tax collectors. In January 1788, St. Catherine's parish said that landlords were raising rents "in proportion to the tax."[17] Such was the opposition that the freeholders of Co. Dublin, who also paid increased taxes to support the police, moved a resolution that called for:

[the] total repeal of the police law in the city of Dublin, and within the limits of the Circular-road to which it extends, … as the taxes under the police establishment are a grievance; and praying that an effectual watch may be established under the constitutional control of the inhabitants.[18]

Four months after Co. Dublin moved this resolution, the *Hibernian Journal* reported that the police were collecting taxes by force:

Though we are ever ready *to give unto Caesar what belongeth to Caesar* yet we cannot entirely approve of tax as being collected with a degree of ferocity and oppression that would disgrace the capital of the Mahometan empire; an instance of this kind occurred, as we are well informed, in this metropolis in the course of last week; the collectors of the police tax having actually levied the tax in several parts of the Earl of Meath's Liberty, literally at the point of the Bayonet, for they went their rounds, attended by a party of the police armed *cap a pie*.[19] This surely may not be unjustly termed a mode rather somewhat forceable, and little *nouvelle* in the collection of taxes in the metropolis of the kingdom.[20]

As this account was published only two weeks after the storming of the Bastille, the sprinkling of italicised French words shows how fearful the citizens of Dublin had become towards the police, whom they believed had usurped the city's traditions and customs.

An additional source of income came from the thousands of traders and vendors in Dublin. The police were given the authority to inspect the licenses of victuallers, or persons selling beer, ale or spirituous liquor.[21] Traders could only procure licenses from the police. Furthermore, the act empowered the police to sell certificates, costing one shilling, to a host of street vendors, including pawnbrokers, watchmakers, buyers of old iron, lead, copper, pewter, tin, dealers in old furniture, old cloth, second-hand goods and stable keepers.[22] In August 1787, the police advised all outside vendors, specifically penny boys, porters and messengers, to register for badges at a cost of five shillings.[23] The police sent 1,000 notices to porters on the Dublin quays warning them about the consequences of disobeying the badging law.[24] Vendors who did not procure their proper badges were liable to be arrested as vagrants.

Indeed, it was reported that the "poor creatures who ply with baskets at the different markets" were out in force begging for the money to purchase their badges. A spate of violent confrontations broke out between the police and porters on the docks. In early August, a policeman was injured at Ormond Market in an attempt to enforce the badging law.[25] Soon after, over 100 horse and foot policemen raided the lower Liffey quays for badges.[26] In September 1787, at the beginning of the winter season, a number of coal porters were arrested without badges, some paying for their badges on the spot. In December, the last report of such a confrontation was reported, indicating that the police had their way on the quays.

In a word, the regulatory functions of the police became so unpopular with the public that their efforts to prevent crime almost went unnoticed. This problem was reinforced by the fact that newspaper printers did not systematically collect information on crime from contemporary court records. Henry Grattan MP appears to have been the only contemporary who collected reliable evidence about crime in Dublin. In 1789, he asked Mr Taylor and Mr Allen, who were court clerks for the Dublin Quarter Sessions, to provide him with data on the number of examinations which had been lodged before city magistrates in the two years before and the two years after the new police had started patrolling the streets of Dublin. He did this to refute Attorney General John Fitzgibbon, who argued that crime in Dublin had diminished with the establishment of the new police. In the end, Grattan produced two sets of figures before the House of Commons. The figures showed that the number of examinations lodged had increased dramatically in 1787–88.

The data provided by Taylor and Allen showed that 2,470 examinations (pre-trial indictments) had been returned to the Dublin Quarter Sessions in 1784 and 1785, compared to 7,452 examinations returned in 1787 and 1788—an increase of nearly 200 percent.[27] While the implications of the Grattan/Fitzgibbon debate are important, the official figures themselves may shed some light on the reliability of the *Hibernian Journal* as a source. The newspaper reported that 152 prosecutions took place in 1784–85, compared with 531 in 1787–88, an increase of 250 percent. The data derived from the *Hibernian Journal*, therefore, diverged only slightly from the Taylor and Allen data and reinforces the validity of newspapers as a reliable source.

Henry Grattan's interpretation of the evidence, however, was politically motivated by his opposition to the police. In the parliamentary debate, Grattan did not take into account the effects of demobilisation after the American War of Independence.[28] Dublin Castle, on the other hand, was well aware of the domestic tensions caused by the return of peace. Transportation was immediately resumed in 1784. Dublin Corporation was also aware of an increase in crime. Arrests nearly doubled in 1785 compared to the previous year, suggesting that Dublin Corporation jolted the parish watch into action.

The four new divisional justices lodged prisoners in Newgate with vigour. Two were especially noteworthy: Thomas Emerson, who lived in the Liberties, and John Exshaw, who lived in the prosperous Stephen's Green division. Emerson himself made more arrests than the north-east Divisional Justice Richard Moncrieffe and the north-west Divisional Justice Henry Hart combined.[29] One of Emerson's first actions was to put down a riot in Francis Street by workers who had thrown a warp into the River Liffey.[30] He also arrested Edward Dowling, a broad weaver, for not finishing work commissioned on behalf of John Kearney, a clothier in Pool Street.[31] Over the years, he tried to strike a balance in a community beset by tense labour relations. In May 1789, he attempted to settle a prosecution out of court by embarking on face-to-face negotiations with a journeyman tanner named John Fitzpatrick, who was imprisoned in Newgate. Fitzpatrick had been prosecuted by Richard Wildridge, a master tanner in James Street, for causing the ruination of perishable calf skins worth £150. Fitzpatrick had simply refused to finish the job on them. Although Emerson was unsuccessful in preventing the prosecution, the Commission of Oyer and Terminer fined the journeyman only £10 and remitted a gaol sentence due to bad health.[32]

Some masters did not take kindly to Emerson's interventions on behalf of artisans. In June 1792, Thomas Abbot and two policemen arrested a female silk-winder for embezzlement, alleging that she had defrauded him of £4. Emerson apparently sided with the woman as he failed to commit her to prison to stand her trial. Abbot became furious at the delay and, in his anger, publicly humiliated the divisional justice by thrusting a copy of a relevant parliamentary statute in his hand to read. An incensed Emerson arrested the silk manufacturer and, in turn, Abbot charged Emerson with false imprisonment. In July 1792, the Commission of Oyer and Terminer convicted Emerson and fined him. (It is not clear what happened to the woman silk weaver.)[33]

John Exshaw was the divisional justice of the Stephen's Green division, which covered the entire southeast quarter of the city. His career in the police force was ruined by one event. On 13 May 1787, Exshaw and a party of policemen forcibly prevented a group of "gentleman's servants" from amusing themselves with "innocent recreations" in Merrion Square.[34] It was a Sunday and the servants were in violation of ancient Sabbatarian laws preventing such events from taking place on that day. When Exshaw arrived in Merrion Square, a match of football and a wrestling match were in progress. Exshaw ordered his men to clear the field, but the players did not disperse quickly enough to satisfy him. In the fray, insults and angry words flew in the direction of Exshaw.

Amongst the spectators were Richard Griffith and two of his friends, John Freke and Henry Hatton. Griffith was a Member of Parliament well-known for his outspoken views. He challenged Exshaw over the justification of the police action and questioned whether the Sunday gathering was indeed illegal. Viewing this as a provocation, Exshaw had Griffith and his two companions arrested. According to their indictment, Griffith and the other two men had "wilfully and maliciously ... made use of several opprobrious and contemptuous expressions—questioned his authority as a magistrate to dispense the riot—and finally, that they did molest, obstruct, and hinder him [Exshaw] from dispersing the persons concerned in the said riot."[35]

Because Griffith, as a Member of Parliament for the Borough of Askeaton, had vigorously opposed the passing of the 1786 Police Act in the House of Commons, the riot took on a political dimension. In his speech before Parliament, Griffith had said he "imagined himself transported to the regions of Indostan ... that if this bill passed, the city of Dublin would be in a more oppressive situation in regard to its government, than the city of Delhi."[36]

Exshaw himself came to regret pressing charges against Griffith. He suddenly resigned his position from the police force as divisional justice just as Griffith's trial came to court in May 1788. At the King's Bench, Griffith was found guilty of insulting Exshaw, but managed to secure a re-hearing with respect to the punishment. At this second hearing in June, Exshaw almost apologised to the court, telling the presiding judge that the jury in the first trial ought to have acquitted Griffith. This volte-face suggests that the two sides had reached a compromise. While the guilty verdict against Griffith was not set aside, no punishment was ordered due to an arrest of judgement. The entire episode suggests that the laws which upheld Sunday as a religious rest-day no longer enjoyed widespread public favour in late eighteenth-century Dublin.

John Carleton, who took over as divisional justice of the Stephen's Green division, was assaulted shortly after his appointment.[37] His assailant, Allen Stewart, was convicted at the Dublin Quarter Sessions and sentenced to three months in Newgate and three public whippings.[38] After his second whipping from Newgate prison to College Green and back again, Stewart petitioned the Lord Lieutenant for a remission of his third whipping. According to surgeon John Whiteway, who was Inspector of Prisons, Stewart's health had been nearly destroyed by the whippings and the incarceration.[39]

In 1788, Parliament passed new legislation to increase the size of the force by 100 new policemen and eight new inspectors, two inspectors in each of the four divisions. The act also mollified some complaints by reducing the police tax on houses with a yearly rent of £5 or under from 1s. 6d. to 1s. in the pound.[39]

William Shea was one of the eight new inspectors assigned to the Stephen's Green division in October 1788.[40] In his first reported action, Shea arrested 32 prostitutes and, on the following night, arrested another 14. A week later, Shea testified against 21 prostitutes at the Dublin Quarter Sessions. Denis George, the Recorder, rejected Shea's testimony out of hand, pointing to "the cruelty of confining persons in prison, without sufficient charge being produced against them."[41] Shea was more successful in arresting thieves. In April 1794, Francis Bennet, a merchant, was attacked and robbed within steps of his door at 84 Fleet Street. He was knocked down, punched, severely cut, beaten and bruised. Bennet recognized one of his attackers as Michael O'Berne, a man whom he had known for 15 years. O'Berne forcibly stole Bennet's gold watch, a gold chain and two gold seals, biting Bennet's finger in order to obtain the valuable items. He also stole his hat and all the money he had about him. After the attack, Bennet received an anonymous letter indicating where his watch, chain and seals could be found.

Based on the information contained within the anonymous letter, Shea proceeded to a public house in Chancery Lane owned by Joseph Sallary, aged 70. Shea confiscated a watch, chain and seals from the publican, but only the watch proved to be Bennet's property. Accompanied by a party of police, Shea then returned to the public house to recover Bennet's chain and seals, which were found on a watch, and to arrest Sallary.[42] The publican in turn lodged examinations against a man named Horish, who had given him the stolen watch, chain and seals. To avoid prosecution, Horish fled to Liverpool. On 23 July 1794, the Commission of Oyer and Terminer heard the trial of O'Berne and Sallary. Shea's testimony eliminated any hope either defendant might have entertained of being acquitted.[43] The jury returned guilty verdicts against both men, recommending O'Berne as an object of mercy. On Monday 28 July 1794, O'Berne was sentenced to hang and Sallary to be transported for seven years.[44]

Despite O'Berne's initial fears, his well-connected friends and his brother exerted pressure on "several members of administration."[45] This had the desired effect and his hanging was respited twice in the space of two months.[46] Meanwhile, upon Sallary's conviction, Horish returned to Dublin from Liverpool. O'Berne's brother tracked down Horish, who was then arrested and remanded in gaol to stand trial.[47] Sallary, in turn, petitioned the Lord Lieutenant for a free pardon, claiming that Shea and Horish were on terms of "mutual friendship."[48] Dublin Castle endorsed the petition "to be laid by 17 October 1794." By February 1795, O'Berne's hanging had been respited seven times. He was finally pardoned on condition that he transport himself out of Europe. On Sunday, 16 August 1795, O'Berne sailed in a ship bound to America.[49]

Shea was also well-acquainted with the garrison in Dublin, which was growing in size since the start of the French Wars in 1793. In the early hours of Sunday morning 20 October 1794, William Wittenham, a serjeant, violently assaulted and robbed James Bardin Palmer of a gilt metal watch, a chain and a gold seal in Fishamble Street. On the preceding Saturday night, Palmer had dined with his brother and sister at a friend's house in William Street, the three family members leaving just before midnight. Palmer accompanied his brother and sister for part of the way to their home near the Royal Barracks in the north-west quadrant of the city until he "considered them out of danger" from robbers. On the way back to his home in Bishop Street, Palmer walked up Fishamble Street until he came to St. John's Church just above Copper Alley. A group of soldiers who were "making a riotous noise" attacked him, but as "the lamps of St. John's

Church burned very clear," he "threw his eye sharply" upon the face of Wittenham.

On the following Monday morning, the victim called upon the police to investigate the robbery. William Shea took over the case and "proposed to go to the barracks and have all the soldiers there drawn up in order to examine" them. An officer assembled the soldiers at Shea's request, giving Palmer the opportunity to identify the man who robbed him. Wittenham was arrested the following day and committed to prison. At Wittenham's trial at the Commission of Oyer and Terminer, a juror requested that Shea give testimony.[50] This request was disallowed by the judge to protect Wittenham, as Shea's testimony would have been "dangerous ... to the life of the unfortunate prisoner." Nevertheless, the jury found Wittenham guilty and he was sentenced to be executed on Saturday 29 November 1794. The judge, however, reassured the soldier that, on application to government, his sentence would be remitted.[51] At the following Commission of Oyer and Terminer in December 1794, Wittenham pleaded a royal pardon on the condition that he be shipped abroad by his regiment.[52]

In October 1788, Bernard Kelly was indicted for stabbing Simon Halfpenny with a bayonet. On his deathbed in Dublin's House of Industry, Halfpenny lodged an examination against Kelly with John Carleton, the divisional justice of Stephen's Green division. It was revealed in court that after Carleton had taken the examination, he then read it back to Halfpenny who swore to its veracity. At the Commission of Oyer and Terminer, Denis George, the presiding judge on this occasion, lectured Carleton on the proper way of taking examinations. George said that the defendant had not been brought face-to-face with his accuser before he died, "nor should the magistrate have entered into a mere conversation with the person; but have sworn him first to speak the truth, and nothing but the truth, and then to have taken his examination." In the end, the jury did not return a guilty verdict.[53] Had Kelly been convicted, he would be certain to hang.

If the Recorder believed that certain policemen were incompetent, so too did jury panels. In October 1789, Patrick Rigbey was indicted at the Commission of Oyer and Terminer for the burglary of William Montgomery's house in Dominick Street the previous July.[54] The police arrested Rigbey and an accomplice after the two had packed up several items of furniture in the house. Rigbey's accomplice subsequently escaped from Newgate. At the trial, a police man named Denis Baynham said "that he saw the prisoner at the bar coming into the house, and that he assisted in apprehending him in the house." The policeman's testimony corroborated the testimony of a prosecution witness. No evidence was produced on behalf of the defendant. Even though the prosecution's case was incontestable, the jury acquitted Rigbey.

Did juries find the police to be ineffectual witnesses? There were similar reports of unsuccessful prosecutions despite police evidence at the Dublin Quarter Sessions. In September 1788, the testimonials of two policemen were given in separate burglary trials at the Dublin Quarter Sessions, but despite their almost watertight evidence, the same jury returned verdicts of not guilty.[55]

The credibility of the police was further called into question when a top-ranking police officer, who had been convicted of manslaughter, held onto his position within the force. In February 1790, Chief Constable Philip Henry Godfrey beat a man, who was described as a stranger, to death in William Street. The policeman was conveyed to Newgate to stand his trial.[56] In the following July, the Commission of Oyer and Terminer tried Godfrey for murder, but in the end convicted him of manslaughter. He was sentenced to be burned in the hand and discharged.[57] Despite his conviction, Godfrey retained his position as Chief Constable of the Barrack Division on the north-west side of Dublin. He was transferred to the Workhouse Division on the south-west side of Dublin in 1793.[58]

On Saturday 25 April 1789, Sir Henry Cavendish, the chairman of a parliamentary committee appointed to inquire into the finances of the new police, delivered the committee's report to the House of Commons.[59] The report was deeply critical of the police commissioners, particularly Nathaniel Warren. It took issue with how the commissioners spent £51,000 of tax-payers' money in only 30 months. Among the criticisms, Cavendish reproached the police commissioners for spending £900 on legal fees, money he claimed was wasted largely on unsuccessful prosecutions.[60]

A revealing debate followed the delivery of the Cavendish report in which John Fitzgibbon, the Attorney General, pointed out to the House of Commons that anarchy had reigned on the streets of Dublin before the 1786 Police Act was passed:[61]

I call upon gentlemen to recollect the year 1784. Was any man
safe in bed? Was any man safe in his house? Were not gangs of
ruffians going about, ready to carry to the Tenter-fields, and
subject to the American patriotic discipline of tar and feathers,
any man that had the misfortune to fall under their displeasure. I
know, sir, a great cry has been raised against the police establishment; it has been a fatal blow to the mobocracy in Dublin. I
know that majestic power will never raise its head, till the civil
power is abolished; but in truth, I am not extremely anxious for
its revival. I recollect the year 1784, when a riotous mob burst
into this house, when their leader took that chair in which you
sit, sir; and when they passed unanimous resolutions against the
lives of the most valuable members of this house, the very best
and ablest friends of this country, I recollect, sir, that my right
honourable friend [Mr Grattan] was himself indebted for his
safety to a strong military guard—does he prefer that to the civil
power? The civil power of that day was unequal to his protection;
the Lord Mayor declared his inability, and it therefore had become necessary to increase the civil power, or depend upon the
military.[62]

John Fitzgibbon also said that the number of capital convictions in the
city had been "daily diminishing" and asked if anyone could remember
the last time there had been a "maiden" Commission of Oyer and
Terminer (one without a death sentence).[63] Serjeant John Toler argued
along similar lines, saying "that within the last two years, the average
proportion of convictions in the court where he presided [Kilmainham
Quarter Sessions], had fallen short one third at least of what they had
been in any similar period of his experience."[64] In a statement after the
Cavendish debate, Dublin Castle also followed the same line, claiming
that "the number of criminal prosecutions in the city and county of
Dublin had diminished in a degree equal to the most sanguine hope."[65]

As Fitzgibbon was speaking, convicted felon John Cowan was being
hanged at the front of Newgate prison. Three days before Cowan's
execution, John Egan was hanged at Newgate. Both had been tried at
the most recent Dublin Quarter Sessions: Egan had been convicted
for the robbery of Patrick Keefe in Patrick Street and John Cowan had
been convicted of stealing two black gelding horses from their owners
in Co. Down.[66]

Cavendish's criticism of the £900 spent on lawsuits by the commissioners was prompted by a belief that the police were too heavy-handed and even broke the law in some cases. An opposition spokesman, Arthur Browne, the Regius Professor of Laws at Trinity College, told Parliament in February 1788 that "a very considerable expense had accrued from defending policemen who were indicted for several crimes and this expense ultimately fell on the citizens of Dublin; and from the information of several very respectable persons, the police were in general the aggressors of the law."[67]

The Cavendish report's criticism of Police Commissioner Nathaniel Warren focused on the fact that one of the largest initial costs for the police was the expense of buying the house that became the central police headquarters at 8 William Street. As the house had also become the residence for the Warren family, it appeared to some that Warren had benefited personally from the purchase. The house cost £500 to purchase, but it cost £3,000 to furnish. In rebutting accusations, Warren said that "it was necessary for him to leave his own dwelling, which was extremely well furnished, and go to live in the police house without any furniture at all." Indeed, he said that he "had paid, at his own private cost, much larger bills for furnishing the house, than that charged to the public."[68] Warren also criticised the Cavendish committee for failing to examine people who supported the police. He said that "no person had been examined (though the whole city was raked for evidence) but such as were supposed hostile to the police."[69] Fitzgibbon concurred with Warren, stating that the Cavendish committee had written a report which was "founded on *ex parte* evidence, founded on partial investigation, founded on garbled and selected evidence."[70] In the end, Fitzgibbon moved that the report be rejected because it "had deviated from the order of reference."[71]

Most of Cavendish's findings seem to have been based on the research of Ambrose Leet, the chief accountant of the police. In October 1789, six months after the Cavendish report was debated in the House of Commons, the police commissioners informed Leet that his position was being terminated along with those of his personal clerk and two other clerks. Leet's dismissal attracted widespread attention. After notice was given of his dismissal, Leet found his office door padlocked and guarded by two policemen, even though his personal possessions were still in the office.[72] With the dismissal of Leet, the police force had effectually purged itself of its most prominent whistle-blower.

The Blackrock Felons Association was a far less significant agency than the police and it enjoyed no specific legal status. The association derived its powers solely from William Beckford, in his capacity as a magistrate. In July 1792, Beckford opened a magistrate's office at the house of one Mrs Whitworths in Blackrock at a cost of 50 guineas a year. He had four constables under him.[73] In August 1792, William Butler, one of the four constables, arrested a robber and conveyed him to Kilmainham gaol. On his return to Blackrock, Butler was waylaid by other members of the robber's gang who wounded him fatally. He was the first and only policeman employed by the Blackrock Felons Association known to have been killed in the line of duty. Bridget Butler, the widow, petitioned the association for compensation on the grounds that her husband was in the employment of Beckford at the time of his death. The petition resulted in an award of five guineas.[74] Given that the association's preamble offered no such arrangement, this case may have set an important precedent in protecting the rights of all surviving family members of police officers who died in the line of duty.

Butler's death apparently caused a weakening of morale among the three remaining constables. In May 1793, constable William Haskins refused to obey Beckford's order "to quell a violent riot" that had erupted following a funeral wake.[75] As a result, Beckford himself arrested two of the rioters, provoking a violent confrontation which forced him and his two captives to seek refuge at the Byrne's Arms Tavern in Blackrock. Eventually, a cavalry regiment from Dublin was called in to prevent the mourners from breaking down the tavern.[76] In the aftermath of the affair, Beckford prosecuted his disobedient constable for neglect of duty. While the outcome of the prosecution against Haskins is not known, Beckford seemed to survive the crisis, although his role in the association changed.

In the changed political climate after 1795, Beckford became involved in political policing. He was called upon to ask every householder in Blackrock to sign an "oath of allegiance" to king and constitution and to "return to this association the names of the persons in the said parishes (if any) who shall decline to sign the said declaration."[77] As a result, Beckford compiled a list of 93 loyal supporters who signed the oath. In July 1797, he received his final payment for the upkeep of the magistrate's office.[78] The Blackrock Felons Association for the prevention of crime had been dominated by one man for 15 years. With its changed direction, it had moved too far from the goals set out in its preamble to justify its continued existence.

On 12 February 1795, Henry Grattan MP moved a bill in the Irish House of Commons to repeal the statutes which had created the new police.[79] What prompted him to put forward the bill at this particular time? For years, the parliamentary opposition had proposed the repeal of the police acts, but with no luck whatsoever and in March 1792, Dublin Castle rejected Grattan's attempts to repeal the acts as "hardly worth mentioning."[80] Three years later, however, Grattan received support from an unexpected quarter, the new Lord Lieutenant, the Whig Earl Fitzwilliam.[81]

In the House of Commons, Grattan cited four main factors that made it necessary to abolish the police: (1) the enormous expense of keeping the force running, (2) the huge debts incurred by the police, (3) the heavy burden of taxation on the householders of Dublin, and (4) the failure of the force to recruit enough policemen to maintain law and order in the city.[82] A week after he introduced the bill, Fitzwilliam was forced out of office.[83] The new Lord Lieutenant, however, remained of the opinion that "the existing police is condemned."[84] On 5 June 1795, the Police Act of 1786 was quietly abolished. The loyal police force continued to patrol the streets of Dublin until the end of September, dignified to the end.[85]

Under the 1795 Police Act, the police bureaucracy was reduced to a fraction of its former size. The four districts were collapsed into two divisions—the North Division and the South Division.[86] A superintendent magistrate replaced the three previous police commissioners and two divisional justices replaced the four previous ones. The new superintendent magistrate had an annual income of £600 and the two divisional justices an annual income of £300. The three remaining salaried positions were filled by aldermen, who were nominated by the upper house of Dublin Corporation (subject to the approval of the lower house). Furthermore, each division was placed under the control of only one inspector or "peace officer," who exercised control over 25 constables. (William Shea himself was appointed as one of the peace officers under the 1795 Police Act.) Thus a whole layer of administrative staff was wiped out, reducing the police establishment to two inspectors and 50 constables. The new police patrolled the streets of Dublin alongside a reconstituted parish watch system.

The 1795 Police Act resolved the major bone of contention for

Grattan and the Whigs because it returned to the local parishes a full measure of control over the running of the watch. Each parish selected nine residents to become directors of the watch with the responsibility for employing their own watchmen.[87] What pleased many householders about the new act was that the police tax on houses valued at over £5 was reduced from 1s. 6d. to 1s. 3d., a decrease of 17 per cent. Finally, the watchmen themselves were happy with the arrangement; they were to receive an annual income of £18, the same wages paid to the former policemen.[88]

At noon on 29 September 1795, the parish watch reappeared on the streets of Dublin for the first time in nine years. They gathered first at their respective watch-houses and then paraded through the city in a show of unity and support.[89] A few weeks later, the parish directors joined together to establish a uniform set of rules to govern the activities of the watch in both districts.[90] Cracks, however, began to emerge over the issue of funding. At a meeting of the church wardens and directors of the watch on 13 October 1795, it was reported that the Lord Lieutenant had not paid the promised funds (amounting to £3,332) to finance the watch. The parish leaders repeatedly called on the Lord Mayor to put pressure on Dublin Castle to make good its promise.[91] The complaints over police financing must have sounded like a familiar refrain to the former police commissioners, whose hard work and relentless efforts to create a modern police force came to nothing as a result of financial pressures. Dublin would have to wait anther 40 years before this lost opportunity was remedied with the formation of the Dublin Metropolitan Police in 1838.[92]

In summary, after the American War of Independence the parish watch system was unable to cope with the crime wave unleashed by the demobilisation of troops. It was almost inevitable that a new police force was necessary and, indeed, the 1786 Police Act survived for nine years in the face of fierce factional politics. It fell victim to the Whig opposition led by Grattan and to the city's propertied classes, who were opposed to both the increase in police taxes and the high cost of settingup the first centralised police force in Dublin. The heavy-handed manner in which the police collected the taxes also worked against their survival. In the end, the new police became a political liability for the government. The transition back to a parish watch system in 1795 predictably followed a smooth course. The crime wave of the mid-1780s was long over, but so was the economic boom and, for those artisans who had not already emigrated, the French wars relieved Dublin of a large section of its young male population. By 1795, Dublin had become a less violent, and perhaps a less spirited, city.

CHAPTER EIGHT

Transportation

Most histories of transportation from Ireland are marked by fixed points of reference: they examine either the transportation of convicts to North America from 1703 to 1775 or the transportation of convicts to Australia from 1791 to 1868. Few, if any, historians have researched the transportation of Irish convicts in the period immediately following the American War of Independence.[1] Transportation to the mainland colonies was suspended during the war and, as the war drew to an end, it was understood that the United States would not be prepared officially to receive convicts. Nevertheless, the practice continued.

England resumed transporting convicts to the Americas in 1783, but only two transport vessels sailed before the operation was permanently shut down less than a year later. In July, a transport ship called the *George* sailed with about 125 convicts from London. Its destination was falsely reported as Nova Scotia, a necessary precaution to avoid alerting the authorities in the United States. Likewise, the *George* changed its name to the *Swift* as an added precaution. It ran aground in a convict rebellion off the Sussex coast, where about 25 prisoners escaped, and finally reached Baltimore, Maryland where, after a considerable delay, most of the convicts were sold. In April 1784, a second ship, the *Mercury*, sailed from London with 179 convicts, but was refused entry by all American ports along the Atlantic coast. In the end, the convicts landed in the British Honduras, to the alarm of the residents, whose protests brought an end to English transportation to the Americas.[2] England resumed transportation only in 1786, when she embarked on an ambitious plan to establish a convict colony in New South Wales.[3]

In her research, Portia Robinson estimates that 62 per cent of all women transported to Botany Bay from Ireland in the five years between 1791 and 1795 were from Dublin.[4] (This finding is remarkable in that Dublin's share of the national population was never more than 4–6 per cent in this period.)[5] According to the *Hibernian Journal*, the vast majority of female transports from Dublin were sentenced by the

Table 4: Post-war Transportation
Convicts transported from
Dublin and Ireland, 1784–1795

Departure	Transport Vessels	Destination	Dublin	Ireland
Nov. 1784	Nancy	St. Kitts-Nevis	100	200
Sept. 1785	Ann Mary Ann	Maryland	126	176
June 1786	Dragon	Virginia	145	190
June 1787	Providence	Maces Bay	*91	183
Oct. 1787	Chance	Bahamas	*59	118
June 1788	Nancy	Connecticut	*100	200
Oct. 1788	Providence	Cape Breton Is.	*63	126
June 1789	Duke of Leinster	Newfoundland	*57	115
Nov. 1789	Duke of Leinster	Leeward Isles	*44	89
Apr. 1791	Queen	Port Jackson	85	153
Dec. 1792	Boddingtons	Port Jackson	61	152
Dec. 1792	Sugar Cane	Port Jackson	62	153
Aug. 1795	Marquis Cornwallis	Port Jackson	*119	238
1784-1795	13 Transport Vessels		1,112	2,093

(*estimated) Sources: Vessels 1–3: *H.J.*, 07.09.88; Vessels 4-9: *Commons' jn. Ire.*, vol 13, p. cccli; Vessel 10: Robinson, *The Women of Botany Bay* p. 91; Vessels 11-13: Shaw, *Convicts & the Colonies* p. 363.

Dublin Quarter Sessions. The three Dublin courts sentenced a total of 101 women to transportation between 1785 and 1795 and, of these, the Dublin Quarter Sessions sentenced 84, which is 83 per cent of the total. This finding has been reinforced by an examination of sentencing patterns for male transports from Dublin. The three Dublin courts sentenced 312 men to transportation in the same period, and of these the Dublin Quarter Sessions sentenced 250, which is 80 per cent of the total.

During the same period, the three Dublin courts hanged an estimated 242 felons, and of these the Dublin Quarter Sessions hanged an estimated 45 felons, which is 19 per cent of the total. These figures suggest that the Recorder of the Dublin Quarter Sessions favoured transportation to capital punishment. In contrast, the Commission of Oyer and Terminer sentenced only 31 men and 3 women to transportation. At the same time, the Commission sentenced an estimated 97 felons to death, which is 40 per cent of the total. Likewise, the

Kilmainham Quarter Sessions sentenced 35 men and 32 women to transportation, but hanged an estimated 82 felons, which is 34 per cent of the Dublin hanged. Clearly, the Commission and the Kilmainham Quarter Sessions favoured the gallows to the transport vessels.

What happened when Ireland resumed transportation to the Americas has never been addressed. Roger Ekirch, an American convict historian who has accounted for the last two transport vessels from England to the Americas, fails to entertain the possibility that Ireland resumed transportation to the Americas and thus is incorrect when he states that transportation to the Americas ended in 1784.[6] The *Duke of Leinster*, not the *Mercury*, was the last transport vessel to sail with convicts from the British Isles to North America. With it nearly a century of transportation to the Americas came to an end. By adding Ekirch's figures to the *Hibernian Journal's* figures, one can now estimate how many convicts were transported in the eighteenth century. Excluding the suspension period between 1775 and 1784, the total number transported from Ireland to the Americas from 1718 to 1789 was 14,400 people.[7]

Transportation offered judges an alternative to capital punishment, thereby saving many lives from the hangmen's noose. It relieved the problem of over-crowding in gaols while at the same time giving offenders a chance to start a new life after several years of servitude. An inexpensive way to dispose of unwanted convicts, costing an average of £1,247 per transport ship including clothing, victualling and passage, Irish transportation turned a handy profit for shipmasters, who sold convicts "as slaves or workmen" for terms ranging from three to seven years at a price of between £8 and £9 each.[8]

The Lord Mayor of Dublin held the responsibility for contract negotiations with Dublin's merchants for the transportation of convicts since 1726, when the Irish Parliament began to pass laws to facilitate this form of secondary punishment.[9] Those merchants who were awarded the lucrative contracts were, according to Audrey Lockhart, "chiefly interested in the profits to be made" from the business.[10] Lockhart discovered that after rival groups of merchants petitioned Parliament for the transport contract in 1739, one group undercut the rest by half with a price of £3 per head, which subsequently became the official rate.[11]

Between 1703 and 1775, George's Quay and Sir John Rogerson's Quay on the south side of the River Liffey were the usual places where convicts were boarded onto waiting vessels.[12] When Ireland resumed transportation to the Americas in 1784, the embarkation site for convicts was transferred to the North Wall. This change was necessitated by the closure of the former city prison on the south side of the city and the opening of Newgate prison on the north side in September 1780. Newgate served as a collection depot for convicts from all over Ireland who were escorted in carts to the North Wall. Once they left Dublin, the transport vessels occasionally called in at Cork to pick up convicts: in September 1785, the *Ann Mary Ann* picked up 50 convicts in Cork and in June 1786, the *Dragon* picked up 45.[13]

In the period 1718–75, Ekirch estimates that Ireland transported about 13,000 people, an average of 227 people per year.[14] In the six years between November 1784 and November 1789, the *Hibernian Journal* reported approximately 1,397 men and women transported on nine vessels to different ports in the Americas, an average of 233 people per year.[15] The average number of people transported from Ireland to the Americas before the war was remarkably similar to that in the period 1784–89. Lockhart discovered that the province of Leinster accounted for nearly half of all Irish transports sentenced between 1737 and 1743.[16] Although the proportion of Leinster transports is not known during the 1780s, there is no reason to suppose that the proportion would have changed.

When the number of convicts awaiting transportation reached a critical figure, the Lord Mayor would negotiate a contract with a ship owner, paying 5–10 guineas per head. Between May 1787 and November 1789, six transport vessels left Dublin. Convicts were indentured as servants by the Lord Mayor in order to increase their market value on their arrival in the colonies.[17] Some captains managed to reach their destination, unload their human cargo and return to Dublin within two months, expecting more convicts to be available.

Transportation lacked mechanisms to safeguard the basic human rights of convicts. Once the ship left port, the role of the Lord Mayor ended. An open-ended clause in the contract gave masters the right to land convicts at any "port or ports in North America" of their choice. The only definite clause in the contract stated that captains "shall not permit any of said convicts or passengers to return back with said ship." The system was, therefore, left wide open to abuse. Indeed, some ship commanders contracted by Dublin Corporation displayed a complete disregard for the safety and well-being of Irish convicts, landing them without food or clothing in the middle of nowhere, even in the dead of winter.

Characterised by lack of planning and organisation, transportation was not immune from disaster. Eight months after the *Mercury* sailed from London in April 1784, the *Nancy* sailed from Dublin. The first transport vessel since the American war left Dublin in the third of November with approximately 200 convicts on board at a total cost of £500 to the Irish Treasury.[18] About 100 convicts, or half the total, came from Dublin gaols. Although the Dublin grand jury bought clothes for the convicts, there was not enough food and water on board the vessel.[19] On the day of departure, a detachment of soldiers escorted the convicts to the North Wall and the convicts boarded lighters to ferry them to the *Nancy* in Dublin Bay. The *Hibernian Journal* falsely reported (just as the English newspapers were known to do) that the *Nancy* was destined for the island of Great Abaco in the Bahamas.[20] Before crossing the Atlantic, Captain Michael Cunnim sailed to the Canary Islands off the north-west coast of Africa to buy provisions. According to the *Hibernian Journal*, new arrivals to the islands must wait for clearance from the health office or else face harsh reprisals. Without waiting for clearance, Cunnim landed 46 convicts in three boats on the island of "Ferro" (probably Hierro)[21] and a horrific massacre took place. All 46 convicts were "surrounded and put to death by the army."[22] With the remaining convicts, Cunnim proceeded across the Atlantic to St. Kitts-Nevis, part of the Leeward Islands.

In the wake of this fiasco, the Lord Mayor negotiated a contract with a master, who sailed directly to the former British colonies and sold his cargo as indentured servants in much the same way as transport merchants had always done throughout the eighteenth century. In September 1785, a second vessel called the *Ann Mary Ann* sailed with 126 convicts from Dublin and 50 from Cork. The *Hibernian Journal* again falsely reported the destination of the transport vessel. Instead of going to Nova Scotia, as reported, Captain Duncan Nevin sold his cargo as indentured servants at Georgetown, Maryland, a port with a long history of trading transports.[23] (Between 1746 and 1775, almost 10,000 transports from England had disembarked in Maryland.[24] According to Ekirch, the overwhelming majority of convicts were transported to three colonies: Virginia, Maryland and Pennsylvania.)[25]

The Lord Mayor then arranged a contract with a third vessel, the *Dragon* of Dublin, which sailed in June 1786. As the convicts were waiting to be transported on the *Dragon*, riots broke out at Newgate.[26] The cause of the violence was no doubt the harsh and over-crowded conditions at this the main collection depot, which would fill with transports from other gaols in Ireland in the weeks and months prior to sailing. The *Hibernian Journal* reported that the vessel was going to the West Indies, now a familiar false destination. In August 1786, after collecting 145 convicts from the North Wall and 45 convicts in Cork, Captain Hamilton sailed to Alexandria, Virginia, where he sold the convicts "in a lump" to Mr John Fitzgerald, a merchant. The mass of 190 convicts was probably set to work at a local factory. In 1770, 55 Irish convicts were sold from a single shipload to work at an ironworks factory in Maryland.[27]

In October 1786, Whitehall informed Dublin Castle that it was planning to transport convicts to Australia, news that aroused the interest of the Lord Lieutenant.[28] At that time about 100 men and women in Irish prisons were awaiting transportation to the Americas. Thinking England had a better idea, Dublin Castle offered to convey the Irish convicts to either Portsmouth or Plymouth, where they could join up with the first English fleet on the long voyage to Botany Bay, but Whitehall rebuffed the offer.[29]

On 3 May 1787, the *Providence* transported 133 men and 50 women to North America at a cost of £1,888.[30] Typically, early reports about their destination were misleading. It was stated that part of the cargo would travel to Botany Bay, after landing some of their number in the United States. Captain Napper sailed for Shelburne, a town on the lower east side of Nova Scotia, but the residents refused to allow the vessel to land, some of them no doubt remembering an incident which occurred just over 50 years earlier in 1735, when a cargo of 40 Irish convicts "ran their vessel aground off Nova Scotia, murdered the entire ship's company, and ran off among local Indians and French settlers."[31] Napper then sailed round the southern tip of the island, depositing the convicts at Maces Bay, an unsettled part of mainland Canada about 50 kilometres north of the American border.[32] Having survived the Atlantic crossing on board the *Providence*, the convicts were then forced to hike over rough terrain into the United States, where it was said that those who survived the ordeal became servants.[33]

Yet another example of the disastrous policy of transporting convicts to North America in the post-war period occurred in October 1787, when Captain Stafford of Barmouth, Wales, transported 118

convicts from Dublin on board the *Chance* for £944. On 12 October
1787, the *Hibernian Journal* reported that the *Chance* sailed for Africa,
but in fact the ship sailed for the Bahamas. After landing on the island
of Inagua, the convicts lost 69 of their number due to the "extremist
hardships" on the "totally desolate" isle.[34] A vessel from New England
rescued the 49 survivors, attended to their needs and deposited them
in Massachusetts.[35]

It was the British provinces on the north Atlantic that began to take
action against arrivals from Ireland. In July 1788, the town of St. John's
on the eastern coast of Newfoundland not only expelled two Irish
convicts, but sent a messenger to Dublin Castle to collect their return
trip fare. William Condron, "an incorrigible rogue and vagrant," and
Elinor Kennery, "a common prostitute" who exposed her infant on a
Newfoundland wharf, were shipped back to Ireland on the brig *Ann
and Francis*, bound for Waterford in June 1788. Dublin Castle took the
attitude that Newfoundland was an insubordinate colony impudently
sending convicts back before the expiration of their sentences and
demanded "a stop to a practice of this nature [returning convicts]; the
illegality and inexpediency of which are sufficiently obvious."[36]

In June 1788, Captain Robert Winthrop transported 200 convicts at
a price of £1,754 on the *Nancy*, the first vessel to sail from Dublin after
the American war.[37] As transports from all over Ireland arrived at
Newgate in May to await shipment on the *Nancy*, fighting broke out
between the country and city (Dublin) transports. Describing it as an
"alarming and serious" riot, the *Hibernian Journal* laid the blame on
the country transports, who had tried to get over a wall separating the
men from the women.[38] Although some prisoners joined the military
in putting down the riot, soldiers shot dead two convicts.

On a quick journey across the Atlantic, the vessel lost "but very few
[convicts] on the voyage."[39] Captain Winthrop confined the convicts
in separate holds on the ship: men were "bolted and properly secured," while women were "only kept locked up."[40] In mid-July 1788,
the *Nancy* arrived at Winthrop's native town of New London, Con-
necticut, where he broke the cargo up for sale. Dublin Corporation
paid Winthrop £7 10s. per convict, but Winthrop increased his profits
by selling some convicts as indentured servants for three years in New
London. He hired a smaller vessel to re-transport the remaining
convicts southward as indentured servants.[41] It was not long before
Winthrop's ploy was found out. A loyalist who served in the British

army during the war, Winthrop paid some form of compensation (the details of which were not clear) "to appease the wrath of his fellow-citizens."

On 18 October 1788, Captain Debenham left the North Wall of Dublin with about 150 convicts after having been escorted from Newgate by a squadron of horse and two companies of foot soldiers.[42] Dublin Corporation paid Debenham £1,106, including a flat rate of £6 per head. This was £1 10s. below Winthrop's price. Despite tight security precautions, one prisoner managed to escape. He was Anthony Molloy and he managed to escape by bribing the captain of the *Providence* to allow him to jump overboard where a lighter was waiting to collect him.[43] Six months later, Justice of the Peace Robert Wilson arrested Molloy in Francis Street for possession of two pistols and detailed directions for coining. Wilson committed him to Newgate, where he waited for the next transport vessel.[44]

A convict who should have also sailed on the *Providence*, but did not, was Frederick Lambert.[45] Lambert's story began in July 1783, when the Commission of Oyer and Terminer convicted the young man of robbing Paul Ham of his watch, a hat and eight shillings in Arran Street.[46] Three men had committed the robbery, but Ham could only recognise Lambert because he had a pronounced limp.[47] The son of a deceased counsellor, Lambert was sentenced to hang, but the Lord Lieutenant reprieved him on condition that he transport himself out of the country within six months and not return for 14 years.[48] Three years later, however, Lambert returned to Dublin, passing himself off as his brother's rent collector. He was eventually arrested for returning before the expiration of his sentence and committed to Newgate to stand trial.[49] In July 1786, at the Commission of Oyer and Terminer, Counsellor William Caldbeck succeeded in postponing his trial, but apparently he was remanded in custody for the next two years.[50] In June 1788, at the Court of King's Bench, Lambert claimed that he had returned to Dublin by sheer accident.[51] In a show of good will, John Fitzgibbon, the Attorney General, accepted his plea of shipwreck and granted him a pardon on condition that he transport himself out of Europe for the rest of his life.[52]

While in Newgate awaiting transportation, Lambert was forced to share a cell with a violent and dangerous offender named Francis Bathurst, who was serving a three-year gaol sentence for throwing a child from a third-storey window.[53] For unknown reasons, a violent dispute broke out between the two prisoners and Bathurst was cut by a razor blade from the chest to the lower abdomen.[54] Bathurst survived the injury and pressed charges against Lambert under the Chalking Act, which required proof of premeditation in cases of murder and maiming (unlike this gaol house brawl, in which there was little or no premeditation).[55]

In October 1788, at the Commission of Oyer and Terminer, Lambert's counsellor argued that his client's actions were not premeditated but were taken in self-defence and, therefore, the indictment upon which Lambert was charged should be withdrawn. Counsel for Bathurst, however, cleverly manipulated the emotions of the jury by asking Bathurst to exhibit his wound before the crowded court. This display shocked the jury into concluding that the crime had indeed come within the scope of the Chalking Act. The jury immediately returned a guilty verdict and Lambert was sentenced to death.[56]

In accordance with the Chalking Act, Lambert was hanged two days after his trial at the front of Newgate on Thursday 30 October 1788. In effect, his hanging turned into a death by torture because the hangman fed the wrong thickness of rope into the pulley. When Lambert dropped, the rope wrenched free of the pulley forcing him to struggle against the rope for several minutes before he finally expired. With difficulty, the hangman lowered his body onto the front steps of Newgate.[57] His death marked an end to over five years of punishment in consequence of a trivial theft from his youth.

The *Providence* had meanwhile set sail on a voyage across the Atlantic Ocean, a journey lasting less than a month. According to the *Hibernian Journal*, 46 passengers perished en route.[58] Due to the inclemency of the weather, Captain Debenham decided against a plan to sail down the St. Lawrence River to an interior part of Quebec province, where he had intended to sell the convicts as indentured servants.[59] Instead, he diverted from his intended course, landing the transports on an uninhabited part of Cape Breton Island in December 1788. Several drowned during the landing, while another 20 died before they reached the nearest town. Those who survived did so because of the generosity and goodwill of the inhabitants of Cape Breton, who maintained them at public expense for the duration of the winter. Lieutenant Governor Macarmick withdrew £787 from the public coffers to cover their expenses. This money that was paid back by Dublin Castle.[60]

Not surprisingly, a few of the convicts committed some atrocious crimes on the island. No specific details were provided as to the nature of these crimes but, where such landings took place, the people feared for their lives and property. It was common knowledge that Irish convicts arrived with almost nothing to sustain them. In July 1789, news reached England that the convicts who had landed on the island of Cape Breton had been "destitute of provisions or clothing" at the beginning of the previous winter. This deeply embarrassed the government. In a letter written on 27 July 1789, Whitehall ordered Dublin Castle "not to direct or authorize the transportation of offenders to the colonies."[61] Dublin Castle ignored Whitehall's instructions, allowing one more transport vessel to leave Dublin on 7 November 1789.

Within two weeks, Dublin Castle was to regret its action. On 23 November, Dublin learned that 79 Irish convicts were on their way back from Newfoundland by way of Portsmouth in a ship that was in effect marked "returned to sender." Newfoundland was still coming to terms with the forced repatriation to Ireland of William Condron, the vagrant, and Elinor Kennery, the prostitute, just a year earlier. After unloading its cargo of 115 convicts,[62] the *Duke of Leinster* beat a fast retreat to Dublin in a seven-week return trip voyage (the ship left Dublin on 12 June 1789), for which the master earned an estimated £500.[63] After the convicts landed, the Governor of Newfoundland arrested all of them, citing the threat they posed to the island's profitable fishery.[64] Several districts in Newfoundland raised £461 to cover almost half of the £917 it cost to send the convicts back. Dublin Castle reimbursed Governor Milbanke, although it objected to paying the £461, claiming this was a gift.[65] Put on board a vessel bound for England, the convicts arrived in Portsmouth on 23 November 1789. It is interesting to note that a list of their names and criminal records had gone to Newfoundland and back again, evidence that Dublin Castle was not remiss in sending the indents of transported convicts to the Americas. Dublin Castle was remiss in sending the indents of convicts transported to Australia in later years.[66] Although no deaths were reported in Newfoundland, only 79 of the 115 convicts returned to Dublin, leaving 36 unaccounted for.

In view of this second major embarrassment, Whitehall was irritated with Dublin Castle for letting matters get out of control and ordered the Castle to stop transporting convicts to the Americas as the practice was "highly improper and is productive of so much expense and inconvenience."[67] But under Irish legislation, specifically the 1786 Police Act, Ireland had acted lawfully in transporting convicts to the former British colonies in the Americas.[68]

The consequences of this policy, however, made it impossible to sustain. The Irish convicts sent back from Newfoundland were impelled to stay in Portsmouth for a month longer than expected while Dublin worked out the legal implications of shipping them back to Ireland. Under Irish law, the courts were obliged to prosecute as a capital felony any persons who returned transported convicts before the expiration of their sentence. Under these conditions, the Irish courts issued a warning to both the captain of the returned transport vessel and the messenger who accompanied the convicts, advising them "to take shelter in some of the neighbouring ports of the British coast."[69] Apparently, the captain and messenger escaped safely, although it is not known where they landed the convicts.

In January 1790, 73 men and six women returned to their former lodgings in Newgate, resulting in a major disturbance at the gaol which spilled over into the city and indeed to other parts of Ireland.[70] Seven months after their unexpected arrival, Newgate was the scene of one of the most dramatic prison riots since the Gordon rioters liberated hundreds of prisoners from London's Newgate prison in June 1780.[71] With the arrival of the returned convicts, Newgate prison contained more than 175 men and 25 women under sentence of transportation.[72] On Tuesday 6 July 1790, hundreds of prisoners staged a roof-top protest and threw slate and timber onto military guards below, who called for reinforcements. A group of prisoners forced the keys from the hands of a deputy gaoler and made themselves the "absolute masters of the interior part of the prison."[73] Dozens managed to escape in the confusion.

To avoid bloodshed, the Lord Mayor ordered the guards back from their positions along the outer walls surrounding Newgate. Rev. Mr Gamble, the Newgate prison chaplain, offered to become a hostage of the prisoners, but the prisoners rejected his offer. At dusk, the Lord Mayor ordered the military to put down the revolt. From positions round the prison and on the tops of houses opposite, soldiers peppered the roof-top with fire, forcing the prisoners to retreat into the gaol where they were secured by the military guards and the gaolers.[74] While the attention of the prison guards was thus occupied, a group of 40 prisoners escaped from Newgate. One knot of 14 prisoners dug their way below the foundation of the gaol into the sewers linking Newgate prison and the River Liffey. Noxious sewer gases poisoned five prisoners, guards captured three at the mouth of the sewer on the bank of the River Liffey and six managed to escape.[75] Some of those who escaped were arrested in the city shortly afterwards, but others managed to return to their families in their native towns. Six executions of escaped prisoners in different towns throughout Ireland were reported in August 1790.[76]

Soon after the takeover and escape, a Dublin grand jury sent a committee to investigate conditions at Newgate.[77] Their investigation resulted in plans for major alterations to the prison, plans that were exhibited at the Royal Exchange in September 1790.[78] After approving the plans, the grand jury presented £1,000 for the construction of an outer wall round the gaol to prevent escapes and £3,000 for the construction of private apartments for the gaoler and his staff.[79] Major internal repairs requiring additional funds were also approved.[80] The work, however, did not begin and conditions at Newgate deteriorated. In October 1790, 100 men and 50 women awaited transportation and 150 prisoners either awaited trial or served time.[81]

Dublin's police commissioners wrote two parliamentary reports which were highly critical of the poor conditions within Newgate.[82] In 1792, the police commissioners recommended that a new prison be built to replace the existing one. According to the report, Newgate had "more the appearance of a ruin than a place for the confinement of felons."[83] In December 1794, Police Commissioner William James demanded an explanation from the Dublin grand jury about the "work that had never been done." James also raised questions about the missing £5,000 that had been approved in 1790, saying that "no account had been returned in what manner that sum had been expended."[84] Over-crowding at Newgate prison also occupied the attention of Dublin Corporation, which approved a plan by Jeremiah Fitzpatrick to transfer 50 convicts to the city Bridewell in James's Street in June 1790.[85]

Although the major modifications to Newgate were never in fact carried out, the Dublin grand jury and Quarter Sessions made key changes in the management and staff of the prison. A series of embarrassments prompted the changes. On 12 April 1790, an American named Redmond escaped from the prison with the aid of Mathew Nulty, aged 35, a messenger employed at Newgate.[86] A member of a gang headed by George Barrington, Redmond had been convicted of picking pockets and was sentenced to transportation.[87] According to the *Hibernian Journal*, Redmond returned to London after his escape from prison.[88] In June 1790, the Dublin Quarter Sessions sentenced Nulty to transportation for aiding and abetting Redmond in his escape.[89]

Although they suffered many indignities in Newgate, the returned transports from Newfoundland would probably have considered themselves fortunate after learning of the plight of yet another cargo of Irish transports. In January 1790, the governors of two islands in the West Indies arrested an entire shipment of convicts along with the commander of their transport vessel. At the centre of this latest fiasco was the *Duke of Leinster*, the same transport vessel whose human cargo had been returned from Newfoundland to Dublin.[90] In this later episode, the *Duke of Leinster* sailed from Dublin with 89 convicts on 7 November 1789. Dublin Corporation paid its captain William Christian £5 5s. per head, the lowest contract rate. In the West Indies, Christian broke up his cargo into two lots, landing them on separate islands. First, he landed 54 convicts on the island of Barbuda "destitute of every necessary." He then sailed to Anguilla, part of the Leeward Islands, but the inhabitants learned of the nature of his visit and arrested him and the 35 convicts.

On Barbuda, the convicts called themselves "redemptioners ... bound to America." The inhabitants of Barbuda gave them food and shelter and even raised a sum of money to support them in their quest. As soon as word reached Barbuda from Anguilla, however, the mood of islanders turned ugly. They arrested all 54 convicts, charging them with stealing 14 watches from a watchmaker's shop and stealing communion plate from a church.[91] The evidence suggests that some of the convicts eventually returned to Dublin. William Dalton was one of the names listed among those transported from Dublin on 7 November 1789.[92] He apparently returned because in October 1791, Police Inspector William Shea arrested him for robbing the Earl of Clanwilliam of his gold watch, three gold seals and a purse containing a five-guinea note on Inchicore Road.[93]

Whitehall, of course, reacted sharply to the news from the West Indies, as it had come just three months after the Newfoundland fiasco. The incident demanded an explanation from Dublin Castle. Had the Castle not followed Whitehall's orders not to transport convicts to British possessions in the Atlantic? The answer may never be known because responsibility for transportation was not effectively in the hands of the Lord Lieutenant. Whitehall did write two letters ordering Dublin Castle to stop transporting convicts to the Americas, the first dated 27 July and the second 25 November 1789.[94] According to the official correspondence, Dublin Castle claimed that orders not to transport convicts to the colonies in the Americas were received on the "25th of November; 18 days after the vessel [*Duke of Leinster*] had sailed from hence."[95]

In April 1790, the Lord Lieutenant took control over the transportation of convicts away from Dublin Corporation.[96] A delay of almost 18 months took place before the first cargo of convicts from Irish prisons sailed for Australia. This caused considerable anxiety in Dublin, where people were accustomed to more frequent departures. In April 1791, Whitehall finally organised the transportation of 133 men and 22 women on the *Queen*, which sailed from Cove [Cobh] and arrived at Port Jackson on 26 September 1791.[97] Seven men died on the *Queen* and the entire cargo landed in a feeble and emaciated state. An inquiry into the condition of the convicts found that the second mate on the *Queen* had cheated the convicts of their rations.[98] After the first sailing, Whitehall suggested that Dublin Castle find Irish shipping to transport its convicts to Australia as English shippers were "adverse at the taking out Irish convicts without a military guard, and we have no such guard to furnish."[99] As no Irish shippers came forward, it was not until October 1792 that English vessels were contracted to make the voyage from Cove.

Consequently, there was another long delay between the first sailing to Botany Bay and the second. By March 1792, the gaols in Ireland were over-flowing, with 250 men and 60 women awaiting transportation.[100] There was considerable concern in Ireland as it appeared to Dublin Corporation that the English government would no longer empty Ireland's gaols on a regular basis. By August 1792, Dublin Castle estimated that the 400 prisoners awaiting transportation were becoming "so numerous as to create considerable danger of infection—their turbulence renders it difficult to guard them from escape."[101] On the last Sunday in September 1792, a riot erupted in Newgate, sparked by prisoners who grumbled that the time confined in Newgate was not "deducted from the time they were to be transported for."[102] They attempted to escape, but a military guard at Newgate prevented them, killing one and wounding another.[103] By October 1792, 200 prisoners were confined in Newgate waiting to be transported, many having been delayed for anything up to five years from the start of their sentences.[104]

Against this background, Dublin Corporation seized the initiative on transportation, as it had done after the American war. On 1 September 1792, Lord Mayor Henry-Gore Sankey proposed a four-point plan to Dublin Castle, underlining the determination of the Corporation to resume transportation of Irish convicts to the Americas. The Lord Mayor promised to "procure a vessel every way well appointed, capable of accommodating 300 passengers and … with sound wholesome provisions, and every accommodation befitting men in their situation (clothing excepted) to be examined and approved of by competent judges."

First, fixed destinations were assigned where Irish convicts would be received, a departure from the former system of transporting convicts willy-nilly across the Atlantic to addresses unknown. Sankey's chosen destinations extended over three continents: Sierra Leone on the western coast of Africa; Baltimore, Maryland, Savannah, Georgia, and ports in North and South Carolina, all in North America; and Cartagena, Columbia, in South America. The proposed destinations did not represent much of a change to previous landing points over the past century. British and Irish convicts were transported across a large area, including 18 mainland colonies in North America, six islands in the Caribbean and the island of Bermuda.[105]

Second, this diaspora was to be properly controlled. Sankey promised to regulate the system, ensuring that ship commanders were to land convicts at agreed destinations where they would be "humanely treated." Third, Sankey proposed to transport convicts twice a year at a cost of only 10 guineas a head, which was more frequent and less costly than the cost of transporting convicts to Port Jackson. Finally, the Lord Mayor promised a period of seven years of uninterrupted transportation, a contract which the government could break in the event of Dublin Corporation not complying with the agreed terms.[106] Dublin Castle apparently supported this plan, as it sent Whitehall copies of the Sankey's letters. But the English government did not respond to his proposals, indicating once and for all that transportation to the Americas was over.

Despite the rejection, Dublin Corporation's plan did nudge

London into action regarding Irish convicts. On 20 October 1792, Whitehall "discovered by accident a few soldiers at Chatham belonging to the New South Wales corps, which can be spared as a guard to the [Irish] convicts during their passage."[107] Dublin Castle, however, wanted a firm guarantee that Whitehall would not waste any more time in organising another shipment of convicts and cited political tensions in Ireland for the urgency of their request. Dublin Castle said that "it is of much importance to us to get them away as soon as possible ... the scenes before us in Europe and the questions presented to the public may possibly agitate the multitudes."[108] On 3 December 1792, Whitehall reassured Dublin Castle that it had engaged the services of William Richards, the contractor for the first fleet, to transport convicts in Ireland.[109] Whitehall said that two transport vessels, the *Boddingtons* and the *Sugar Cane*, were ready to sail from Cove after 15 December 1792. This proved to be an underestimation of the time necessary to organise the ships.[110]

In the second week of December 1792, two troops of horse and two companies of foot soldiers escorted 92 male and 31 female convicts in carts from Newgate to the North Wall, where they were put on board a lighter. They were then transferred to a waiting ship called the *Hibernia*, chartered to deliver them to Cork. Three men and four women did not make the journey due to sickness. During the operation two prisoners, "Jemmy the Schemer" and Andrew Morgan, managed to escape while they were being tied into the carts just outside Newgate. Another convict tried to escape, but he was shot through the shoulder and then put on board the *Hibernia*. A company of foot soldiers were also put on board the *Hibernia* for the journey to Cork.[111]

The convicts waited in Cork for over a month before the first transport vessels sailed. They waited aboard the *Hibernia*, which was not equipped for that purpose and many of them were sick by the time the transport vessels arrived at Cork. Before the *Boddingtons* embarked, two surgeons restored most of the convicts to a fair degree of health. Only one of the sick convicts died aboard the *Boddingtons*, which sailed with 125 men and 20 women on February 15, 1793. The *Sugar Cane* sailed with 110 men and 50 women on the 12 April. One of its convicts was shot dead after he was found without leg irons on. The *Boddingtons* arrived in Port Jackson on 7 August 1793 and the *Sugar Cane* on 17 September 1793.[112]

In October 1794, Dublin Castle reminded Whitehall that it had been nearly two years since the last two transport vessels had left Cove. 160 men and 40 women were now awaiting transportation in Irish gaols, causing considerable over-crowding once again.[113] Conditions in Newgate worsened in the following year. In May 1795, eight prisoners attempted to escape from the gaol, and two were successful, including one Ralph, who had been awaiting transportation for five years.[114] In June 1795, Whitehall responded to pressure from Dublin Castle by sending a transport vessel to Cork. When the *Marquis Cornwallis* arrived, however, a minor mutiny was in progress aboard the ship. The 26 soldiers, who were to act as convict guards on the vessel, had become "riotous and discontented" because they had "no officer with them nor ... arms or ammunition." They also had not been paid bounty money and allowances and the food provided to them was inedible.[115]

Riots also swept London in 1795. E.P. Thompson describes the riots in London of 1795–96 as the last time the labouring poor were to rise up against high food prices; he calls this period the end of the "moral economy."[116] In Dublin, there were riots as well. Military detachments were posted at warehouses located near the Grand Canal Harbour in Rainsford Street to prevent looting of corn meal and flour.[117] The riots aboard the *Marquis Cornwallis* delayed its departure until August. Meanwhile, convicts began arriving in Cork. From Dublin, two transport vessels arrived with 80 prisoners, half of whom were women. The relatively high proportion of women was due to the French wars since, according to reports, the government encouraged convicted felons to enlist in the military.[118] Meanwhile, the courts showed a greater enthusiasm to sentence women to transportation.[119] According to the *Hibernian Journal*, the three Dublin courts sentenced 32 women to transportation between 1785 and 1789, but sentenced 57 women from 1790 to 1794, an increase of 78 per cent.

When the *Marquis Cornwallis* sailed, 168 men and 70 women filled her hold. The occupational status of some of the convicts is made evident in the working implements put on board the ship: six looms for making sail cloth and "sundry articles for the manufacture of coarse linens," costing £127.[120] The convicts were obviously labouring people.[121] Given the pre-existing tensions aboard the vessel before she sailed, the journey to Australia was not a pleasant one and seven convicts "died of wounds in mutiny" during the voyage.[122]

In summary, after the American War of Independence, Dublin

Corporation resumed transportation to the Americas as an economical solution to the problem of over-crowding in gaols. Neither the United States nor the remaining British colonies, however, were prepared to receive Irish convicts officially. Previously, ship masters could expect to make handsome profits from the sale of the convicts as indentured servants. This made it worth their while to safeguard the lives and health of the convicts. After the war, however, the climate was more uncertain and prospects of sales were eroded. Ship masters suddenly saw their human cargo as a liability with the result that untold suffering, hardship and death characterised the final six years of transportation to the Americas. In the 68 years between 1718 and 1789 (excluding 1776–83), it is estimated that 14,400 convicts were transported to the Americas, an average of 212 people per year. It is not known how many convicts died before they reached their destinations, but the evidence from the last six years of transportation to the Americas suggests that a sizeable percentage did not survive the ordeal.

Conclusion

The hundreds of Dubliners who were hanged in the late eighteenth century have been forgotten. The great fire in the Public Record Office at the Four Courts in 1922, which destroyed virtually all the official court records in Ireland, certainly contributed to this oversight. But at a small park where Newgate gaol once stood, nothing reminds the visitor of the vast spectacles that once took place there. No memorial recalls the torture and punishment suffered by men, women and children. Only certain condemned prisoners from that era, such as Robert Emmet, are remembered for their revolutionary ideals and a long-standing exhibition at Kilmainham gaol is dedicated solely to the founding fathers of the Free State who were imprisoned and executed in the prison.

During the latter half of the eighteenth century, Dublin became one of the great European capitals. The city's main streets and quays were adorned with elegant houses and fine stately buildings. As the city grew in size and density, however, the gap between the rich and the poor widened. Destructive social pressures began to exert themselves on the ruling elite. The city's crime problems—murder, rape, robbery, burglary, assault, as well as child prostitution, vagrancy and drunkenness—stood out as unsightly stains against the Georgian background and the city's great accomplishments. Parliament's solution to this striking contradiction was to pass more severe legislation; the Irish *Statute Book* and the gallows served as the main weapons in the war against crime.

There is no danger of history repeating itself. In April 1954, the last felon was executed in Ireland and, in 1990, the death penalty was entirely abolished from the Irish *Statute Book*. The Irish courts have indeed softened the severity of their punishments; all crimes committed in Ireland which were once punishable by death are now punishable by prison sentences of varying lengths including life in prison. Clearly, Ireland was far more severe on crime in the late eighteenth century than today.

The Dublin Hanged, 1780–1795

242 total hangings; 199 verified hangings, 43 unverified hangings (latter marked *)

1. Mr Duffy Court: O&T	18 Mar. 1780 Burglary of house	Stephen's Green Volunteers escorted him
2. Mr Reed Court: O&T	18 Mar. 1780 Burglary of house	Stephen's Green Volunteers escorted him
3. Thomas Keams* Court: O&T	19 Aug. 1780 Robbery	Unknown Victim: W. Osbrey
4. Charles Hannigan* Court:O&T	19 Aug. 1780 Robbery	Unknown Victim: John Millikin
5. Edward Kinshelagh Court: O&T	21 Oct. 1780 Robbed a dairyman	Stephen's Green Mob grabbed his body
6. Timothy Sinnot* Court: O&T	9 Dec. 1780 Murder	Unknown Victim: Geo. Fitzharris
7. George Lowe Court: O&T	23 Dec. 1780 Burglary of house	Stephen's Green Confessed guilt
8. Robert Varsoe Court: O&T	10 Mar. 1781 Robbed an attorney	Stephen's Green Confessed a murderer
9. Peter Murphy Court: O&T	17 Mar. 1781 Burglary	Stephen's Green Co. Dublin
10. Peter O'Hara Court: O&T	11 Aug. 1781 Burglary of house	Stephen's Green Linked with Nugent
11. John Larney Court: O&T	11 Aug. 1781 Burglary of house	Stephen's Green Linked with Nugent
12. Michael Nugent Court: O&T	11 Aug. 1781 Robbed a carman	Stephen's Green Alias Nicholas
13. Valentine Pluck Court: O&T	29 Dec. 1781 Burglary of house	Stephen's Green Pluck's gang
14. Thomas Fannin Court: O&T	29 Dec. 1781 Burglary of house	Stephen's Green Fannin's gang
15. Michael Troy Court: O&T	29 Dec. 1781 Burglary of house	Stephen's Green Fannin's gang
16. Alexander Martin Court: O&T	26 Jan. 1782 Burglary of house	Stephen's Green Fannin's gang
17. John Porter Court: O&T	26 Jan. 1782 Burglary of house	Stephen's Green Pluck's gang

18.	John Doyle	27 Feb. 1782	Stephen's Green
	Court: O&T	Street robbery	A watchman
19.	Wife (Unnamed)	2 Mar. 1782	Stephen's Green
	Court: O&T	Murdered husband	Fire at hanging
20.	John Rorke	20 Jul. 1782	Stephen's Green
	Court: O&T	Uttered forged drafts	Place: High Street
21.	John Cotter	20 Jul. 1782	Stephen's Green
	Court: O&T	Burglary, North-side	Victim: Mr Dobson
22.	Edward Curley	20 Jul. 1782	Stephen's Green
	Court: O&T	Street robbery	Unknown
23.	John Wall	20 Jul. 1782	Stephen's Green
	Court: O&T	Robbed Houghton	alias "Jack the Smasher"
24.	John Murdock	20 Jul. 1782	Stephen's Green
	Court: O&T	Robbed Houghton	Two boys reprieved
25.	Michael Greet	2 Nov. 1782	Stephen's Green
	Court: O&T	Street robbery	Lynch's gang
26.	Thomas Heney	2 Nov. 1782	Stephen's Green
	Court: DQS	Burglary of dealman	Mr McCutchen's house
27.	John Murray	2 Nov. 1782	Stephen's Green
	Court: DQS	Burglary of merchant	Mr McCutchen's house
28.	Patrick Dougherty	21 Dec. 1782	Stephen's Green
	Court: O&T	Street robbery	Mob grabbed body
29.	Patrick Lynch	4 Jan. 1783	Newgate
	Court: DQS	Street robbery	1st Newgate hanging
30.	James Kennedy	18 Jan. 1783	Kilmainham
	Court: KQS	Burglary of house	1st Kil. drop hanging
31.	Patrick Farrell	18 Jan. 1783	Kilmainham
	Court: KQS	Burglary of house	1st Kil. drop hanging
32.	James Gaynor	18 Jan. 1783	Kilmainham
	Court: KQS	Burglary of house	1st Kil. drop hanging
33.	Mr Mathews	15 Mar. 1783	Newgate
	Court: O&T	Robbed £200	Fled to England
34	Mary Purfield	22 Mar. 1783	Kilmainham
	Court: O&T	Arson Blanchardstown	Strangled and burned
35.	Patrick Kane	14 May 1783	Kilmainham
	Court: KQS	Stole bank notes	Led a gang of five
36.	James Kelly	14 May 1783	Kilmainham
	Court: KQS	Burglary at the Barn	Place: Dolphin's Barn
37.	Owen Carroll	14 May 1783	Kilmainham
	Court: KQS	Burglary at the Barn	Arrested in Co. Carlow
38.	Charles Burgess	2 Aug. 1783	Newgate
	Court: DQS	Warehouse burglary	Died instantly
39.	Patrick Godfrey	2 Aug. 1783	Newgate
	Court: DQS	Warehouse burglary	25 minutes of torture

40.	Michael Lenhan Court: KQS	6 Aug. 1783 Unknown offence	Kilmainham Unknown
41.	Mr Brennan Court: KQS	6 Aug. 1783 Unknown offence	Kilmainham Unknown
42.	James Egan Court: O&T	9 Aug. 1783 Highway robbery	Newgate Victim: J. M. Davis
43.	John Short Court: O&T	9 Aug. 1783 Highway robbery	Newgate Boy, aged 13-14
44.	Mr Woods Court: ???	9 Aug. 1783 Unknown offence	Newgate Unknown
45.	Hugh Quinn Court: O&T	20 Mar. 1784 Murdered co-soldier	Newgate (?) Weapon: Bayonet
46.	James Blake O&T	20 Mar. 1784 Stole mare	Newgate (?) Victim: Francis Shaw
47.	James Murphy Court: O&T	20 Mar. 1784 Burgled silversmith	Newgate (?) Victim: A. Borradale
48.	John Kelly Court: O&T	20 Mar. 1784 Burgled silversmith	Newgate (?) 36 gold rings
49.	Hugh Feeney Court: O&T	20 Mar. 1784 Burglary of house	Kilmainham Reprieved mins. too late
50.	John Murphy Court: O&T	20 Mar. 1784 Burglary of house	Kilmainham Reprieved mins. too late
51.	Name Not Known Court: ???	15 May 1784 Unknown offence	Newgate 7 mins. of torture
52.	John Keenan Court: O&T	17 Jul. 1784 Robbery	Kilmainham Promised to haunt gaol
53.	Philip Duffy Court: O&T	21 Jul. 1784 Murder of watchman	Kilmainham Admitted his guilt
54.	Michael Hughes Court: O&T	24 Jul. 1784 Murder of watchman	Newgate Declared his innocence
55.	George Cruise Court: O&T	24 Jul. 1784 Murder of watchman	Newgate Declared his innocence
56.	John Mullen Court: ???	24 Jul. 1784 Street robbery	Kilmainham Declared his innocence
57.	Peter Mullen Court: ???	24 Jul. 1784 Street robbery	Kilmainham Declared his innocence
58.	Henry Binns Court: ???	24 Jul. 1784 Street robbery	Kilmainham Declared his innocence
59.	Mary Fairfield Court: O&T	21 Aug. 1784 Murder	Stephen's Green Strangled & burned
60.	Captain Lemon Court: ???	11 Sept. 1784 Burglary of house	Newgate (?) Attempted to escape
61.	Mr Reilly Court: ???	18 Sept. 1784 Burglary	Newgate Attempted to escape

62.	James Farran Court: O&T	6 Nov. 1784 Mail theft	Kilmainham Place: Rathcool Road
63.	Name Not Known Court: ???	6 Nov. 1784 Sheep stealer	Kilmainham Unknown
64.	Name Not Known Court: ???	6 Nov. 1784 Prison Robber	Kilmainham Unknown
65.	Mary Sutton Court: ???	6 Nov. 1784 Bleach green theft	Kilmainham Declared his innocence
66.	Richard Walsh Court: O&T	29 Dec. 1784 Burglary of house	Kilmainham Victim: Dorothy Napper
67.	William Warble Court: O&T	13 Jan. 1785 Robbed servant	Newgate (?) Soldier
68.	Edward Doyle Court: KQS	22 Jan. 1785 Burglary of house	Kilmainham Victim: Chr. Nash
69.	Roger Mathews Court: KQS	22 Jan. 1785 Burglary of house	Kilmainham Victim: Tho. Murphy
70.	Nicholas Eager Court: KQS	22 Jan. 1785 Burglary of house	Kilmainham Place: Goatstown
71.	Charles Davis Court: DQS	29 Jan. 1785 Street robbery	Newgate (?) Victim: Mr McDonnell
72.	James Hickey Court: DQS	29 Jan. 1785 Street robbery	Newgate (?) Pistoled-whipped victim
73.	James Farral Court: KQS	2 Feb. 1785 Burglary of house	Kilmainham Victim: Patrick Bryan
74.	Mr Foye Court: KQS	9 Mar. 1785 Murdered Mrs Foye	Kilmainham Blackrock Felons Assn
75.	Thomas Kean* Court: KQS	9 Mar. 1785 Murder	Kilmainham (?) Place: Tenter Fields
76.	John Hughes Court: ???	18 Mar. 1785 Burglary of house	Newgate Place: Cornmarket
77.	Thomas Keogh* Court: KQS	7 May 1785 Stole Bullocks	Kilmainham (?) Victim: Eliz. Shiels
78.	William Curry* Court: KQS	7 May 1785 Highway Robbery	Kilmainham (?) Unknown
79.	Mr Meaghan Court: ???	18 Jun. 1785 Street robbery	Newgate (?) Victim: Hon. Mr Agar
80.	Mr Reilly Court: ???	18 Jun. 1785 Street robbery	Newgate (?) Victim: Hon. Mr Agar
81.	Thomas Cartwright Court: KQS	23 Jul. 1785 Robbed bleach green	Kilmainham Gallows collapsed
82.	M. Shoughnessy Court: KQS	23 Jul. 1785 Robbed bleach green	Kilmainham Gallows collapsed
83.	Jeremiah Reily Court: KQS	23 Jul. 1785 Robbed bleach green	Kilmainham Gallows collapsed

84.	Charles Fallon Court: KQS	23 Jul. 1785 Robbed bleach green	Kilmainham No kin to wake body
85.	James McMahon Court: KQS	23 Jul. 1785 Robbed bleach green	Kilmainham No kin to wake body
86.	Michael Friel* Court: KQS	6 Aug. 1785 Robbery	Kilmainham (?) Victim: Abra. Beamish
87.	James Keegan* Court: KQS	6 Aug. 1785 Highway robbery	Kilmainham (?) Victim: James Clark
88.	John Crowley* Court: KQS	27 Sept. 1785 Stole 2 Saggard cows	Kilmainham (?) Victim: Mark Byrne
89.	John Hugon Court: KQS	22 Oct. 1785 Street robbery	Kilmainham Confessed guilt
90.	Daniel Devay Court: KQS	22 Oct. 1785 Street robbery	Kilmainham Victim: Thomas Bolts
91.	William Shanley Court: KQS	22 Oct. 1785 Street robbery	Kilmainham Place: Glasnevin
92.	James Ennis Court: O&T	15 Oct.1785 Murdered his mother	Newgate Crowds injured
93.	Mr Mooney Court: DQS	24 Oct. 1785 Street robbery	Newgate (?) Victim: Mrs Leathley
94.	William Ready Court: O&T	5 Nov. 1785 Theft	Newgate Unknown
95.	Maurice Fitzgerald Court: O&T	5 Nov. 1785 Street robbery	Newgate Victim: Rob. Ahmuty
96.	Thomas Lynch* Court: O&T	5 Nov. 1785 Robbery	Newgate (?) Victim: Ed. Creaton
97.	Mary Hardy Court: DQS	12 Nov. 1785 Street robbery	Newgate Victim: John Nevil
98.	Ed. McDonough Court: DQS	12 Nov. 1785 Street robbery	Newgate Penknife and 12s.
99.	John Farrell Court: O&T	31 Dec. 1785 Murdered victim	Tallaght Hanged and gibbeted
100.	Peter Rigney Court: KQS	25 Jan. 1786 Sheep killing	Kilmainham Skinned sheep alive
101.	Nicholas Fagan* Court: O&T	14 Jan. 1786 Murder	Kilmainham (?) Hanged and quartered
102.	Mary Hart* Court: KQS	18 Feb. 1786 Burglary	Kilmainham (?) Victim: Thom. Moulds
103.	Mary Farrell* Court: KQS	18 Feb. 1786 Burglary	Kilmainham (?) Place: Ward's Hill
104.	Bryan Mcevers* Court: KQS	18 Feb. 1786 Cow Theft	Kilmainham (?) Returned Transport
105.	James Stewart* Court: KQS	18 Feb. 1786 Burglary	Kilmainham (?) Place: Shankill

106. Mary Smith* Court: KQS	18 Feb. 1786 Burglary	Kilmainham (?) Place: Shankill
107. Robert Jameson Court: O&T	18 Mar. 1786 Murdered J. Kelly	Chapelizod Hanged and gibbeted
108. Alex. McClivery Court: KB	18 Mar. 1786 Robbed mails	Newgate Postal worker
109. Thomas Dillon Court: KQS	3 May 1786 Theft of silver	Kilmainham Aged 19
110. John Lyons Court: DQS	5 Aug. 1786 Street robbery	Newgate (?) Victim: H. Maguire
111. Edward Hyland* Court: KQS	2 Sept. 1786 Burglary of house	Kilmainham (?) Victim: Paul J. Burke
112. William English* Court: KQS	2 Sept. 1786 Burglary of house	Kilmainham (?) Victim: Paul J. Burke
113. William Wilkinson* Court: KQS	2 Sept. 1786 Burglary of house	Kilmainham (?) Victim: Paul J. Burke
114. Patrick Boyle* Court: KQS	2 Sept. 1786 Burgled P.J. Burke	Kilmainham (?) Place: Lucan
115. Roger McCowley* Court: KQS	16 Sept. 1786 Bleach-green theft	Kilmainham (?) Victim: James Field
116. Thomas Brady Court: KQS	2 Dec. 1786 Stole 11 sheep	Kilmainham Victim: Richard Byrne
117. James Manly Court: KQS	2 Dec. 1786 Hanlon bleach green	Kilmainham Place: Blue Bell
118. Robert Kearney* Court: O&T	2 Dec. 1786 Robbery of purse £57	Newgate (?) Victim: John Smith
119. Samuel Watson* Court: O&T	2 Dec. 1786 Burglary of house	Newgate (?) Victim: W. Radford
120. Edward Keefe* Court: O&T	2 Dec. 1786 Burglary	Newgate (?) Place: Exchange Alley
121. Owen Rafferty Court: DQS	23 Dec. 1786 Robbed mistress	Newgate Money later returned
122. John King* Court: O&T	27 Jan. 1787 Murder	Newgate (?) Victim: A. Dougherty
123. Fr. Thompson* Court: O&T	27 Jan. 1787 Murder Dougherty	Newgate (?) Hanged and quartered
124. William Hackett Court: KQS	28 Apr. 1787 Burglary of house	Kilmainham Returned transport
125. John Maguire Court: KQS	28 Apr. 1787 Burglary of house	Kilmainham Judge: John Toler
126. Caleb Fitzpatrick Court: KQS	28 Apr. 1787 Burglary of house	Kilmainham Multiple hanging
127. Daniel Flinn Court: KQS	28 Apr. 1787 Burglary of house	Kilmainham Multiple hanging

128. John Byrne* Court: KQS	19 May 1787 Stole 7 sheep	Kilmainham (?) Victim: Henry Smith
129. James Hickey* Court: KQS	19 May 1787 Stole a mare	Kilmainham (?) Victim: James Segrave
130. James Mcgarry Court: O&T	28 Jul. 1787 Street robbery	Newgate Aged 20; cried innocent
131. Richard Troy Court: O&T	28 Jul. 1787 Street robbery	Newgate Declared his innocence
132. George Wild Court: KQS	8 Oct. 1787 Street robbery	Kilmainham Alias Ree-Raw
133. James Darby Court: O&T	21 Oct. 1787 Murdered Pat Lynch	Newgate (?) Bailiff kills debtor
134. Margaret Savage Court: DQS	17 Nov. 1787 Street robbery	Newgate Habitual offender
135. Philip Reilly Court: DQS	24 Nov. 1787 Robbed customer	Newgate Publican
136. Daniel Connor Court: DQS	24 Nov. 1787 Robbed customer	Newgate Reilly's waiter
137. John Conlan Court: O&T	22 Dec. 1787 Burglary of house	Kilmainham (?) Victim: Peter Callage
138. Thomas Robinson Court: O&T	22 Dec. 1787 Burglary of house	Kilmainham (?) Place: Bonnybrook
139. James Kelly Court: O&T	22 Dec. 1787 Mail theft	Kilmainham Place: Bromore
140. Mrs Dignam Court: KQS	26 Jan. 1788 Burglary of house	Kilmainham Ch. Dignam's mother
141. Charles Dignam Court: KQS	26 Jan. 1788 Burglary of house	Kilmainham Son of Mrs Dignam
142. John Maguire Court: KQS	26 Jan. 1788 Burglary of house	Kilmainham brothers
143. Terence Maguire Court: KQS	26 Jan. 1788 Burglary of house	Kilmainham brothers
144. Charles Gallagher Court: KQS	26 Jan. 1788 Burglary of house	Kilmainham Victim: James Froode
145. John Kelly Court: KQS	26 Jan.1788 Burglary of house	Kilmainham Victim: Patrick Gracy
146. John Raferty* Court: O&T	2 Feb. 1788 Robbed £3	Kilmainham (?) Victim: Francis Molloy
147. James Sherlock* Court: DQS	23 Feb. 1788 Stole & killed horse	Newgate (?) Victim: T. Dougherty
148. Charles Echlin Court: KB	12 Mar. 1788 Mail theft	Kilmainham Detected in Liverpool
149. Edward Kearney Court: O&T	12 Jul. 1788 Highway robbery	Kilmainham Victim: Daniel Scott

150. James Bryne Court: O&T	12 Jul. 1788 Highway robbery	Kilmainham Place: Hermitage
151. Patrick Reilly Court: O&T	12 Jul. 1788 Highway robbery	Newgate Victim: W. Dwyer
152. James Moghan* Court: KQS	9 Aug. 1788 Callage burglary	Kilmainham (?) Alias: James Maughan
153. Joseph Smith Court: DQS	23 Aug. 1788 Burglary	Newgate (?) Victim: Michael Askins
154. John Kenny Court: DQS	23 Aug. 1788 Burglary	Newgate (?) Place: Donnybrook
155. Fr. Lambert Court: O&T	30 Oct. 1788 Stabbed Fr. Bathurst	Newgate Place: Newgate cell
156. Pat. McCormick Court: DQS	15 Nov. 1788 Burglary of house	Newgate (?) Servant
157. James Wade Court: DQS	10 Jan. 1789 Burglary of house	Newgate (?) Brothers
158. John Wade Court: DQS	10 Jan. 1789 Burglary of house	Newgate (?) Brothers
159. George Stalker Court: KQS	31 Jan. 1789 Cow theft	Kilmainham Sold skin of calf
160. John Egan Court: DQS	22 Apr. 1789 Street robbery	Newgate (?) Victim: Patrick Keefe
161. John Cowan Court: DQS	25 Apr. 1789 Stole 2 black geldings	Newgate (?) Place: Co. Down
162. Daniel Dowling O&T	27 Jul. 1789 Murder: Charles Tyndal	Newgate (?) Hanged and be headed
163. Thomas Fitzgerald Court: O&T	29 Jul. 1789 Street robbery	Newgate (?) Victim: Peter Dunn
166. Francis Gore Court: O&T	29 Jul. 1789 Burglary of house	Newgate (?) Victim: Robert Gray
167. James Ford Court: O&T	1 Aug. 1789 Burglary	Newgate Resisted hanging to last
168. James Cochlan Court: DQS	15 Aug. 1789 Burglary of house	Newgate (?) Victim: Daniel Farrel
169. Thomas Kelly Court: DQS	24 Oct. 1789 Burglary of house	Newgate (?) Victim: John Corry
170. Michael Delany Court: DQS	24 Oct. 1789 Robbed a police man	Newgate (?) Victim: James Gernon
171. Terence Smith Court: O&T	7 Nov. 1789 Embezzled linen	Newgate (?) Linen hall porter
172. Mr Hastler Court: KQS	11 Nov. 1789 Bleach-green theft	Kilmainham Aged 60
173. Mr Rooney* Court: KQS	12 Dec. 1789 Horse theft	Kilmainham (?) Kept diary in Dublin

174.	William Martin Court: O&T	2 Jan. 1790 Street robbery	Newgate Victim: Samuel Perry
175.	Robert Keating Court: DQS	24 Apr. 1790 Street robbery	Newgate Victim: Joseph Holt
176.	James Byrne Court: DQS	24 Apr. 1790 Stole six hams	Newgate Victim: Patrick Keely
177.	Mr Robinson Court: ???	19 Jun. 1790 Highway robbery	Newgate Unknown
178.	Mr Finlay Court: ???	19 Jun. 1790 Burglary of house	Newgate Place: Chancery Lane
179.	John Read Court: O&T	7 Jul. 1790 Intent to murder	Newgate Combinator: sawyer
180.	Th. McDermott Court: O&T	7 Jul. 1790 Intent to murder .	Newgate Combinator: sawyer
181.	Mr Sky Court: KQS	8 Jul. 1790 Assaulted Crowder	Kilmainham Combinator: weaver
182.	Michael Sullivan Court: O&T	24 Jul. 1790 Raped A. Fitzgerald	Newgate Combinator: weaver
183.	Thomas Coleby Court: O&T	24 Jul. 1790 Highway robbery	Newgate Unknown
184.	Andrew Doreen Court: O&T	30 Oct. 1790 Highway robbery	Kilmainham (?) Victim: Daniel Lyons
185.	James Murphy Court: O&T	30 Oct. 1790 Burgled shoe shop	Newgate (?) Victim: John Dooley
186.	Terence Byrne* Court: KQS	3 Nov. 1790 Burgled John Brady	Kilmainham (?) Place: Brittas Bay
187.	James Cadden Court: DQS	20 Nov. 1790 Burglary	Newgate (?) Victim: William Kelly
188.	James Kelly Court: DQS	20 Nov. 1790 Robbed a labourer	Newgate (?) Victim: R. Dowdal
189.	Philip Smith* Court: DQS	5 Feb. 1791 Robbed carrier	Newgate (?) Victim: D. Holland
190.	Laurence Lynch Court: DQS	23 Apr. 1791 Street robbery	Newgate Declared his innocence
191.	John McDermot Court: DQS	23 Apr. 1791 Street robbery	Newgate Declared his innocence
192.	Mr Doran Court: KQS	1 Oct. 1791 Robbed carriage	Kilmainham Victim: J Dunn
193.	Mr Donaghoe Court: KQS	1 Oct. 1791 Robbed carriage	Kilmainham Place: Green Hills
194.	Michael Dooley Court: KQS	1 Oct. 1791 Bleach-green theft	Newgate Victim: Jacob Sisson
195.	John Watson Court: DQS	29 Oct. 1791 Street robbery	Newgate Pleaded innocence

196. Alexander Nesbitt Court: O&T	2 Nov. 1791 Murdered chairman	Newgate Victim: John Gordon
197. John Reilly* Court: KQS	19 Nov. 1791 Burglary	Kilmainham (?) Receiver acquitted
198. James Pallas Court: KQS	31 Dec. 1791 Burglary	Kilmainham (?) Victim: Pat. McGowen
199. James Kelly* Court: O&T	13 Jan. 1792 Burglary	Newgate (?) Victim: Ed. Graham
200. Edward Byrne Court: O&T	14 Jan. 1792 Mail theft	Newgate (?) Place: Leeson Street
201. John Philips Court: DQS	14 Jan. 1792 Theft of hat and coat	Newgate Sailor, aged 50
202. Martin Mccarthy Court: O&T	22 Aug. 1792 Street robbery	Kilmainham (?) Victim: John Flinn
203. George Robinson Court: KQS	12 Sept. 1792 Street rob. & murder	Kilmainham Robinson led gang
204. Charles Brooks Court: KQS	12 Sept. 1792 Street rob. & murder	Kilmainham Victim: Benj. Lyneal
205. John Cunningham Court: KQS	12 Sept. 1792 Street rob. & murder	Kilmainham Place: Dolphin's Barn
206. William Norton Court: KQS	12 Sept. 1792 Street rob. & murder	Kilmainham Robinson's gang
207. Patrick Malone Court: DQS	27 Oct. 1792 Highway robbery	Newgate (?) Victim: J. Haughton
208. Thomas S. Walsh Court: O&T	15 Dec. 1792 Mail theft	Newgate Received money
209. Thomas Walsh Court: O&T	15 Dec. 1792 Mail theft	Newgate Postal worker
210. Mary Blake Court: DQS	5 Jan.1793 Murder	Newgate Victim: Mary Ryan
211. Bridget Monks Court: DQS	5 Jan. 1793 Murder	Newgate Victim: Mary Ryan
212. Patrick Boyle* Court: DQS	10 Jan. 1793 Highway robbery	Newgate (?) Victim: Patrick Ward
213. Patrick Segrave Court: ???	?? Apr. 1793 Street robbery	Newgate Place: Exchequer Street
214. Francis Moore* Court: KQS	15 Jun. 1793 Burglary of house	Kilmainham (?) Victim: School Master
215. John Delany Court: O&T	1 Jul. 1793 Murder of W. Grady	Newgate Defender
216. Laurence Penrose Court: O&T	1 Jul. 1793 Murder of W. Grady	Newgate Quakers and brothers
217. Patrick Penrose Court: O&T	1 Jul. 1793 Murder of W. Grady	Newgate Quakers and brothers

218.	Edward Boyce Court: O&T	1 Jul. 1793 Murder of W. Grady	Newgate Defender
219.	Henry Grogan Court: O&T	8 Jul. 1793 Murder shopowner	Newgate Hanged and dis sected
220.	Patrick Heydon Court: O&T	20 Jul. 1793 Mail theft	Newgate Postal worker
221.	Michael Connolly Court: O&T	20 Jul. 1793 Highway robbery	Kilmainham Victim: Sir J. Erskine
222.	James Cregan Court: O&T	20 Jul. 1793 Highway robbery	Kilmainham Victim: Sir J. Erskine
223.	Richard Farrell Court: KQS	3 Aug. 1793 Bleach-green theft	Kilmainham Alias Blake
224.	Thom.Plunkett Court: KQS	3 Aug. 1793 Bleach-green theft	Kilmainham Arrested by Wm. Shea
225.	Thomas Archbold Court: KQS	3 Aug. 1793 Bleach-green theft	Kilmainham Place: Glasnevin
226.	John Collins Court: KQS	31 Aug. 1793 Burglary & robbery	Kilmainham Place: Tallaght
227.	Name Unknown Court: KQS	31 Aug. 1793 Admitted murder	Kilmainham Victim: RC clergy man
228.	William Lynch* Court: DQS	7 Sept. 1793 Highway robbery	Newgate (?) Robbed two women
229.	Shaunghnessey* Court: DQS	7 Sept. 1793 Highway robbery	Newgate (?) Robbed two women
230.	Name Unknown Court: ???	19 Oct. 1793 Offence not known	Kilmainham Hanged and dissected
231.	Name Unknown Court: ???	19 Oct. 1793 Offence not known	Kilmainham Hanged and dissected
232.	Miles Burke Court: O&T	2 Nov. 1793 Highway robbery	Kilmainham (?) Place: Fox and Geese
233.	Michael Connolly Court: DQS	15 Feb. 1794 Burglary of house	Newgate (?) Declared his innocence
234.	Fitzharris Court: KQS	31 May 1794 Burgled dairyman	Kilmainham Northumberland Street
235.	Mathew Reilly Court: DQS	17 Jun. 1794 Street robbery	Newgate (?) Unknown
236.	John Kinlan Court: DQS	17 Jun. 1794 Street robbery	Newgate (?) Unknown
237.	Darby Walsh Court: KQS	5 Jul. 1794 Burglary in Fairview	Kilmainham Victim: Mr Gordon
238.	John Brennan* Court: KQS	6 Sept. 1794 Highway robbery	Kilmainham (?) Victim: J. Farringdon
239.	Garret Keating* Court: KQS	6 Sept. 1794 Highway robbery	Kilmainham (?) Alias John Byrne

240. John Smith*
     Court: KQS

18 Mar. 1795
Robbed watch & guinea

Kilmainham (?)
Victim: M. Dougherty

241. Mr Connolly
     Court: KQS

25 Apr. 1795
Theft of cow

Kilmainham
Brothers

242. Mr Connolly
     Court: KQS

25 Apr. 1795
Theft of cow

Kilmainham
Brothers

243. Sarah Delany
     Court: O&T

22 Aug. 1795
Rape of girl, aged 10

Newgate
Victim: Ann Mathews

244. John Toole
     Court: DQS

7 Nov. 1795
Burglary

Newgate (?)
Advertised reward

Source: *Hibernian Journal, Walker's Hibernian Magazine, Dublin Evening Post,*
1780-1795. Abbreviations: DQS: Dublin Quarter Sessions; KB: King's Bench; KQS:
Kilmainham Quarter Sessions; O&T: Commisson of Oyer and Terminer.

Notes

INTRODUCTION
1. See Brian Henry, "Crime, Law Enforcement and Punishment in Dublin, 1780–95," (Ph D thesis, Trinity College, Dublin, 1992), p. 16.
2. Doorly, Bernadette, "Newgate Prison," in David Dickson (ed.) *The Gorgeous Mask, Dublin 1700–1850* (Dublin, 1987), p. 122.
3. *Hibernian Journal* (hereafter *H.J.*), 27.09.80.
4. *H.J.*, 11.10.80.

THE DUBLIN HANGED
1. *H.J.*, 03.10.81.
2. *H.J.*, 18.07.81.
3. Bartlett, Thomas *The Fall and Rise of the Irish Nation, The Catholic Question, 1690–1830* (Dublin, 1992), pp. 92–117.
4. O'Connell, Maurice R., *Irish Politics and Social Conflict in the Age of the American Revolution* (Philadelphia, 1965), p. 89; for references to Volunteer interventions on hanging days, see Pádraig O Snodaigh, "Some police and military aspects of the Irish Volunteers," *Irish Sword* vol. 13, no. 52, (1978–79), pp. 223–224.
5. Rex -v- Duffy and Reid, Comm., in *H.J.*, 25.02.80.
6. *H.J.*, 17.01.80.
7. *H.J.*, 27.10.80; also see *Dublin Evening Post* (hereafter *D.E.P.*), 31.10.80.
8. *H.J.*, 27.12.80.
9. Mr. Norclift (Nordleigh) -v- George Lowe, Comm., in *H.J.*, 18.12.80.
10. *Statutes* (Ire.), 3 Geo. II, c. 15 (1729).
11. Miss Hamilton -v- Hall Fitzsimons, Comm., in *H.J.*, 12.07.80.
12. *H.J.*, 04.03.82.
13. Rex -v- Husband-killer, Comm., in *H.J.*, 20.02.82; also *H.J.*, 01.03.82.
14. *H.J.*, 22.07.82; *H.J.*, 03.07.82.
15. *H.J.*, 11.11.82; and *Walker's Hibernian Magazine* (hereafter *W.H.M.*), Nov. 1782, p. 607.
16. George McCutchen -v- Thomas Heney and John Murray, Dublin Quarter Sessions (hereafter D.Q.S.), in *H.J.*, 01.11.82.
17. *H.J.* 11.11.82.
18. *H.J.*, 14.08.82.
19. *H.J.*, 07.10.82.
20. Thomas Moran -v- Patrick Dougherty and George Coffey, Comm., in *H.J.*, 18.12.82.
21. *H.J.*, 20.12.82.
22. Linebaugh, Peter, "The Tyburn riot against the surgeons," in Douglas Hay, *et al.*, *Albion's Fatal Tree: crime and society in eighteenth-century England* (London, 1975), p. 117.
23. *H.J.*, 15.06.87.
24. *H.J.*, 05.12.81.

25. *H.J.*, 27.12.82.
26. Mr. Dowling -v- Patrick Lynch, D.Q.S., in *H.J.*, 03.01.83.
27. *Statutes* (Ire.) 17 & 18 Geo. III, c. 11 (1778).
28. *Statutes* (Ire.) 17 & 18 Geo. III, c. 11 (1778), which stipulated dissection by the surgeons.
29. *H.J.*, 06.01.83.
30. *H.J.*, 20.01.83.
31. For an old photograph of Dublin's Newgate gallows, see Maurice Craig, *Dublin 1660–1860* (Dublin, 1980), plate 33, following p. 352.
32. *H.J.*, 20.05.83.
33. *H.J.*, 15.01.83; and *H.J.*, 14.03.83.
34. *H.J.*, 20.01.83.
35. Mary Leigh -v- Peter O'Hara and John Larney, Comm., in *H.J.*, 23,07.81; McKennan -v- Michael, otherwise Nicholas Nugent, Comm., in *H.J.*, 27.07.81.
36. *H.J.*, 03.03.83.
37. *H.J.*, 03.03.83.
38. *H.J.*, 07.03.83.
39. *H.J.*, 14.03.83.
40. *H.J.*, 12.03.83.
41. *H.J.*, 14.03.83.
42. *H.J.*, 20.11.82.
43. Rex -v- Christopher Burgess, Comm., in *H.J.*, 18.12.82.
44. *H.J.*, 17.02.83.
45. *H.J.*, 19.03.83.
46. Report of burglary: *H.J.*, 09.05.83; Simon Christie -v- Christopher Burgess and Patrick Godfrey, D.Q.S., in *H.J.*, 25.07.83.
47. *H.J.*, 30.07.83.
48. *H.J.*, 01.08.83.
49. *H.J.*, 08.08.83.
50. James Moore Davis -v- James Egan and John Short, Comm., in *H.J.*, 28.07.83.
51. *H.J.*, 08.08.83.
52. *H.J.*, 22.03.84.
53. Luke Gardiner -v- Hugh Feeney and John Murphy, Comm., in *H.J.*, 05.03.84.
54. *H.J.*, 14.01.84.
55. *H.J.*, 14.01.84.
56. *H.J.*, 28.07.84.
57. *H.J.*, 14.09.85; Thomas Bolts -v- John Hugan, Daniel Devay and William Shanley, K.Q.S., in *H.J.*, 10.10.85; and *H.J.*, 26.10.85.
58. *H.J.*, 31.10.85.
59. Rex -v- Michael Shoughnessy, Jeremiah Reily, Charles Fallon, James McMahon, (K.Q.S.), in *W.H.M.*, Aug. 1785, p. 447.
60. Mr. Monaghan -v- Thomas Cartwright, K.Q.S., in *H.J.*, 18.07.85.
61. *W.H.M.*, Aug. 1785, p. 447; Christian Nash -v- Edward Doyle, K.Q.S., in *H.J.*, 19.01.85; Thomas Murphy -v- Roger Mathews and James Egan (or Nicholas Eager), K.Q.S., in *H.J.*, 19.01.85.
62. *H.J.*, 27.07.85.
63. *H.J.*, 29.07.85.
64. *H.J.*, 21.03.91.
65. Jonathan Taylor -v- Laurence Farrell (name spelled Lynch in *H.J.*, 27.04.91) and John McDermot, D.Q.S., in *H.J.*, 04.04.91.
66. *H.J.*, 27.04.91.
67. *W.H.M.*, Sept. 1792, pp. 286–87.

68. Thirty female convicts, including Margaret Savage, and two male convicts to Lord Lieutenant, 27 August 1782: National Archives, Dublin, Prisoners' petitions and cases, MS 10.
69. *H.J.*, 17.09.87.
70. Mary Purcell -v- Margaret Savage, D.Q.S., in *H.J.*, 31.10.87.
71. *H.J.*, 21.11.87.
72. Patrick McGowen -v- John Philips, D.Q.S., in *W.H.M.* Jan. 1792, p. 91; see also *H.J.*, 26.12.91.
73. John Philips to Lord Lieutenant, January 1792: National Archives, Dublin, Prisoners' Petitions and cases, MS 17.
74. *H.J.*, 16.09.85; *H.J.*, 19.10.85.
75. *H.J.*, 09.11.85.
76. *H.J.*, 31.08.85.
77. *H.J.*, 07.10.85.
78. Rex -v- William Ready and Thomas Deacon, Comm., in *H.J.*, 19.10.85.
79. *H.J.*, 07.09.85.
80. *H.J.*, 30.09.85.
81. Robert Ahmuty -v- Maurice Fitzgerald, Comm., in *H.J.*, 19.10.85.
82. *H.J.*, 09.11.85.
83. *H.J.*, 14.11.85.
84. *H.J.*, 05.05.86.
85. *H.J.*, 19.05.86.
86. *H.J.*, 30.11.85.
87. *H.J.*, 12.12.85.
88. Rex -v- John Farrell, Comm., in *H.J.*, 19.12.85.
89. Two needle-makers -v- John Farrell, Comm., in *H.J.*, 09.12.85.
90. *H.J.*, 30.12.85.
91. *H.J.*, 30.12.85.
92 *H.J.*, 04.01.86.
93. *H.J.*, 19.09.85.
94. *W.H.M.*, Mar. 1786, pp. 166-167.
95. *H.J.*, 13.03.86.
96. *H.J.*, 26.09.85.
97. Rex -v- Robert Jameson, Comm., in *H.J.*, 06.03.86.
98. *D.E.P.*, 30.03.86.
99. *D.E.P.*, 11.04.86.
100. *H.J.*, 23.03.85.
101. June Haughton -v- Patrick Malone, D.Q.S., in *H.J.*, 10.10.92.
102. *H.J.*, 29.10.92.
103. Enlistment riots and mutinies: *H.J.*, 26.04.93; and *H.J.*, 03.05.93.
104. Food riots: *H.J.*, 07.06.93; *H.J.*, 19.08.93; and *H.J.*, 23.08.93.
105. McLynn, Frank, *Crime and Punishment in eighteenth-century England* (London, 1989), p. 335.
106. Police operation: *H.J.*, 29.03.93.
107. For references to Defenderism in March 1793, see James Smyth, "Dublin's political underground in the 1790s," in Gerard O'Brien, *Parliament, Politics & People, essays in eighteenth-century Irish history* (Dublin, 1989), p. 137.
108. *H.J.*, 13.03.93; and *H.J.*, 18.03.93.
109. *H.J.*, 20.03.93.
110. Rex -v- John Delany, Laurence and Patrick Penrose, Comm., in *H.J.*, 01.07.93.
111. Rex -v- Edward Boyce, Comm., in *H.J.*, 01.07.93.
112. *Statutes* (Ire.) 31 Geo. III, c. 17 (1791).

113. *H.J.*, 03.07.93.
114. MacNevin, Thomas, *Lives and trials* (Dublin, 1846), pp. 299-479.
115. Rex -v- James Weldon, Comm., in *H.J.*, 23.12.95.
116. *H.J.*, 04.03.96.
117. Smyth, "Dublin's political underground in the 1790s", p. 147.
118. Kelly, James "Scarcity and poor relief in eighteenth-century Ireland: the subsistence crisis of 1782-4", *Irish Historical Studies* vol. 28, no. 109, (May 1992), p. 54.
119. McLynn, *Crime and Punishment*, p. 260.
120. Data supplied by John Beattie in a personal communication.
121. Toler succeeded Robert Sipthorp in 1782; Toler was himself succeeded by Robert Day in 1789; see *Wilson's Dublin Directory*, 1782-89.

WOMEN AND CRIME
1. *H.J.*, 18.05.81.
2. *H.J.*, 23.07.81.
3. *H.J.*, 25.07.81.
4. *H.J.*, 16.04.83.
5. *H.J.*, 05.05.83.
6. *Dublin Morning Post* (hereafter *M.P.*), 09.09.90.
7. *H.J.*, 09.07.90.
8. *H.J.*, 17.09.81.
9. *H.J.*, 22.10.94; see also James Kelly, "Infanticide in eighteenth-century Ireland", in *Irish Economic and Social History* vol. XIX, (1992), pp. 5-26.
10. *H.J.*, 09.07.81; see also *H.J.*, 21.03.91.
11. *H.J.*, 17.04.86.
12. *H.J.*, 13.12.90; see also *M.P.*, 10.12.90.
13. *H.J.*, 03.12.87.
14. *H.J.*, 05.08.89.
15. *H.J.*, 10.12.90.
16. *H.J.*, 27.09.90.
17. *W.H.M.*, June 1790, pp. 574–575.
18. *H.J.*, 31.05.90.
19. *H.J.*, 30.07.88.
20. *H.J.*, 24.10.88.
21. *H.J.*, 13.07.95; *W.H.M.*, Aug. 1795, pp. 187–189.
22. *W.H.M.*, Aug. 1795, pp. 187–189.
23. *H.J.*, 08.07.95.
24. *H.J.*, 16.02.81.
25. *H.J.*, 15.10.81.
26. *H.J.*, 08.07.82.
27. *H.J.*, 27.04.91.
28. *H.J.*, 27.07.91.
29. *H.J.*, 13.06.95.
30. *H.J.*, 15.06.95.
31. *H.J.*, 02.06.86.
32. Mary Hogg -v- Morgan Donnelly, Thomas Keating, and James King, D.Q.S., in *H.J.*, 25.08.86.
33. Mary Neal -v- Maria Lewellin, Comm., in *H.J.*, 02.07.88.
34. *H.J.*, 19.01.89. Ironically, three months after an inquiry was launched into Roe's abuse of Anne Neal, George Roe, 24, died of "an apoplectic fit," thus ending the Roe's family decade-long control over Newgate: see *H.J.*, 18.03.89.
35. For more information about the Mary Neal case, see Leslie Hale, *John Philpot*

Curran (London, 1958), pp. 73-74; Hale blamed Lord Carhampton for the rape of Mary Neal but typically, no footnotes were given to substantiate the allegation.

36. *H.J.*, 12.11.88.
37. Anne Molyneux -v- Robert Edgeworth, Comm., in *H.J.*, 12.12.88.
38. *H.J.*, 19.12.88.
39. *H.J.*, 13.07.89.
40. Michael Walsh -v- William Byrne, Comm., July 1792, in Dowling, *Trials at large* vol. 632, part 1 and 2, R.I.A., (Dublin, 1792); NB: vol. 632, part 1, is missing pages 209–216, which are found in vol. 631, part 5, R.I.A., (Dublin, 1792); this reference in part 1, p. 60.
41. Letitia Morgan -v- Charles Morgan, D.Q.S., Aug. 1792, in Dowling, *Trials at large* part 2, p. 84.
42. *H.J.*, 24.08.92.
43. *H.J.*, 24.08.92.
44. *H.J.*, 01.09.84.
45. *H.J.*, 03.09.84.
46. *H.J.*, 09.09.89.
47. *H.J.*, 11.09.89.
48. At least two newspapers published Parvisol's letter and deposition: see *H.J.*, 04.04.85, and also *Freeman's Journal*, 02–05 Apr. 1785.
49. Anne Parvisol -v- Robert Parvisol, K.Q.S., in *H.J.*, 11.04.85.
50. *Morning Post* (hereafter *M.P.*), 09.04.85.
51. Anne Parvisol -v- Robert Parvisol, K.Q.S., in the *D.E.P.*, 12.04.85.
52. Up to 1783, *Wilson's Dublin Directory* listed Robert Parvisol's address as 32 Prussia Street. From 1784 to 1794, the directory stopped printing his name and address. In 1795, it listed his address as 34 Manor Street, a continuation of Prussia Street.
53. *M.P.*, 11.12.90.
54. *H.J.*, 11.07.88.
55. *H.J.*, 09.10.80.
56. *W.H.M.*, Oct. 1780, p. 519.
57. *H.J.*, 05.01.85.
58. *Minute Book of the Blackrock Association*, 4 Mar. 1785: N.L.I., Manuscripts Collection, Dublin, MS 84
59. Rex -v- Foye, KQS, in *H.J.*, 04.03.85.
60. *H.J.*, 12.12.91.
61. *H.J.*, 19.01.91.
62. Dowling, *Trials at large* part 1, p 84.
63. *H.J.*, 13.04.92.
64. Dowling, *Trials at large* part 1, pp. 37–49.
65. John Groves -v- John Echlin, Comm., in *H.J.*, 23, 07.94.
66. *H.J.*, 23.01.86.
67. Dickson, "The place of Dublin," p. 182.
68. *Commons' jn. Ire.*, vol. 7, part 2, p. dciv.
69. *H.J.*, 27.12.86.
70. *H.J.*, 28.01.88.
71. *H.J.*, 21.07.90.
72. *H.J.*, 26.10.89.
73. *H.J.*, 10.01.91.
74. *H.J.*, 14.01.91.
75. *W.H.M.*, Jan. 1791, pp. 102–103.
76. *W.H.M.*, Mar. 1786, pp. 166–167.
77. *H.J.*, 04.05.81.

78. *H.J.*, 09.10.80.
79. *H.J.*, 12.02.90.
80. *W.H.M.*, Nov. 1784, pp. 678-679.
81. Mrs. Spear and Bray -v- Rapists, Comm., in *W.H.M.*, Dec. 1784, pp. 742-743.
82. Mrs. Spear and Bray -v- Rapists, Comm., in *H.J.*, 17.12.84.
83. Dowling, *Trials at large*, part 1, p. 62.
84. *H.J.*, 27.06.88.
85. Elizabeth Knox -v- William Crane, Mathew Denison and unnamed, Comm. (postponed twice), in *H.J.*, 29.10.88; and *H.J.*, 10.12.88.
86. *H.J.*, 31.07.86.
87. *H.J.*, 30.06.88.
88. *H.J.*, 02.06.88.
89. Elizabeth Egan -v- Captain Robert Kindillan and Ann Carol, Comm., in *H.J.*, 16.12.89.
90. Watts, Henry (Printer), *A Report of the Action of Seduction, wherein Barnaby Egan, Esq. was Plaintiff and Rob. Kindillan, Esq., Defendant* Court of Exchequer Michaelmas Term, 1791, vol. 631, part 4, R.I.A., (Dublin, 1792), *passim*.
91. *D.E.P.*, 15.11.85.
92. John Travers -v- Denis McCarthy, Court of Exchequer, in *W.H.M.*, Feb. 1791, pp. 189-191.
93. Denis McCarthy to House of Commons, 28 Apr. 1795: *Commons' jn. Ire.*, vol. 16, p. 109.
94. *H.J.*, 31.03.90.
95. *M.P.*, 31.03.90.
96. *M.P.*, 06.12.90.
97. *D.E.P.*, 16.12.90.
98. Dowling, *Trials at Large*, part 2, pp. 16–43.
99. *H.J.*, 25.04.81.
100. *H.J.*, 27.04.81.
101. For female receivers in London, see Peter Linebaugh, *The London Hanged, crime and civil society in the eighteenth century* (London, 1991), p. 145.
102. Adjutant Withers -v- John Keenan, Comm., in *H.J.*, 19.07.84.
103. *H.J.*, 23.07.84.
104. Patrick Keefe -v- John Egan, Robert Fisher, and John Whelan, D.Q.S., in *H.J.*, 20.04.89.
105. *H.J.*, 22.04.89.
106. *H.J.*, 12.07.93.
107. *H.J.*, 29.10.87.
108. *H.J.*, 03.03.83.
109. *H.J.*, 21.03.83.
110. *H.J.*, 17.12.83; name also reported as Mary Fairhill.
111. *H.J.*, 23.08.84.
112. *H.J.*, 21.07.84.
113. Linebaugh, *The London Hanged* p. 143.
114. Beattie, John M., *Crime and the courts in England* (Oxford, 1986), p. 532.

INDUSTRIAL VIOLENCE
1. *Statutes* (Ire.) 33 Hen VIII. [Session 1], Chapter IX (1542)
2. *Statutes* (Ire.) 3 Geo. II, c. 14 (1729); see Andrew Boyd, *The Rise of the Irish Trade Unions* (Dublin: Anvil Books, 1972), p. 11; see also John William Boyle, *The Irish labour movement in the nineteenth century* (Washington D.C., 1988), p. 7.
3. *Statutes* (Ire.): 17 Geo. II, c. 8 (1743); 31 Geo. II, c. 10 (1757); 33 Geo. II, c. 5 (1759);

3 Geo. III, c. 17 (1763); 3 Geo. III, c. 34 (1763); 11 & 12 Geo. III, c. 18 (1771–2); 11 & 12 Geo. III, c. 33 (1771–2); for discussion of the combination acts, see Seán Daly, *Cork: a city in crisis, a history of labour conflict and social misery 1870-1872* (Cork, 1978), pp. 254–280; also see John V. Orth, *Combination and Conspiracy, A Legal History of Trade Unionism, 1721-1906* (Oxford, 1991), pp. 203–204.

4. *Statutes* (Ire.) 17 Geo. II, c. 8 (1743).

5. *Statutes* (Ire.) 19 & 20 Geo. III, c. 19 (1780) [general]; 19 & 20 Geo. III, c. 24 (1780) [silk industry]; 19 & 20 Geo. III, c. 36 (1780) [butter trade and provisions].

6. *Statutes* (Ire.) 19 & 20 Geo. III, c. 19 (1786); for a discussion see Fergus A. D'Arcy and Ken Hannigan (eds), *Workers in Union, documents and commentaries on the history of Irish labour*, (Dublin, 1988), pp. 2,3; also see Maurice O'Connell, "Class conflict in a pre-industrial society: Dublin in 1780," *Irish Ecclesiastical Record* vol. 103–104, (1965), p. 105.

7. O'Connell, "Class conflict in a pre-industrial society," p. 106.

8. Clarkson, Jesse Dunsmore, *Labour and Nationalism in Ireland* (New York, 1925), p. 51.

9. *Statutes* (Ire.) 31 Geo. II, c. 10. s. 13 (1757).

10. *Statutes* (Ire.) 3 Geo. III, c. 34. s. 25 (1763); it has been assumed that "death without benefit of clergy" meant that a hanging took place without a clergyman being present at the gallows; in this period the medieval expression had become a crude form of shorthand for a felony carrying the death penalty. Clergymen were almost always present at hangings, see Daly, *Cork: a city in crisis* p. 280.

11. Sir Lucius O'Brien, "Report of the Grand Committee for Trade," Feb., 1780: *Commons'jn. Ire.*, vol. 10, part 1, pp. cxi–cxviii.

12. Clarkson, *Labour and Nationalism in Ireland*, p. 47–49.

13. According to one historian, however, this was merely "yet another inquiry" by the House of Commons Grand Committee for Trade, see Boyd, *The Rise of the Irish Trade Unions* p. 23.

14. Sir Lucius O'Brien, "Report of the grand committee for trade", February, 1780: *Commons'jn. Ire.*, vol. 10, part 1, pp. cxi-cxviii.

15. Dobson, *Masters and journeymen* p. 140.

16. Linebaugh, *The London hanged* pp. 333–334.

17. *Statutes* (Ire.) 19 & 20 Geo. III, c. 19 (1780); also see O'Connell, "Class conflict in a pre-industrial society," p. 103.

18. "Letter from Dublin, June 17," *Lloyd's Evening Post*, 23–26 June 1780, cited in Dobson, *Masters and journeymen* p. 140.

19. O'Connell, *Irish politics and social conflict* p. 263; also see Stanley Palmer, "The Irish police experiment: The beginnings of modern police in the British Isles, 1785–1795," *Social Science Quarterly* vol. 56, (1975), pp. 413–14.

20. Journeyman committees helped to create an artificial labour shortage in Dublin in 1780, thereby forcing up wages in the linen weaving industry by as much as 50 percent; see C. R. Dobson, *Masters and Journeymen: A Prehistory of Industrial Relations, 1717–1800* (London, 1980), p. 140.

21. *Statutes* (Ire.) 25 Geo. III, c. 17 (1785).

22. *H.J.*, 18.04.88; and *H.J.*, 30.04.88.

23. Rex -v- Joseph Harrington, King's Bench, in *H.J.*, 30.05.88.

24. Rex -v- Thomas Philpot, King's Bench, in *H.J.*, 28.05.88.

25. George Holmes, "Report on the state of gaols and prisons," 3 Mar. 1788: *Commons' jn. Ire.*, vol. 12, part 2, pp. dccxxxiii-dccxxxvi.

26. Joseph Harrington to Lord Lieutenant, Aug. 1789: National Archives, Dublin, Prisoners'petitions and cases, MS 19.

27. Sam Baird -v- 19 Pin-makers, Comm., in *H.J.*, 29.10.87.

28. *H.J.*, 30.07.88.
29. *H.J.*, 17.09.88.
30. Anthony McKinley, Michael Rorke, Hudson Hampden and Richard Barber to Lord Lieutenant, December 1788: National Archives, Dublin, Prisoners' petitions and cases, MS 23.
31. *H.J.*, 10.12.88.
32. *H.J.*, 12.06.80.
33. *H.J.*, 22.05.80.
34. *H.J.*, 27.04.81.
35. *H.J.*, 09.10.80.
36. *H.J.*, 30.10.80.
37. *H.J.*, 30.10.80.
38. *H.J.*, 13.11.80; and *H.J.*, 15.12.80; see Boyle, *The Irish labour movement in the nineteenth century* p. 20.
39. *H.J.*, 01.12.80.
40. *H.J.*, 01.12.80; *H.J.*, 19.12.80.
41. *H.J.*, 05.01.81.
42. *H.J.*, 09.02.81.
43. Kelly, James J., "Napper Tandy," in James Kelly and Uáitéar Mac Gearailt (eds.), *Dublin and Dubliners* (Dublin, 1990), p. 4.
44. Ferguson, K.P., "The Volunteer movement and the government, 1778-1793," *Irish Sword* vol. 13, no. 52, (1978–79), p. 215.
45. Rutland to Sydney, 2 Jun. 1784: P.R.O. H.O. 100/13/97.
46. Thomas Orde to Nepean, 7 Apr. 1784: P.R.O. H.O. 100/12/268–270.
47. Rutland to Sydney, 21 June 1784: P.R.O. H.O. 100/13/159–160.
48. It is possible that Alexander Clarke was a government informer: in August 1784, Thomas Orde mentioned the name of one Clark as such, see Orde to Whitehall, 21 Aug. 1784: P.R.O. H.O. 100/14/80–82.
49. *H.J.*, 25.06.84.
50. *W.H.M.*, July 1784, p. 413; also see *H.J.*, 28.06.84.
51. Rutland to Sydney, 21 July 1784: P.R.O. H.O. 100/14/7–8.
52. *H.J.*, 11.08.84.
53. *H.J.*, 16.08.84.
54. Orde to Lord Mayor Thomas Greene, 13 Aug. 1784: P.R.O. H.O. 100/14/34-35; also see *H.J.*, 13.08.84.
55. Rex -v- Gosson, D.Q.S., July 1784, in *H.J.*, 09.08.84; also see Rutland to Sydney, 19 Aug. 1784: P.R.O. H.O. 100/14/56–59.
56. Thomas Orde to Lord Mayor Thomas Greene, 13 August 1784: P.R.O. H.O. 100/14/34–35.
57. Rutland to Sydney, 19 Aug. 1784: P.R.O. H.O. 100/14/56–59.
58. *W.H.M.*, August 1784, pp. 485–488.
59. Patrick Flaskey -v- Patrick Dignam, D.Q.S., Aug. 1784, in *H.J.*, 25.08.84.
60. Rutland to Sydney, 24 Aug. 1784: P.R.O. H.O. 100/14/85–86.
61. *H.J.*, 30.08.84.
62. *H.J.*, 23.06.90.
63. *D.E.P.*, 21.10.90.
64. *H.J.*, 15.04.89.
65. *H.J.*, 17.04.89.
66. Rex -v- Richard Patten, Robert Campbell, Thomas Cassidy, James Byrne, John Lobden, and Thomas Geary, Comm., July 1789, in *H.J.*, 15.07.89.
67. Rex -v- Michael Brien, Comm., Oct. 1789, in *H.J.*, 28.10.89.
68. *H.J.*, 21.06.90; see also C.R. Dobson, *Masters and Journeymen*, p. 165.

69. *H.J.*, 14.06.90.
70. *H.J.*, 16.06.90.
71. *H.J.*, 30.06.90.
72. *Statutes* (Ire.), 23 & 24 Geo. III, c. 56 s. 4 (1784).
73. Patrick Wall -v- John Read and Thomas McDermott, Comm., in *H.J.*, 07.07.90; see also *W.H.M.*, July 90, pp. 94–96.
74. *H.J.*, 09.07.90.
75. Linebaugh, "The Tyburn riot against the surgeons," pp. 102, 117.
76. Dobson, *Masters and journeymen* p. 165.
77. *H.J.*, 04.06.90.
78. Sir Lucius O'Brien, "Report of the grand committee for trade", Feb., 1780: *Commons' jn. Ire.*, vol. 10, part 1, pp. cxi–cxviii.
79. *H.J.*, 04.06.90.
80. *H.J.*, 09.06.90; see also *H.J.*, 11.06.90.
81. *W.H.M.*, July 1790, pp. 94-96.
82. *H.J.*, 30.06.90.
83. Crowder -v- Sky, K.Q.S., in *H.J.*, 12.07.90.
84. Alice Fitzgerald -v- Michael Sullivan, Comm., in *H.J.*, 12.07.90.
85. James Lightholder -v- Thomas Whelan, Comm., July 1792, in Dowling, *Trials at large*, part 1, pp. 90-91; also see *H.J.*, 18.07.92.
86. *H.J.*, 24.10.92.
87. *H.J.*, 16.11.92.
88. *Statutes* (Ire.) 23 & 24 Geo. III, c. 17 (1784).
89. John Armit to Mr. Fitzpatrick; May-June 1782: P.R.O. H.O. 100/1/241–262.
90. *D.E.P.* 05.11.85; also see *H.J.*, 30.12.85.
91. Post Office -v- Alexander Maclivery, Comm., in *D.E.P.*, 17.12.85.
92. Post Office -v- Alexander Maclivery, King's Bench, in *D.E.P.*, 02.03.86.
93. *D.E.P.*, 18.03.86.
94. *H.J.*, 20.04.92.
95. *H.J.* 23.07.87.
96. The Commission of Oyer and Terminer was created under *Statutes* (Ire.) 3 Geo. II, c. 15 (1729).
97. Post Office -v- Thomas Styles Walsh and Thomas Walsh, in *W.H.M.*, Oct. 1792, pp. 382-383; also in *H.J.*, 24.10.92.
98. *W.H.M.*, Dec. 1792 p. 567; also see *H.J.*, 12.12.92.
99. Post Office -v- Patrick Hayden, Comm., in *H.J.*, 28.06.93; also see *H.J.*, 18.02.93.
100. *H.J.*, 29.07.93.
101. *H.J.*, 29.07.93.
102. Henry, "Crime, Law Enforcement and Punishment in Dublin, 1780-95," p. 93.
103. Samuel Dixon -v- Thomas Casey and William Trevor, Comm., July 1792, in Dowling, *Trials at large* Section 1, p. 157.
104. Samuel Dixon -v- John McArdell, Comm., in *H.J.*, 19.12.94.
105. *H.J.*, 22.06.92.
106. *H.J.*, 30.04.94.
107. *H.J.*, 02.05.94.
108. *H.J.*, 25.07.94.
109. Miles Keogh -v- Charles White, John Shortal, John Millally, and Adam Murphy, Comm., in *H.J.*, 30.07.94.
110. *H.J.*, 15.10.90.
111. John Dooley -v- James Murphy, Comm., in *H.J.*, 22.10.90.
112. D'Arcy, Fergus A., "Wages of labourers in the Dublin building industry, 1667–1918," *Saothar* vol. 15, (Dublin, 1990), see tables 3 and 4 on pp. 24–25; see also

D'Arcy, "Wages of labourers," *Saothar* vol. 14, (Dublin, 1989), pp. 17–32.

113. Speaking before a British Parliamentary Committee in London in 1824, Patrick Farrell, a journeyman carpenter from Dublin, did his best to recall the date of this bill and the demonstrations against it. He was only three years off the exact date, it was 1792 not 1789; see *U.K. Parl. papers: First Report from the Select Committee appointed to Inquire into the State of the Law Regarding Artizans and Machinery*, Vol. 5, 1824, pp. 431–432.

114. *H.J.*, 23.03.92.

115. Mr. Graydon and Mr. Vandeleur, "A bill to prevent unlawful combinations of journeymen artificers," 10 Mar. 1792: *Commons' jn. Ire.*, vol. 15, part 1, pp. 90, 93, 93, 101, 103.

116. Farrell put the number of those demonstrating in Phoenix Park at between 15,000 and 20,000, and a monthly magazine in Dublin put the number demonstrating in the Liberties in the thousands; see *First Report from the Select Committee*, p. 432, and *W.H.M.*, July 1792, pp. 95–96.

117. O'Connor, Emmet, *A Labour History of Ireland 1824–1960* (Dublin, 1992), *passim*.

MURDER AT LARGE

1. *H.J.*, 11.02.80.; also see *W.H.M.*, Feb. 1780, pp. 118–119.
2. *H.J.*, 28.02.80.
3. *H.J.*, 24.04.80.
4. *H.J.*, 11.10.80.
5. *H.J.*, 04.10.82.
6. *H.J.*, 06.12.82.
7. *H.J.*, 16.06.80.
8. O'Farell: *H.J.*, 05.07.80; Boylan: *H.J.*, 01.11.80; Conolly: *H.J.*, 31.12.80.
9. Stone, Lawrence, *The family, sex and marriage in England 1500–1800* (London, 1978), p. 28.
10. *H.J.*, 16.10.80.; also see *W.H.M.*, Oct. 1780, p. 519.
11. *H.J.*, 06.12.80.
12. *H.J.*, 27.12.80.
13. *H.J.*, 03.09.81.
14. *H.J.*, 24.10.81.
15. *H.J.*, 21.09.85.
16. *H.J.*, 29.08.85.
17. *W.H.M.*, Sept. 1785, pp. 502–503; also cited as William Elliot.
18. Rex -v- William Fullarton, Comm., in *D.E.P.*, 28.02.86.
19. *H.J.*, 16.09.85.
20. *W.H.M.*, Oct. 1785, p. 559.
21. *H.J.*, 21.10.85.
22. Samuel Gamble -v- James Ennis, Comm., in *H.J.*, 12.10.85.
23. *H.J.*, 19.10.85.
24. *H.J.*, 27.03.89.
25. *W.H.M.*, Mar. 1789, pp. 164-167.
26. Rex -v- Anthony Dempsey, Comm., in *H.J.*, 17.07.89.
27. *H.J.*, 20.07.89.
28. *M.P.*, 07.10.90.
29. *H.J.*, 17.04.82.
30. Rex -v- Samuel Forster, Comm., in *H.J.*, 21.10.82.
31. *W.H.M.*, Feb. 1787, p. 111.
32. *H.J.*, 16.02.87.
33. Rex -v- Dominick Trant, Comm., in *H.J.*, 23.07.87; also in *W.H.M.*, July 1787, pp. 388-91.

34. *H.J.*, 29.02.92.
35. Rex -v- Roderick O'Connor, Comm., July 1792, in Dowling, *Trials at large*, part 1, p. 9.
36. *H.J.*, 16.07.90; also see *M.P.*, 15.07.90.
37. Debt: *H.J.*, 16.07.90; Poems: *H.J.*, 03.09.90 and *H.J.*, 15.09.90.
38. Craig, *Dublin 1660-1860*, pp. 221-223.
39. Ann Kelly -v- William Whaley, Comm., (postponed), in *H.J.*, 22.10.90.
40. Ann Kelly -v- William Whaley, Comm., in *H.J.*, 15.12.90.
41. *H.J.*, 04.05.85.
42. *H.J.*, 20.01.90; Cunningham spelled Conyngham.
43. *W.H.M.*, Sept. 1792, pp. pp. 286–287.
44. *H.J.*, 26.10.91; William Dalton's name appears on list of convicts, 7 Nov. 1789: P.R.O. H.O. 100/29/198.
45. *H.J.*, 08.09.90.
46. William Shea -v- John Cunningham, D.Q.S., in *H.J.*, 04.10.90.
47. John Kealy -v- Terence McDaniel, John Cunningham and Joshua McDonough, Comm., in *H.J.*, 22.10.90.
48. Report of shop burglary: *H.J.*, 30.12.91; robbery at Goldenbridge in *H.J.*, 03.09.92; robbery of George Sturgeon in *H.J.*, 16.07.92, and in Dowling, *Trials at large*, part 1, pp. 74–78; robbery of Blair and Magee in *H.J.*, 23.03.92; murder of Benjamin Lyneal in Dowling, *Trials at large*, part 1, pp. 165–199; dying declarations of George Robinson, William Norton, Charles Brooks, John Cunningham in *W.H.M.*, Sept. 1792, pp. 286–287.
49. *M.P.*, 24.02.90.
50. Dying declaration of William Norton, in *W.H.M.*, Sept. 1792, pp. 286–287.
51. *H.J.*, 30.01.84.
52. Rex -v- George Robinson *et. al.* in Dowling, *Trials at large*, part 1, pp. 169.
53. Ibid., p. 168.
54. Ibid., p. 171.
55. Ibid., p. 189.
56. George Sturgeon -v- George Robinson *et. al.*, Comm., July 1792, in Dowling, *Trials at large*, part 1, p. 78.
57. *W.H.M.*, July 1792, pp. 95-96.
58. *H.J.*, 31.08.92.
59. Dying declaration of John Cunningham, in *W.H.M.*, Sept. 1792, pp. 286-287.
60. Condran [Conran] discharged by proclamation, D.Q.S., in *H.J.*, 03.10.92.
61. Rex -v- John Farrell, Comm., in *H.J.*, 25.07.94.
62. For a discussion of this tabular information for England see J.S. Cockburn, "Patterns of violence in English society: Homicide in Kent 1560–1985," *Past & Present*, no. 130, (1991), pp. 70–106.
63. *H.J.*, 05.07.93.
64. *Statutes* (Ire.) 31 Geo. III. c. 17 (1791).
65. Rex -v- Henry Grogan, Comm., in *H.J.*, 10.07.93.
67. Hugh Purcell -v- William Whaley, Comm., in *H.J.*, 28.10.91.
68. *H.J.*, 27.04.91.
69. John Callaghan -v- Alexander Nesbitt, Comm., in *H.J.*, 27.07.91.
70. *Statutes* (Ire.) 31 Geo. III c. 17 (1791).
71. *H.J.*, 04.11.91.
72. *H.J.*, 25.07.81.
73. *H.J.*, 28.09.91.
74. *H.J.*, 02.01.88.

75. Rex -v- Nicholas McCann, Comm., in *H.J.*, 02.07.88.
76. Rex -v- Nicholas McCann and James McClean, Comm., in *H.J.*, 04.07.88.
77. *H.J.*, 07.11.88.
78. Rex -v- Thomas McNamee, Comm., in *H.J.*, 29.10.88.
79. Thomas McNamee to Lord Lieutenant, Oct-Nov 1788: National Archives, Dublin, Prisoners' petitions and cases, MS 22.
80. *H.J.*, 02.01.88.
81 *H.J.*, 07.11.88.
82. *H.J.*, 10.11.88; see also *H.J.*, 19.11.88.
83. *H.J.*, 10.12.88.
84. *H.J.*, 30.12.89.
85. Unnamed man: *H.J.*, 01.01.90; *H.J.*, 04.01.90.
86. Drummond, William Hamilton, *Autobiography of Archibald Hamilton Rowan* (Dublin, 1840), pp. 103-106.
87. Rex -v- Sheriff Vance, King's Bench, in *H.J.*, 03.03.90.
88. Henry Neill -v- Edward Wingfield Dowse and Robert Darlington, Comm., July 1792, in Dowling, *Trials at large* part 1, p. 208; see also H.J., 25.07.92.
89. James Ryan -v- Henry and Peter Egglesoe, (and Rev. Mr. Byrne), Comm., in *H.J.*, 11.12.93.
90. James Ryan -v- Henry and Peter Egglesoe, Court of Exchequer, in *H.J.*, 06.08.94.
91. Peter Egglesoe -v- Ann Foy, D.Q.S., in *H.J.*, 15.08.94.
92. *H.J.*, 29.05.95.
93. Robinson, Portia, *The Women of Botany Bay*, (Maquarie Library, 1988), see appendix B-1, pp. 312–313.
94. Andrew Carty -v- Thomas Ward, Comm., in *H.J.*, 23.07.94.
95. *H.J.*, 30.07.94.
96. Thomas Ward pleads his Majesty's pardon, Comm., in *H.J.*, 31.10.94.

PROPERTY THEFT
1. Hay, Douglas, "War, dearth and theft in the eighteenth century: The record of the English courts," *Past & Present* no. 95, (1982), p. 126.
2. *H.J.*, 26.05.86.
3. *W.H.M.*, Feb. 1790, p. 190; *H.J.*, 15.02.90.
4. *H.J.*, 24.12.87.
5. *H.J.*, 01.12.94.
6. *H.J.*, 24.09.84.
7. *W.H.M.*, Oct. 1787, pp. 557–559.
8. *H.J.*, 01.11.84.
9. *H.J.*, 15.09.86.
10. James Frood -v- Hugh McGowran, alias the Morning Star, Comm., in *H.J.*, 02.11.87.
11. Report of Callage burglary in *H.J.*, 12.11.87; statement exonerating McGowran in *H.J.*, 26.12.87.
12. *H.J.*, 05.12.87.
13. Peter Callage -v- James Maughan, K.Q.S., in *H.J.*, 23.07.88.
14. Peter Callage -v- Joseph MacDaniel or McDonnell, K.Q.S., in *H.J.*, 15.10.88.
15. Peter Callage -v- Joseph MacDaniel, John Conlan, and Thomas Robinson, Comm., in *H.J.*, 14.12.87.
16. James Frood -v- John and Terence Maguire, and Charles Gallagher, K.Q.S., in *H.J.*, 21.01.88.
17. Report of Booth burglary in *H.J.*, 05.12.87; John Booth -v- Man (Charles Dignam) and Woman (Mrs. Dignam), K.Q.S., in *H.J.*, 18.01.88; but see also John Booth

(and Peter Callage) -v- Charles Dignam, K.Q.S., in *H.J.*, 21.01.88.

18. Report of Gracy burglary in *H.J.*, 05.12.87; Patrick Gracy -v- John Kelly, K.Q.S., in *H.J.*, 21.01.88.

19. For report of the execution of the six, including two brothers and a mother and her son, see *W.H.M.*, Feb. 1788, pp. 109–110.

20. Rex -v- Daniel Flinn, K.Q.S. (report not clear), in *H.J.*, 25.04.87.

21. According to the *Hibernian Journal*, the original estimate of building Kilmainham prison was put at £12,000, but the final cost rose to £22,000, or nearly double the original estimate (*H.J.*, 25.04.87 and 16.10.95.) The newspaper also reported that the architectural plans of Kilmainham prison were taken from the design of Reading gaol, a design which Lord Carhampton brought forward (*H.J.*, 31.08.89). It was also said that one Captain Jones supervised the construction of Kilmainham gaol (*H.J.*, 29.08.87).

22. Peter Keefe -v- William Hacket, John Maguire, Caleb Fitzpatrick, K.Q.S., in *H.J.*, 25.04.87.

23. Jane Brady -v- James and John Wade, D.Q.S., in *H.J.*, 26.12.88.

24. *H.J.*, 25.04.88.

25. William Dwyer -v- Patrick Reilly, Thomas Sheridan, and Richard Murphy, Comm., in *H.J.*, 02.07.88.

26. *W.H.M.*, May 1789, pp. 286-288.

27. *H.J.*, 24.04.82.

28. *H.J.*, 01.05.82.

29. Benjamin Houghton -v- John Wall, alias Jack the Smasher, John Murdock (or Mordaunt), James Rooney, and Barnaby Ledwith, Comm., in *H.J.*, 03.07.82.

30. *H.J.*, 28.10.85.

31. *Wilson's Dublin Directory*, 1791.

32. *H.J.*, 23.09.82.

33. *H.J.*, 30.03.87

34. *H.J.*, 23.04.87.

35. *H.J.*, 26.12.92.

36. *H.J.*, 01.11.86.

37. Linebaugh, *The London Hanged* p. 82.

38. Sir Frederick Flood -v- William May, Comm., in *H.J.*, 29.10.87; William May pleads his majesty's pardon, Comm., in *H.J.*, 02.07.88.

39. This mistake did not appear in *H.J.*, 07.07.88.

40. Frederick May, watch maker, 138 Capel Street; see *Wilson's Dublin Directory*, 1791.

41. Sir Frederick Flood -v- Michael Delany, Comm., in *H.J.*, 31.10.88.

42. Malton, James, *A Picturesque and Descriptive View of the City of Dublin* (London 1792–99), *passim*.

43. *H.J.*, 01.07.82.

44. *H.J.*, 10.07.82.

45. Linebaugh, *The London Hanged* p. 256.

46. *H.J.*, 28.12.82.

47. *H.J.*, 24.10.88.

48. *H.J.*, 20.09.80.

49. For the only known depiction of a bleach-green in Dublin, see an illustration called "Tarring and Feathering" in *W.H.M.*, July 1784, (this is attributed to William Esdall), also found in Brian Henry, "Crime, Law Enforcement and Punishment in Dublin, 1780–95," p. 72.

50. Bleach-green owner -v- Hastlers (father and son), K.Q.S., in *H.J.*, 13.11.89.

51. *H.J.*, 27.07.91.

52. Jacob Sisson -v- Michael Dooley, K.Q.S., in *H.J.*, 21.09.91.

53. Jacob Sisson -v- Thomas Hughes, K.Q.S., in *H.J.*, 09.12.91.
54. Glasnevin bleach-green owner -v- Richard Farrell, alias Blake, Thomas Plunkett, and Thomas Archbold, K.Q.S., in *H.J.*, 26.07.93.
55. *H.J.*, 15.09.83.
56. *H.J.*, 07.04.80.
57. *H.J.*, 01.12.84.
58. *H.J.*, 02.02.84.
59. *H.J.*, 01.04.85.
60. Rex -v- Peter Rigney, K.Q.S., in *H.J.*, 16.01.86; *W.H.M.*, Feb. 1786, pp. 109–110.
61. *H.J.*, 16.05.87.
62. John Hely Hutchinson -v- William Cooper, Comm., in *H.J.*, 23.07.87.
63. Rex -v- Connolly brothers and Clarke, K.Q.S., in *H.J.*, 22.04.95.
64. *H.J.*, 15.01.87.
65. *W.H.M.*, Jan. 1787, p. 55.
66. *H.J.*, 10.01.81.
67. *H.J.*, 02.01.84.
68. Northington to Sydney, 17 Jan. 1784: P.R.O. H.O. 100/12/52–53.
69. Beattie, *Crime and the Courts* p. 223.
70. Post Office -v- James Farran, Comm., in *H.J.*, 03.11.84.
71. Post Office -v- Byrne, Comm., in *H.J.*, 20.12.84.
72. *H.J.*, 27.12.84.; and *H.J.*, 03.01.85.
73. *H.J.*, 29.12.84.
74. *H.J.*, 24.09.87.
75. *W.H.M.*, November 1787, pp. 612-615; also see *H.J.*, 09.11.87.
76. Post Office -v- Charles Echlin, King's Bench., Feb. 1788, in *W.H.M.*, Mar. 1788, pp. 162-165; also see *H.J.*, 05.03.87.
77. *H.J.*, 12.12.85.
78. Benjamin Watson -v- Mary Newman, D.Q.S., in *H.J.*, 05.10.92; and Mathew West -v- Mary Lloyd, D.Q.S., in *H.J.*, 10.10.92.
79. Benjamin Watson -v- Mary Newman, D.Q.S., Oct. 1792, in Dowling, *Trials at large* part 2, pp. 128-129.
80. Mathew West -v- Mary Lloyd, D.Q.S., Oct. 1792, in Dowling, *Trials at large* part 2, p. 149.
81. *H.J.*, 03.08.92.
82. *H.J.*, 25.03.82.
83. *H.J.*, 01.04.82.
84. *H.J.*, 18.10.86.
85. *H.J.*, 20.11.86.
86. Rex -v- John Clarke, Comm., in *H.J.*, 27.10.86.
87. For more detail on the subject of coining, see John Styles, "'Our traitorous money makers': The Yorkshire coiners and the law, 1760–83," in John Brewer and John Styles (eds.), *An Ungovernable People: The English and their law in the seventeenth and eighteenth centuries* (London, 1980), pp. 172–249.

THE PARISH WATCH

1. Anon., *Animadversions on the street robberies in Dublin*, King's Inns Library, Dublin, pamphlet collection, vol. 332, (Dublin, 1765); reprinted with an introduction by Brian Henry, *Irish Jurist* (Winter, 1988), pp. 347–356.
2. "Heads of a bill for improving the police of the City of Dublin, June 1778": N.L.I., Dublin, *Bolton Papers*, MS 15,927 (1); see also MS 15,926 (1–17) for a break-down of the parish watch system six years after the 1778 Bill; also see "Sir Henry Cavendish Report" and debate on the police finances, 25 Apr. 1789: *Parl. reg. Ire.*, vol. 6, p. 397.

3. *H.J.*, 29.10.81.
4. Also see Pádraig O Snodaigh, "Some police and military aspects of the Irish Volunteers," p. 224.
5. *H.J.*, 27.04.81.
6. *H.J.*, 28.02.80; and *H.J.*, 25.09.80.
7. *H.J.*, 07.04.80.
8. Rex -v- John Eagan, Comm., in *H.J.*, 12.07.80.
9. *Statutes* (Ire.) 7 Will. III, c. 17 (1695); also see W.N. Osborough, "Sport, Freedom and the Criminal Law" in Anthony Whelan (ed.), *Law and Liberty in Ireland* (Dublin, 1993), fn. 38, p. 47.
10. *H.J.*, 17.11.80.
11. *H.J.*, 11.12.80.
12. *H.J.*, 23.10.80.
13. *H.J.*, 27.10.80.
14. Definition of night-houses found in Mary Amyott -v- Francis Amyott, D.Q.S., Aug. 1792, in Dowling, *Trials at large* part 2, pp. 16–43.
15. *H.J.*, 08.01.81; also see *W.H.M.*, Dec. 1780, pp. 686-687
16. *H.J.*, 11.12.80.
17. *H.J.*, 22.12.80.
18. *H.J.*, 05.01.81.
19. *H.J.*, 24.01.81.
20. *H.J.*, 08.11.80.
21. *H.J.*, 10.10.81.
22. Richard Gladwill to Thomas Orde, return of St. Andrews parish, 24 Dec. 1785: N.L.I., Dublin, *Bolton papers*, MS 15,926 (1).
23. *H.J.*, 20.08.81; the Volunteers were involved in another more famous incident involving 1,500 wreckers and a ship that had run aground at Malahide, see *H.J.*, 05.01.80, and *D.E.P.*, 01.01.80.
24. *H.J.*, 26.09.81.
25. *H.J.*, 13.05.82; also see *Wilson's Dublin Directory*, 1782.
26. *H.J.*, 26.09.81; *H.J.*, 01.10.81.
27. *H.J.*, 26.10.81.
28. *H.J.*, 26.09.81.
29. Craig, *Dublin 1660–1860* p. 89.
30. *H.J.*, 08.08.81.
31. Craig, *Dublin 1660–1860* pp. 239–240.
32. *H.J.*, 16.11.81.
33. *H.J.*, 09.11.81.
34. House of Industry: Petition no. 450 in favour of Benjamin Houghton, 15 Feb. 1774: *Commons' jn. Ire.*, vol. 9, part 1, pp. 95–96.
35. *H.J.*, 15.07.82.
36. Richard Gladwill to Thomas Orde, return of St. Andrews parish, 24 Dec. 1785: N.L.I., Dublin, *Bolton Papers*, MS 15,926 (1).
37. Rutland to Sydney, 21 June 1784: P.R.O., H.O. 100/13/159–160.
38. "Account of the number of watch-men employed in the several parishes in the County of the City of Dublin collected from the returns to parliament & watch houses", for the year ending 25 Mar. 1784: N.L.I., Dublin, *Bolton Papers*, MS 15,926 (1).
39. *H.J.*, 22.10.81.
40. *H.J.*, 7.11.81.
41. Henry Howison and Francis Armstrong to Thomas Orde, return of St. Mary's Parish, 21 February 1785: N.L.I., Dublin, *Bolton Papers*, MS 15,926 (5).

42. Richard Gladwill to Thomas Orde, return of St. Andrews parish, 24 December 1785: N.L.I., Dublin, *Bolton Papers*, MS 15,926 (1).
43. *H.J.*, 19.12.81.
44. *H.J.*, 02.11.85.
45. According to the "Account of the number of watch-men," the eight parishes which sent back reports were: Saints. Paul's, Ann's, Mark's, Mary's, Thomas's, John's, Audeon's, Michan's, for the year ending 25 Mar. 1784: N.L.I., Dublin, *Bolton Papers*, MS 15,926 (1).
46. J. Sparrow to Thomas Orde, return of St. Catherine's parish, 24 Mar. 1785: N.L.I., Dublin, *Bolton Papers*, MS 15,926 (15).
47. Robert Lowther to Orde, return of St. James's Watch, 22 Feb. 1785: N.L.I., Dublin, *Bolton Papers*, MS 15,926 (17).
48. Stanley Palmer said that "the pre-1786 watchmen had earned £7," but this amount seems to have been the wages paid to watchmen at the bottom end of the parochial scale; see Stanley Palmer, *Police and protest in England and Ireland, 1780–1850* (Cambridge, 1988), p. 134; but also see "Account of the number of watch-men", for the year ending 25 Mar. 1784: N.L.I., Dublin, *Bolton Papers*, MS 15,926 (1).
49. The wages paid to the 400 watchmen were reported in "An account of the receipts and expenditures of the commissioners of police from the 29th of September, 1787, to the 29th of September, 1788": *Commons' jn. Ire.*, vol. 13, (1789–90), pp. cl-clv.
50. Snodaigh, " Some police and military aspects," pp. 226–227.
51. Ferguson, "The Volunteer movement and the government", p. 215.
52. Beattie, *Crime and the courts in England* p. 49.
53. *H.J.*, 01.11.82.
54. *H.J.*, 16.12.82; *H.J.*, 18.12.82; *H.J.*, 13.12.82.
55. *H.J.*, 18.12.82.
56. *H.J.*, 03.31.83.
57. *H.J.*, 01.09.83.
58. *H.J.*, 03.12.81.
59. James Moore Davis is listed in a "Return of licensed pawnbrokers," year ending 31 Dec. 1787: *Commons' jn. Ire.*, vol. 12, part 2, pp. dciii–dciv; Davis was selected as a juror in 1794: see *H.J.*, 29.10.94.
60. *H.J.*, 09.09.82.
61. *H.J.*, 09.12.82.
62. *Minute book of the Blackrock association* (hereafter *Minute book*), 9 Dec. 1782: N.L.I., Dublin, MS 84.
63. Ibid., 17 Dec. 1782: N.L.I., Dublin, MS 84.
64. Ibid., 2 Nov. 1784: N.L.I., Dublin, MS 84.
65. Ibid., 7 Sept. 1784: N.L.I., Dublin, MS 84.; the handles of the hangars were engraved with the name of the Blackrock Felons Association.
66. *Minute book*, 27 Jan. 1785: N.L.I., Dublin, MS 84.
67. *H.J.*, 29.10.84.
68. *Minute book*, 9 May 1785: N.L.I., Dublin, MS 84.
69. *H.J.*, 01.08.92.
70. *H.J.*, 25.02.80; see also *W.H.M.*, Mar. 1780, pp. 174–176.
71. *H.J.*, 06.09.80.
72. *H.J.*, 10.01.81.
73. Owen Mitchell -v- Peter Murphy, Comm., in *H.J.*, 09.03.81; also see *W.H.M.*, Mar. 1781, p. 167.
74. *H.J.*, 03.09.81; Stephen Gordon or Charles Gordon, see *W.H.M.*, Nov. 1781, pp. 614-616.

75. *H.J.*, 05.09.81.
76. *H.J.*, 05.09.81.
77. *H.J.*, 03.09.81.
78. Stephen Gordon -v- Daniel McDonagh and Elizabeth Mulhall, Comm., in *H.J.*, 24.10.81.
79. Acquittal of Nicholas Mulhall in *H.J.*, 10.04.82.
80. *H.J.*, 16.01.82.
81. *H.J.*, 21.01.82.
82. *H.J.*, 23.01.82.
83. *H.J.*, 13.02.82.
84. *W.H.M.*, Feb. 1782, p. 109.
85. *H.J.*, 31.05.82.
86. *H.J.*, 08.04.82; also see Connor -v- James Donnelly and Nicholas Mulhall, Cork Assizes, in *W.H.M.*, Apr. 1782, pp. 220–223.
87. *Minute book*, 17 December 1782: N.L.I., Dublin, MS 84;. Beckford could not attend and sent his apologies as he was in pursuit of some armed robbers.
88. John Irwin -v- William Delaney, Comm., in *H.J.*, 20.12.82.
89. *Minute book*, 25 Jan. 1783: N.L.I., Dublin, MS 84.
90. *Ibid.*, 13 Jan. 1783: N.L.I., Dublin, MS 84.
91. Surgeon George Daunt -v- James Kennedy, Patrick Farrell, and James Gaynor, K.Q.S., in *H.J.*, 15.01.83; see also *W.H.M.*, Jan. 1783, p. 53; for an illustration of the execution of Lord Ferrers, see McLynn, *Crime and punishment* illustrations 9–10, pp. 132–33; execution, op. cit. pp. 150–51.
92. *Minute book*, 25 Jan. 1783: N.L.I., Dublin, MS 84.
93. *H.J.*, 30.07.83.
94. *H.J.*, 12.02.83.
95. *H.J.*, 05.03.83.
96. *H.J.*, 14.03.83.
97. James Moore Davis -v- James Egan and John Short, Comm., in *H.J.*, 28.07.83.
98. *H.J.*, 20.09.84.
99. *Minute book*, 20 Aug. 1785: N.L.I., Dublin, MS 84.
100. Ibid.
101. *H.J.*, 25.09.82.
102. *H.J.*, 02.12.82.
103. *H.J.*, 18.10.82.
104. *H.J.*, 26.03.84.
105. Rex -v- Michael Hughes and George Cruise, [Phillip Duffy], Comm., in *H.J.*, 14.07.84; the reference to Duffy was found in George Cruise and Michael Hughes to Lord Lieutenant, 23 July 1784: National Archives, Dublin, Prisoners' petitions and cases, MS 12.
106. George Cruise and Michael Hughes to Lord Lieutenant, 23 July 1784: National Archives, Dublin, Prisoners' petitions and cases, MS 12.
107. *H.J.*, 28.07.84.
108. Ibid.
109. *H.J.*, 28.10.85.
110. *Statutes* (Ire.) 23 & 24 Geo. III. c. 57 (1784); also see Joseph P. Starr, "The enforcing of law and order in eighteenth century Ireland," (unpublished Ph.D. thesis, Trinity College, Dublin, 1968) p. 155.
111. Rutland to Sydney, 21 June 1784: P.R.O., H.O. 100/13/159–160.
112. *H.J.*, 07.02.85.

113. Palmer, "The Irish police experiment," p. 413.
114. Rutland to Sydney, 16 July 1785: P.R.O. H.O. 100/13/194–195
115. "The Police Bill," readings to the House of Commons, Mar. 1786: *Parl. reg. Ire.*, vol. 6, p. 382.
116. "Account of the number of watch-men," for the year ending 25 Mar. 1784: N.L.I., Dublin, *Bolton Papers*, MS 15,926 (1).

THE NEW POLICE

1. For the political and administrative background to the police see Kevin Boyle, "Police in Ireland before the union: I," *Irish Jurist* new series, vol. 7, (1972), pp. 115–137; "Police in Ireland before the union: II," *Irish Jurist* new series, vol. 8, (1973), pp. 90–116; and "Police in Ireland before the union: III," *Irish Jurist* new series, vol. 8, (1973), pp. 323–348.
2. Ekirch, A. Roger, *Bound for America, the transportation of British convicts to the colonies, 1718–1775* (Oxford, 1987), pp. 233–235.
3. On Monday 20 March 1786, the Solicitor-General, Hugh Carleton (in the absence of the Attorney-General, John Fitzgibbon, whose mother had just passed away) read the police bill before the House of Commons for the first time. The bill received the Royal Assent on Monday 8 May. Reading of the Police Bill to the House of Commons, Mar. 1786: *Parl. reg. Ire.*, vol. 6, pp. 326–399; Reading of the Police Bill to the House of Lords, Mar.–Apr. 1786: *Lords' jn. Ire.*, vol. 5, (1776–1786), pp. 729, 737, 740; Royal assent of the Police Bill, May 1786: *Commons' jn. Ire.*, vol. 12, part 1, pp. 141–42.
4. For a discussion of the failed "London and Westminster Police Bill," see Beattie, *Crime and the Courts in England*, pp. 66–67.
5. William Street was not mentioned in the Police Act, see *Statutes* (Ire.) 26 Geo. III, c. 24.
6. For an analysis of the structure of Dublin corporation, see Sean Murphy, "Municipal politics and popular disturbances: 1600–1800," in Art Cosgrove, *Dublin through the Ages* (Dublin, 1988), pp. 77–79; also see Jacqueline Hill, "The politics of privilege: Dublin Corporation and the Catholic question 1792–1823", *Maynooth Review* vol. 7, (1982), pp. 19–21.
7. Nathaniel Warren to Thomas Orde, "Memorandum on the police and city boundaries", 16 Nov. 1784: N.L.I., Dublin, *Bolton Papers*, MS 15,932 (1).
8. Ekirch, *Bound for America* pp. 233–235.
9. *H.J.*, 22.03.86.
10. "An account of the amount of salaries paid to the commissioners of police and divisional justices", from 29 Sept. 1786 to 29 Sept. 1790: *Commons' jn. Ire.*, vol. 14, p. ccxcviii.
11. "Sir Henry Cavendish Report" and debate on the police finances, 25 Apr. 1789: *Parl. reg. Ire.*, vol. 9, p. 397; Leet's salary: "An account of the receipts and expenditures of the commissioners of police", 29 Sept. 1787 to 29 Sept. 1788: *Commons' jn. Ire.*, vol. 13, pp. cl–clv.
12. "An account of the receipts and expenditures of the commissioners of police", 29 Sept. 1787 to 29 Sept. 1788: *Commons' jn. Ire.*, vol. 13, pp. cl–clv.
13. "Account of the number of watch-men", for the year ending 25 Mar. 1784: N.L.I., Dublin, *Bolton Papers*, MS 15,926 (1).
14. "An account of the particulars of the charge made by the commissioners of police for *Hue and Cry*", from 29 Sept. 1786 to 25 Dec. 1787: *Commons' jn. Ire.*, vol. 12, part 2, pp. dcciv–dccix.

15. "An account of the expense of the police establishment" from 29 Sept. 1786 to 29 Sept. 1790: *Commons' jn. Ire.*, vol. 14, pp. cclxxv–cclxxvi.
16. *Statutes* (Ire.) 26 Geo. III, c. 24, cl. 21.
17. *H.J.*, 30.01.88.
18. *H.J.*, 03.04.89.
19. *H.J.*, 29.07.89.
20. *H.J.*, 29.07.89.
21. *Statutes* (Ire.) 26 Geo. III, c. 24, cl. 36.
22. *Statutes* (Ire.) 26 Geo. III, c. 24, cl. 38; see also Palmer, *Police and protest* p. 121.
23. *H.J.*, 02.07.87.
24. "An account of the particulars of the charge made by the commissioners of police for *Hue and Cry*," from 29 Sept. 1786 to 25 Dec. 1787: *Commons' jn. Ire.*, vol. 12, part 2, pp. dcciv–dccix.
25. *H.J.*, 10.08.87.
26. *H.J.*, 13.08.87.
27. *Parl. reg. Ire.*, vol. 9, pp. 399, 422.
28. For effects of demobilisation in England, see Hay, "War, dearth and theft," p. 140.
29. See police establishment in *Wilson's Dublin Directory*, 1787-1795.
30. *W.H.M.*, Oct. 1786, pp. 558–560.
31. *W.H.M.*, Nov. 1786, pp. 613–616.
32. Richard Wildridge -v- John Fitzpatrick, Comm., in *H.J.*, 17.07.89.
33. Thomas Abbot -v- Thomas Emerson, Comm., July 1792, in Dowling, *Trials at large*, part 1, pp. 63–66.
34. *H.J.*, 16.05.87; also see *W.H.M.*, Aug. 1788, pp. 388–91.
35. John Exshaw -v- Richard Griffith, Sir John Freke, and Henry Hatton, King's Bench, in *H.J.*, 09.05.88; *H.J.*, 06.06.88; and *H.J.*, 11.06.88.
36. *H.J.*, 24.03.86.
37. For notice of Fleming's first arrest, see *H.J.*, 04.01.92.
38. Michael Fox and George [John] Carleton -v- Alexander [Allan] Stuart [Stewart], D.Q.S., in *H.J.*, 19.05.88.
39. Allen Stewart to Lord Lieutenant, 18 July 1788: National Archives, Dublin, Prisoners' petitions and cases, MS 16.
39. *Statutes* (Ire.) 28 Geo. III, c. 45 (1788).
40. William Shea is also spelled as William Shee in *Wilson's Dublin Directory*, 1793.
41. Rex -v- 21 prostitutes, D.Q.S., in *W.H.M.*, Oct. 1788, pp. 557–559; also see *H.J.*, 13.10.88, for a list of their names.
42. Joseph Sallary to Lord Lieutenant, 17 Oct. 1794: National Archives, Prisoners' petitions and cases, MS 50.
43. Francis Bennet -v- Michael O'Berne and Joseph Sallary, Comm., in *H.J.*, 25.07.94.
44. *H.J.*, 30.07.94.
45. *H.J.*, 15.08.94.
46. *H.J.*, 22.08.94.
47. *H.J.*, 03.09.94.
48. McDowell, R.B., "The personnel of the Dublin Society of United Irishmen 1791-1794," *Irish Historical Studies* vol. 2 (1940–1), pp. 12–53.
49. *H.J.*, 19.08.95.
50. James Bardin Palmer -v- William Wittenham, Comm., *H.J.*, 29.10.94.
51. *H.J.*, 03.11.94.
52. William Wittenham pleads his majesty's pardon, Comm., in *H.J.*, 22.12.94.
53. Rex -v- Bernard Kelly, Comm., in *H.J.*, 29.10.88.
54. William Montgomery -v- Patrick Rigbey, Comm., in *H.J.*, 28.10.89.

55. See Rt. Hon Robert, Earl of Lanesborough -v- Mark Magrath, D.Q.S., and Daniel Craig -v- Mary Kelly, D.Q.S., in *H.J.*, 10.09.88.
56. *M.P.*, 19.02.90; also *H.J.*, 19.02.90.
57. Rex -v- Godfrey, Comm., in *M.P.*, 10.07.90; also *W.H.M.*, July, pp. 94–96.
58. *Wilson's Dublin Directory*, 1793.
59. Report of Sir Henry Cavendish on the police finances, 25 Apr. 1789: *Parl. reg. Ire.*, vol. 9, pp. 394–424.
60. Sir Henry Cavendish to House of Commons, "Report of the committee appointed to examine the accounts of the commissioners of police," 25 Apr. 1789: *Commons'jn. Ire.*, vol. 13, pp. ccviii–ccix.
61. For a treatment of John Fitzgibbon, see Ann C. Kavanaugh, "John FitzGibbon, Earl of Clare", in David Dickson, Dáire Keogh and Kevin Whelan (eds.), *The United Irishmen, Republicans, Radicalism and Rebellion* (Dublin, 1993), pp. 115–123.
62. Report of Sir Henry Cavendish on the police finances, 25 Apr. 1789: *Parl. reg. Ire.*, vol. 9, pp. 397–98.
63. Report of Sir Henry Cavendish on the police finances, 25 Apr. 1789: *Parl. reg. Ire.*, vol. 9, p. 399.
64. Ibid., p. 407.
65. Hobart to Lord Lieutenant, 27 Apr. 1789: P.R.O. H.O. 100/27/7–9.
66. Patrick Keefe -v- John Egan, Robert Fisher, and John Whelan, D.Q.S., in *H.J.*, 20.04.89; also see *H.J.*, 06.04.89. Horse Owners -v- John Cowan, D.Q.S., in *H.J.*, 20.04.89; see also *H.J.*, 20.05.89.
67. *H.J.*, 20.02.88. In view of this, Browne ordered that the number of such crimes brought to trial be printed from 1786 to 1788. Although such a list of trials does not appear to have been printed, it may have been the basis for the Cavendish report. For more information on crimes committed by police, see Palmer, *Police and protest*, pp. 125–126.
68. Report of Sir Henry Cavendish on the police finances, 25 Apr. 1789: *Parl. reg. Ire.*, vol. 9, p. 416.
69. Ibid., pp. 416–417.
70. Ibid., p. 398.
71. Ibid., p. 424.
72. *H.J.*, 05.10.89.
73. *Minute book*, 13 July 1792: N.L.I., Dublin, MS 84.
74. Ibid., 17 Aug. 1792: N.L.I., Dublin, MS 84.
75. Ibid., 25 July 1793: N.L.I., Dublin, MS 84.
76. *H.J.*, 31.05.93.
77. *Minute book*, 15 Sept. 1796: N.L.I., Dublin, MS 84.
78. *Minute book*, 7 July 1797: N.L.I., Dublin, MS 84; NB: This is the last meeting recorded in the manuscript.
79. *Statutes* (Ire.) 26 Geo. III, c. 24 (1786); 28 Geo. III, c. 45 (1788).
80. Hobart to Bernard, 19 Mar. 1792: P.R.O. H.O. 100/37/36–37; for Grattan's arguments and debate which followed, see *H.J.*, 16.03.92.
81. Fitzwilliam to Portland, 5 January 1795: P.R.O. H.O. 100/56/81–86.
82. "Committee … to enquire into the state of the police of the city of Dublin", 16 Feb. 1795: *Parl. reg. Ire.*, vol. 15, (1795), pp. 110–111.
83. Palmer, *Police and protest*, p. 133.
84. Thomas Pelham to Portland, 30 Mar. 1795: P.R.O. H.O. 100/57/21–28.
85. *Parl. reg. Ire.*, vol. 15, (1795), p. 404.
86. *Statutes* (Ire.) 35 Geo. III, c. 36 (1795).
87. *H.J.*, 24.06.95.
88. *H.J.*, 02.10.95.　　　　　　　　　89. *H.J.*, 02.10.95.

90. Rules for the City of Dublin Watch, 26 Oct. 1795: National Archives, Dublin, Official Papers, series 2, 11/5.
91. *H.J.*, 16.10.95.
92. In 1838, a second centralised police force began patrolling the streets of Dublin. This gap of 43 years between the first and second centralised police forces in Dublin explains why some police historians have mistakenly dated the history of the first centralised police force in the British Isles to the London Metropolitan Police founded by Peel in 1829; see Nigel Cochrane, "Public Reaction to the Introduction of a New Police Force: Dublin 1838-45," in *Police Studies: The International Review of Police Development* Vol. 10, No. 2, (Summer 1787), pp. 72–79.

TRANSPORTATION

1. Lockhart, Audrey, *Some aspects of emigration from Ireland to the North American colonies between 1660 and 1775* (M. Litt. thesis, Trinity College, Dublin, 1971, publ. 1976), pp. 80–97.
2. Ekirch, *Bound for America* pp. 233–235.
3. Beattie, *Crime and the courts in England* p. 223.
4. Robinson, *The women of Botany Bay* pp. 312–313
5. Dickson, "The place of Dublin", p. 178.
6. Ekirch, *Bound for America* pp. 234–236.
7. Ekirch, *Bound for America* p. 25; "Account of the number of convicts transported", Jan. 1790: *Commons'Jn. Ire.*, vol. 13, p. ccli; *H.J.*, 17.09.88.
8. "Account of the number of convicts transported from Ireland in the years 1787, 1788 and 1789 and the number of convicts brought back to Ireland", Jan. 1790: *Commons' jn. Ire.*, vol. 13, p. ccli; also see *H.J.*, 20.10.88.
9. Lockhart, *Some aspects of emigration* p. 83.
10. Ibid., p. 89.
11. Ibid., p. 88.
12. Ibid., pp. 91-92.
13. *H.J.*, 17.09.88.
14. Ekirch, *Bound for America* p. 25.
15. "Account of the number of convicts transported", Jan. 1790: *Commons' jn. Ire.*, vol. 13, p. ccli; also see *H.J.*, 17.09.88.
16. Lockhart, *Some aspects of emigration* p. 89.
17. Ibid., p. 90.
18. *H.J.*, 25.10.84.
19. *H.J.*, 17.09.88.
20. *H.J.*, 19.11.84.
21. Hierro was spelled Ferro in *H.J.*, 17.09.88.; see also *H.J.*, 23.05.85.
22. *H.J.*, 23.05.85.
23. *H.J.*, 16.09.85; *H.J.*, 26.09.85.
24. Ekirch, *Bound for America* p. 73.
25. Ibid., p. 114.
26. *H.J.*, 02.06.86.
27. Ekirch, *Bound for America* p. 145.
28. Whitehall to Sackville Hamilton, 24 Oct. 1786: P.R.O. H.O. 100/18/369–373.
29. Sackville Hamilton to Evan Nepean, 2 Dec. 1786: P.R.O. H.O. 100/18/391.
30. *W.H.M.*, May, 1787, pp. 278-280; also see "Account of the number of convicts transported", Jan. 1790: *Commons'jn. Ire.*, vol. 13, p. ccli.
31. Ekirch, *Bound for America* p. 109.
32. Maces Bay was spelled as Machias Bay; see *H.J.*, 17.09.88.
33. *H.J.*, 17.09.88.

34. Inagua was spelled as Heneaga; see *H.J.*, 17.09.88.
35. *W.H.M.*, Nov., 1787, pp. 612–615; also see *H.J.*, 15.10.87.
36. Buckingham to Sydney, 17 July 1788: P.R.O. H.O. 100/23/298.
37. "Account of the number of convicts transported," Jan. 1790: *Commons' jn. Ire.*, vol. 13, p. cccli; also see *H.J.*, 17.09.88.
38. *H.J.* 23.05.88; *H.J.*, 19.05.88.
39. *H.J.*, 10.09.88.
40. *H.J.*, 16.05.88.
41. *H.J.*, 17.09.88.
42. *H.J.*, 22.10.88.
43. *H.J.*, 21.01.89.
44. *H.J.*, 06.04.89.
45. For a popular account of Lambert, see John Edward Walsh, *Ireland sixty years ago* (Dublin, 1851), pp. 69–70.
46. Paul Ham -v- Frederick Lambert, Comm., in *H.J.*, 28.07.83.
47. *H.J.*, 06.08.83.
48. *H.J.*, 11.08.83.
49. Rex -v- Frederick Lambert, Comm. (trial postponed), in *H.J.*, 19.07.86.
50. *H.J.*, 28.07.86.
51. *H.J.*, 25.04.88.
52. Rex -v- Frederick Lambert, King's Bench, in *H.J.*, 11.06.88.
53. Report of Bathurst's crime: *H.J.*, 25.05.87; Denis Magaray -v- Francis Bathurst, Comm., in *H.J.*, 23.07.87.
54. *H.J.*, 22.08.88; see also *D.E.P.*, 30.10.88.
55. *Statutes* (Ire.) 23 & 24 Geo. III, c. 56 (1784).
56. Francis Bathurst -v- Frederick Lambert, Comm., in *H.J.*, 31.10.88.
57. Much of this information is derived from a short anonymous biography of Lambert, which appeared in *H.J.*, 31.10.88.
58. *H.J.*, 17.06.89.
59. Whitehall to Buckingham, 27 July 1789: P.R.O. H.O. 100/27/216–219.
60. Sackville Hamilton to Bernard, 15 May 1792: P.R.O. H.O. 100/37/132–133.
61. Whitehall to Buckingham, 27 July 1789: P.R.O. H.O. 100/27/216–219.
62. "Account of the number of convicts transported", Jan. 1790: *Commons' jn. Ire.*, vol. 13, p. cccli.
63. *H.J.*, 10.08.89.
64. Whitehall to Lord Lieutenant, 23 Nov. 1789: P.R.O. H.O. 100/27/287–288.
65. Sackville Hamilton to Bernard, 15 May 1792: P.R.O. H.O. 100/37/132–133.
66. Shaw, A.G.L., *Convicts & the colonies: A study of penal transportation from Great Britain & Ireland to Australia & other parts of the British Empire* (Melbourne, 1977), p. 171.
67. Whitehall to the Lords Justices of the King's Bench, 25 Nov. 1789: P.R.O. H.O. 100/27/289–290.
68. *Statutes* (Ire.) 26 Geo. III, c. 24, cl. 64-70 (1786).
69. John Fitzgibbon and John Foster to Lords Justice, 1 Dec. 1789: P.R.O. H.O. 100/27/293–295.
70. "Account of the number of convicts transported": *Commons' jn. Ire.*, vol. 13, p. cccli.
71. Stevenson, John, *Popular disturbances in England, 1700–1870* (London, 1979), pp. 76–90.
72. Hobart to Evan Nepean, 15 July 1790: P.R.O. H.O. 100/30/128.
73. *H.J.*, 09.07.90.
74. *H.J.*, 14.07.90; also see an account in *W.H.M.*, July 1790, pp. 94–96.
75. *H.J.*, 21.07.90.

76. *H.J.*, 18.08.90.
77. *H.J.*, 23.07.90.
78. *H.J.*, 01.10.90.
79. £3,000: *H.J.*, 10.09.90; £1,000: *H.J.*, 01.10.90.
80. *H.J.*, 20.09.90.
81. Quote: *H.J.*, 01.10.90; 300 prisoners: *M.P.*, 02.10.90.
82. "Report from the commissioners of police, of the state of the several gaols and prisons within the district of the metropolis, in which persons charged with or guilty of felony, misdemeanor or breach of the peace are confined, as visited by them the 19th January, 1791", 27 Jan. 1791: *Commons' jn. Ire.*, vol. 14, p. lvii.
83. "Report from the commissioners of police, of the present state of the several gaols, and prisons within the district of the metropolis, wherein persons charged with or guilty of treason, felony, misdemeanor or breach of the peace, are confined", 23 Jan. 1792: *Commons' jn. Ire.*, vol. 15, part 1, p. xii.
84. *H.J.*, 24.12.94.
85. *W.H.M.*, June 1790, pp. 574-5.
86. *D.E.P.*, 16.10.90; also see *W.H.M.*, Apr. 1790, p. 382.
87. *M.P.*, 18 Dec. 1790; see also *H.J.*, 16.04.90.
88. *H.J.*, 07.05.90.
89. Rex -v- Mathew Nulty, D.Q.S., in *H.J.*, 04.06.90; also see *W.H.M.*, Apr. 1790, p. 382; and June 1790, pp. 574-575.
90. The *Duke of Leinster* is also spelled the *Dublin of Leinster* in the "Account of the number of convicts transported," Jan. 1790: *Commons' jn. Ire.*, vol. 13, p. cccli.
91. Extract of letter from Sir William Codrington, 18 Jan. 1790: P.R.O. H.O. 100/29/149-150.
92. Hobart to Evan Nepean, 25 Mar. 1790: P.R.O. H.O. 100/29/198; on a list of transports, the name of William Dalton appeared.
93. *H.J.*, 26.10.91.
94. Whitehall to Buckingham, 27 July 1789: P.R.O. H.O. 100/27/216-219; and Whitehall to the Lords Justices of the King's Bench, 25 Nov. 1789: P.R.O. H.O. 100/27/289-290.
95. Hobart to Evan Nepean, 25 Mar. 1790: P.R.O. H.O. 100/29/192-193.
96. 30 Geo. III, c. 32 (1790).
97. Robinson, *The women of Botany Bay* p. 91; also see Shaw, *Convicts & the colonies* p. 363; Robinson's figures for the *Queen* and Shaw's figures for the *Boddingtons, Sugar Cane* and *Marquis Cornwallis*, are employed here.
98. Bateson, Charles, *The convict ships, 1787-1868* (Australia, 1974), pp. 135-136.
99. Nepean to Hobart, 13 Oct. 1792: P.R.O. H.O. 100/38/28-29.
100. Hobart to Bernard, 13 Mar. 1792: P.R.O. H.O. 100/37/11.
101. Westmoreland to Henry Dundas, 4 Aug. 1792: P.R.O. H.O. 100/37/200-201.
102. *H.J.*, 28.09.92.
103. Hobart to Evan Nepean, 28 Sept. 1792: P.R.O. H.O. 100/37/281.
104. *H.J.*, 19.10.92.
105. Ekirch, *Bound for America* p. 112.
106. Henry-Gore Sankey to Hobart, 1 Sept. 1792: P.R.O. H.O. 100/37/238-239.
107. Nepean to Hobart, 20 Oct. 1792: P.R.O. H.O. 100/38/34-35.
108. Hamilton to Nepean, 27 Nov. 1792: P.R.O. H.O. 100/38/103-104.
109. Whitehall to Hobart, Dec. 1792: P.R.O. H.O. 100/38/150-152; also see Robinson, *The women of Botany Bay* p.86.
110. Hobart to Nepean, 3 Dec. 1792: P.R.O. H.O. 100/38/113.
111. *H.J.*, 14.12.92.
112. Bateson, *The convict ships* pp. 145-147.

113. Westmoreland to Portland, 8 Oct. 1794: P.R.O. H.O. 100/52/220–221.
114. *H.J.*, 01.05.95.
115. Pelham to John King, 26 June 1795: P.R.O. H.O. 100/58/79.
116. Thompson, E.P., *The making of the English working class* (London, 1986 edn), p. 63
117. *H.J.*, 10.06.95.
118. *H.J.*, 17.07.95.
119. *H.J.*, 22.06.95.
120. *H.J.*, 22.06.95; "Invoice of sundry articles shipped by Order of Sackville Hamilton on board the Marquis of Cornwallis Captain Richardson for Botany Bay August 8, 1795": P.R.O. H.O. 100/58/316; Sackville Hamilton to John King, 23 Oct. 1795: P.R.O. H.O. 100/59/56; Sackville Hamilton to John King, 16 Nov. 1795: P.R.O. H.O. 100/59/83.
121. Sackville Hamilton to John King, 16 Sept. 1795: P.R.O. H.O. 100/58/314.
122. Shaw, *Convicts & the Colonies* p. 363.

Bibliography

I. MANUSCRIPTS

a. Bolton Papers
Papers of Thomas Orde, 1st Baron Bolton, National Library of Ireland, Manuscripts Collection, Dublin.

b. Correspondence of Thomas Orde, 1784–87
MS 15,926 (1): Richard Gladwill to Thomas Orde, return of St. Andrews parish, 24 December 1785.
MS 15,926 (1): "Account of the Number of Watch-men employed in the Several Parishes in the County of the City of Dublin Collected from the Returns to Parliament & Watch Houses," for the year ending 25 March 1784.
MS 15,926 (5): Henry Howison and Francis Armstrong to Thomas Orde, return of St. Mary's Parish, 21 February 1785.
MS 15,926 (15): J. Sparrow to Thomas Orde, return of St. Catherine's parish, 24 March 1785.
MS 15,926 (17): Robert Lowther to Thomas Orde, return of St. James's Watch, 22 February 1785.
MS 15,927 (1): [–] to Thomas Orde, "Heads of a Bill for improving the police of the City of Dublin, June 1778," [1784].
MS 15,932 (1): Nathaniel Warren to Thomas Orde, "Memorandum on the police and city boundaries," 16 November 1784.
MS 15,939 (2): Francis Graham to Thomas Orde, Need for a force of mounted constables, 21 February 1787.

c. Minute Book
Minute Book of the Blackrock Association: National Library of Ireland, Manuscripts Collection, Dublin: MS 84.

d. Official Papers: National Archives, Dublin.
Police commissioners Nathaniel Warren, John Rose and William James to Dublin Castle, 13 August 1795: OP/11/4, Carton 507.

e. Prisoners' petitions & cases: National Archives, Dublin.
Petition 10: Thirty female convicts, including Margaret Savage, and two male convicts to Lord Lieutenant, 27 August 1782.
Petition 12: George Cruise and Michael Hughes to Lord Lieutenant, 23 July 1784.
Petition 16: Allen Stewart to Lord Lieutenant, 18 July 1788.
Petition 17: John Philips to Lord Lieutenant, January 1792.
Petition 19: Joseph Harrington to Lord Lieutenant, August 1789.
Petition 21: Patrick Fay to Lord Lieutenant, October 1788.
Petition 22: Thomas McNamee to Lord Lieutenant, Oct.–Nov. 1788.

Petition 23: Anthony McKinley, Michael Rorke, Hudson Hampden and Richard Barber to Lord Lieutenant, December 1788.
Petition 50: Joseph Sallary to Lord Lieutenant, 17 October 1794.

II. PARLIAMENTARY RECORDS

a. Commons' Jn. Ire.
Journals of the House of Commons of the Kingdom of Ireland . . . , (1613–1791, 28 vols., Dublin, 1753–1791; reprinted and continued, 1613–1800, 19 vols., Dublin, 1796–1800).
"Petition in favour of Benjamin Houghton," House of Industry, 15 February 1774: vol. 9, part 1, pp. 95–96.
"Report of the grand committee for trade," Sir Lucius O'Brien, February, 1780: vol. 10, part 1, pp. cxi–cxviii.
"The Police Bill," receives Royal Assent, May 1786: vol. 12, part 1, pp. 141–42.
"Return of licensed pawnbrokers," year ending 31 December 1787: vol. 12, part 2, pp. dciii–dciv.
"Account of the particulars of the charge made by the commissioners of police for incidents, from the commencement of their institution to the 25th of December, 1787": vol. 12, part 2, pp. dccii–dcciii.
"Account of the particulars of the charge made by the commissioners of police for *Hue and Cry* and stationery, from the commencement of their institution to the 25th of December, 1787": vol. 12, part 2, pp. dcciv–dccix.
"Report on the state of gaols and prisons," George Holmes, 3 March 1788: vol. 12, part 2, pp. dccxxxiii–dccxxxvi.
"Account of the particulars of all sums expended by the commissioners of police," from 29 Sept. 1786 to 25 Mar. 1788: vol. 12, part 2, pp. dcccxxxiii–dcccxxxvi.
"Account of the receipts and expenditures of the commissioners of police from the 29th of September, 1787, to the 29th of September, 1788": vol. 13, pp. cl–clv.
"Report of the committee appointed to examine the accounts of the commissioners of police," Sir Henry Cavendish, 25 April 1789: vol. 13, pp. ccviii–ccix.
"Account of the number of convicts transported from Ireland in the years 1787, 1788 and 1789 and the number of convicts brought back to Ireland in January, 1790": vol. 13, p. cccli.
"Account of the sums paid in the Treasury Office for the transportation of convicts within the four last years," January 1790: vol. 13, p. cccli.
"Account of the expense of the police establishment from its first institution to the 29th of September, 1790": vol. 14, pp. cclxxv–cclxxvi.
"Account of the amount of salaries paid to the commissioners of police and divisional justices since the first establishment of the institution to the 29 September 1790": vol. 14, p. ccxcviii.
"Report from the commissioners of police, of the state of the several gaols and prisons within the district of the metropolis, in which persons charged with or guilty of felony, misdemeanor or breach of the peace are confined, as visited by them the 19th January, 1791," 27 January 1791: vol. 14, p. lvii.
"Report on the petition of the governors of the Foundling Hospital," Sir John Blaquiere, 7 February 1791: vol. 14, pp. cci–ccii.
"Report from the commissioners of police, of the present state of the several gaols, and prisons within the district of the metropolis, wherein persons charged with or guilty of treason, felony, misdemeanor or breach of the peace, are confined," 23

January 1792: vol. 15, part 1, p. xii.

"Bill to prevent unlawful combinations of journeymen artificers," Mr Graydon and Mr Vandeleur, 10 March 1792: vol. 15, part 1, pp. 90, 93, 93, 101, 103.

"Petition of Denis McCarthy to the House of Commons," 28 April 1795: vol. 16, p. 109.

b. Lords' jn. Ire.

Journals of the House of Lords [of Ireland], 1634–1800 (8 vols., Dublin, 1779–1800).

"The Police Bill," readings to the House of Lords, March–April 1786: vol. 5, (1776–1786), pp. 729, 737, 740.

c. Parl. reg. Ire.

The Parliamentary Register, or the History of the Proceedings and Debates of the House of Commons of Ireland [1781–97] (17 vols., Dublin, 1782–1801).

"The Police Bill," readings to the House of Commons, March 1786: vol. 6, (1786), pp. 326–399.

"Sir Henry Cavendish Report" and debate on the police finances, 25 April 1789: vol. 9, (1789), p. 394–424.

"Petition by Dublin Corporation against the bill proposed by Sir John Blaquiere for the reform of the Foundling Hospital," 15 March 1791: vol. 11, (1791), p. 307–312.

"Bill proposed by Sir John Blaquiere for the reform of the Foundling Hospital," 2 March 1791: vol. 11, (1791), pp. 257–258.

"Committee . . . to enquire into the state of the police of the city of Dublin," 16 February 1795: vol. 15, (1795), pp. 110–111.

"An act for more effectually preserving the peace within the city of Dublin," receives Royal Assent, 5 June 1795: vol. 15, (1795), p. 404.

d. Statutes (Ire.)

The Statutes at Large, passed in the Parliaments held in Ireland (1310–1800), 20 vols., (Dublin, 1765–1801).

Bull-beating: 19 & 20 Geo. III, c. 36 (1780).

Chalking Act: 13 & 14 Geo. III, c. 45 (1774).

Chalking Act: 17 & 18 Geo. III, c. 11 (1778).

Coining Act: 23 & 24 Geo. III, c. 50 (1784).

Combination Act: 19 & 20 Geo. III, c. 19 (1780).

Combination and Bounty Act: 21 & 22 Geo. III, c. 43 (1781–82).

Commission of Oyer and Terminer at Tholsel: 3 Geo. II, c. 15 (1729).

Commission of Oyer and Terminer at Green Street: 35 Geo. III, c. 25. (1795).

Houghing Act: 23 & 24 Geo. III, c. 56 (1784).

Justice of the Peace: 23 & 24 Geo. III, c. 30 (1784).

Murder Act: 31 Geo. III, c. 17 (1791).

Mutiny: 21 & 22 Geo. III, c. 43 (1781–82).

Parish Watch Act: 17 & 18 Geo. III, c. 43 (1778).

Pawnbroking Act: 28 Geo. III, c. 49 (1788).

Police Act: 26 Geo. III, c. 24 (1786).

Police Act (Amended): 28 Geo. III, c. 45 (1788).

Parish Watch Act: 35 Geo. III, c. 36 (1795).

Post Office Act: 23 & 24 Geo. III, c. 17 (1784).

Post Office Act (Amended): 28 Geo III, c. 13 (1788).

Press Restrictions: 23 & 24 Geo. III, c. 28 (1784).

Press Restrictions (Amended): 31 Geo. III, c. 32 (1791).

Press Restrictions (Amended): 33 Geo. III, c. 43 (1793).
Receivers of Stolen Property Act: 23 & 24 Geo. III, c. 45 (1784).
Riot Act: 27 Geo. III, c. 15 (1787).
Rutland Square Watch, contained in "An act of the more effectually paving, cleansing, and lighting of the streets of the city of Dublin": 23 & 24 Geo. III, c. 57 cl. 82 (1784).
Seduction of Artisans: 25 Geo. III, c. 17 (1785)
St. George's parish: 33 Geo. III, c. 53 (1793).
Transportation to Americas: 26 Geo. III, c. 24 (1786).
Transportation to Australia: 30 Geo. III, c. 32 (1790).

e. U.K. Parliamentary Papers
Journals of the House of Commons [of England, Great Britain, or United Kingdom].
Census of Ireland, 1821; "Abstract of the Answers and Returns": vol. 22, p. 411, (within p. 411, see pp. 11–26).
First Report from the Select Committee appointed to Inquire into the State of the Law Regarding Artizans and Machinery, Vol. 5, 1824, pp. 431–432.

III. PRINTED MATTER

a. Newspapers and Magazines
Dublin Evening Post, (Dublin, . . . – . . .).
Freeman's Journal, (Dublin, 1763–1924)
Hibernian Journal, (Dublin, 1771–1821).
Morning Post, (Dublin, . . . – . . .)
Walker's Hibernian Magazine, (Dublin, 1771–1812).

b. Contemporary Printed Sources
Anon., *The Picture of Dublin* with fold-out *Map of Dublin*, c. 1810, (Dublin, . . .).
Dowling, Vincent, *Trials at large*, vol. 632, part 1 and 2, R.I.A., (Dublin, 1792); NB: vol. 632, part 1, is missing pages 209–216, which are found in vol. 631, part 5, R.I.A., (Dublin, 1792).
Drummond, William Hamilton, *Autobiography of Archibald Hamilton Rowan* (Dublin, 1840).
MacNevin, Thomas, *Lives and trials* (Dublin, 1846), pp. 299–479.
Malton, James, *A Picturesque and Descriptive View of the City of Dublin* (London 1792–99).
McGregor, J.S., *New Picture of Dublin* (Dublin, 1821).
Walsh, John Edward, *Ireland sixty years ago* (Dublin, 1851); reprinted as *Rakes and ruffians: the underworld of Georgian Dublin* (Dublin, 1979).
Warburton, John, James Whitelaw and Rev Robert Walsh, *History of the city of Dublin* 2 vols., (London, 1818).
Watts, Henry (Printer), *A Report of the Action of Seduction, wherein Barnaby Egan, Esq. was Plaintiff and Rob. Kindillan, Esq., Defendant* Court of Exchequer Michaelmas Term, 1791, vol. 631, part 4, R.I.A., (Dublin, 1792).
Wilson's Dublin Directory, in *The Treble Almanack*, bound with the *Almanack* (Watson's) and the *English Registry* (Exshaw's), (Dublin, 1780–95).

c. Secondary Printed Sources
Bartlett, Thomas, *The Fall and Rise of the Irish Nation, the Catholic question, 1690–1830* (Dublin, 1992).

Bateson, Charles, *The convict ships, 1787–1868* (Australia, 1974).

Beattie, John M., *Crime and the Courts in England, 1660–1800* (Oxford, 1986).

Boyd, Andrew, *The Rise of the Irish Trade Unions* (Dublin, 1972).

Boyle, John William, *The Irish Labour Movement in the Nineteenth Century* (Washington D.C., 1988).

Boyle, Kevin "Police in Ireland before the union: I," *Irish Jurist* new series, vol. 7, (1972), pp. 115–137.

———— "Police in Ireland before the union: II," *Irish Jurist* new series, vol. 8, (1973), pp. 90–116.

———— "Police in Ireland before the union: III," *Irish Jurist* new series, vol. 8, (1973), pp. 323–348.

Clarkson, Jesse Dunsmore, *Labour and Nationalism in Ireland* (New York, 1925).

Cochrane, Nigel, "Public Reaction to the Introduction of a New Police Force: Dublin 1838–45," in *Police Studies: The International Review of Police Development* Vol. 10, No. 2, (Summer 1787), pp. 72–79.

Cockburn, J.S., "Patterns of violence in English society: Homicide in Kent 1560–1985," *Past & Present*, no. 130, (1991), pp. 70–106.

Cosgrove, Art (ed.), *Dublin through the Ages* (Dublin, 1988).

Craig, Maurice, *Dublin 1660–1860* (Dublin, 1980).

Daly, Seán, *Cork: A City In Crisis, a history of labour conflict and social misery 1870–1872* (Cork, 1978).

D'Arcy, Fergus A., "Wages of labourers in the Dublin building industry, 1667–1918," *Saothar* vol. 14, (1989), pp. 17–32, and vol. 15, (1990), pp. 21–38.

———— and Ken Hannigan (eds.), *Workers in Union, documents and commentaries on the History of Irish labour*, (Dublin, 1988).

Dickson, David, "The Place of Dublin in the eighteenth-century Irish economy," in T. Devine and David Dickson (eds..), *Ireland and Scotland 1600–1850* (Edinburgh, 1983), pp. 177–189.

———— "The gap in famines: A useful myth?," in E. Margaret Crawford (ed.), *Famine: The Irish Experience, 900–1900, subsistence crises and famines in Ireland* (Edinburgh, 1989), pp. 96–111.

Dobson, C.R., *Masters and Journeymen: a prehistory of industrial relations, 1717–1800* (London, 1980).

Doorly, Bernadette, "Newgate Prison," in David Dickson (ed.) *The Gorgeous Mask, Dublin 1700–1850* (Dublin, 1987), pp. 121–131.

Ekirch, A. Roger, *Bound for America, the transportation of British convicts to the colonies, 1718–1775* (Oxford, 1987).

Ferguson, K.P., "The Volunteer movement and the government, 1778– 1793," *Irish Sword* vol. 13, no. 52, (1978–79), pp. 208–216.

Gilbert, J.T. and R., *Calendar of Ancient Records of the City of Dublin*, 19 vols., (Dublin, 1889–1944).

Hale, Leslie, *John Philpot Curran* (London, 1958).

Hay, Douglas, and Peter Linebaugh, and E.P. Thompson, (eds..), *Albion's Fatal Tree: crime and society in eighteenth-century England* (London, 1975).

———— "Property, authority and the criminal law," in Douglas Hay, *et. al.*, *Albion's Fatal Tree: crime and society in eighteenth-century England* (London, 1975), pp. 17–63.

———— "Crime and justice in the eighteenth and nineteenth century England," in Norval Morris and Michael Tonry (eds..), *Crime and Justice, an annual review of research* vol. 2, (Chicago, 1980), pp. 45–84.

———— "War, dearth and theft in the eighteenth century: The record of the English courts," *Past & Present* no. 95, (1982), pp. 117–60.

Henry, Brian, *Animadversions on the Street Robberies in Dublin*, King's Inns Library, Dublin, vol. 332, (Dublin, 1765), reprinted with an introduction in *Irish Jurist* (Winter, 1988), pp. 347–356.

––––––– "Crime, Law Enforcement and Punishment in Dublin, 1780–95" (Ph.D. thesis, Trinity College, Dublin, 1992).

Hill, Jacqueline, "The politics of privilege: Dublin Corporation and the Catholic question 1792–1823," *Maynooth Review* vol. 7, (1982), pp. 17–36.

Kavanaugh, Ann C., "John FitzGibbon, Earl of Clare," in David Dickson, Dáire Keogh and Kevin Whelan (eds..), *The United Irishmen, Republicans, Radicalism and Rebellion* (Dublin, 1993), pp. 115–123.

Kelly, James J., "Napper Tandy," in James Kelly and Uáitéar Mac Gearailt (eds..), *Dublin and Dubliners* (Dublin, 1990), pp. 1–24.

––––––– "Infanticide in eighteenth-century Ireland," in *Irish Economic and Social History* vol. XIX, (1992), pp. 5–26.

––––––– "Scarcity and poor relief in eighteenth-century Ireland: the subsistence crisis of 1782–4," *Irish Historical Studies* vol. 28, no. 109, (May 1992), pp. 38–62.

Linebaugh, Peter, "The Tyburn riot against the surgeons," in Douglas Hay, *et al.*, *Albion's Fatal Tree: crime and society in eighteenth-century England* (London, 1975), pp. 65–118.

––––––– *The London Hanged, crime and civil society in the eighteenth century* (London, 1991).

Lockhart, Audrey, *Some Aspects of Emigration from Ireland to the North American Colonies between 1660 and 1775* (M. Litt. thesis, Trinity College, Dublin, 1971, publ. 1976).

McDowell, R.B., "The personnel of the Dublin Society of United Irishmen," 1791–4, *Irish Historical Studies* vol. 2 (1940–1), pp. 12–53.

McLynn, Frank, *Crime and Punishment in Eighteenth-Century England* (London, 1989).

Murphy, Sean, "The Dublin anti-union riot of 3 December 1759," in Gerard O'Brien (ed.), *Parliament, Politics & People, essays in eighteenth-century Irish history* (Dublin, 1989), pp. 49–68.

O'Brien, Gerard (ed.), *Parliament, Politics & People, essays in eighteenth-century Irish history* (Dublin, 1989).

O'Connell, Maurice, *Irish Politics and Social Conflict in the Age of the American Revolution*. (Philadelphia, 1965).

––––––– "Class conflict in a pre-industrial society: Dublin in 1780," *Irish Ecclesiastical Record* vol. 103–104, (1965), pp. 93–106.

O'Connor, Emmet, *A Labour History of Ireland 1824–1960* (Dublin, 1992).

Orth, John V., *Combination and Conspiracy, a legal history of trade unionism, 1721–1906* (Oxford, 1991).

Osborough, W.N., "Sport, Freedom and the Criminal Law" in Anthony Whelan (ed.), *Law and Liberty in Ireland* (Dublin, 1993) pp.38–66.

Palmer, Stanley H., "The Irish police experiment: The beginnings of modern police in the British Isles, 1785–1795," *Social Science Quarterly* vol. 56, (1975), pp. 410–424.

––––––– *Police and Protest in England and Ireland, 1780–1850* (Cambridge, 1988).

Reynolds, Mairead, *A History of the Irish Post Office* (Dublin, 1983).

Robinson, Portia, *The Women of Botany Bay* (Maquarie Library, 1988).

Shaw, A.G.L., *Convicts & the Colonies: a study of penal transportation from Great Britain & Ireland to Australia & other parts of the British Empire* (Melbourne, 1977).

Shubert, Adrian, "Private initiative in law enforcement: Associations for the prosecution of felons, 1744–1856," in Victor Bailey (ed.), *Policing and Punishment in Nineteenth-Century Britain* (London, 1981), pp. 25–41.

Smyth, James, "Dublin's Political Underground in the 1790s," in Gerald O'Brien, *Parliament, Politics & People, essays in eighteenth-century Irish history* (Dublin, 1989), pp. 129–148.

Smyth, Peter D.H., "The Volunteers and parliament, 1779–84," in Thomas Bartlett and D.W. Hayton, (eds..), *Penal Era and Golden Age: essays in Irish history, 1690–1800* (Belfast, 1979), pp. 113–136.

Snodaigh, Pádraig O, "Some police and military aspects of the Irish Volunteers," *Irish Sword* vol. 13, no. 52, (1978–79), pp. 217–229.

Starr, Joseph P., "The enforcing of law and order in eighteenth century Ireland," (unpublished Ph.D. thesis, Trinity College, Dublin, 1968).

Stevenson, John, *Popular Disturbances in England, 1700–1870* (London, 1979).

Stone, Lawrence, *The Family, Sex and Marriage in England 1500–1800* (London, 1978).

Styles, John, "'Our traitorous money makers': The Yorkshire coiners and the law, 1760–83," in John Brewer and John Styles (eds.), *An Ungovernable People: the English and their law in the seventeenth and eighteenth centuries* (London, 1980), pp. 172–249.

Thompson, E.P., *The Making of the English Working Class* (London, 1986 edn.).

Index of Names

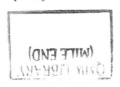